## Praise for *Foundations of Gree*

D1305226

"There's a lot of talk about green these days, but Marty takes us from ideas and ideals to actions and accountability. Information Technology (IT) might only account for two percent of the earth's carbon emissions, but its ability to have broad impact well beyond IT is huge. This book gets us thinking and acting in the right direction."

**Marie Hattar**, Vice President of Marketing, Cisco

"Companies of all sizes are interested in ways that they can reduce their energy consumption and have a more efficient data center. Marty's book does a great job explaining why customers should consider adopting a green approach to their data center, the multiple ways they can achieve critical IT efficiencies that are good for the environment and save them money, and how to optimize their return on investment."

**Gregg Ambulos**, Vice President, Americas Channel Sales, EMC Corporation.

"In this book, Marty Poniatowski comprehensively discusses design considerations for the truly energy-efficient data center, achievable only through virtualization and the advanced data center automation . . ."

**Scott Davis**, Chief Data Center Architect, Office of the CTO, VMware, Inc.

"Marty Poniatowski assembles a powerful and compelling presentation for server consolidation and virtualization with detailed technical descriptions. The cost and power savings as summarized by Mr. Poniatowski are crystal clear. The entire book shows a mastery of current technology from which every CIO, Data Center Manager, and Network Administrator will benefit."

**Peter Stankov**, IT Industry Consultant

# Foundations of Green IT

# Foundations of Green IT

## Consolidation, Virtualization, Efficiency, and ROI in the Data Center

Marty Poniatowski

PRENTICE
HALL

Upper Saddle River, NJ • Boston • Indianapolis • San Francisco
New York • Toronto • Montreal • London • Munich • Paris • Madrid
Capetown • Sydney • Tokyo • Singapore • Mexico City

Many of the designations used by manufacturers and sellers to distinguish their products are claimed as trademarks. Where those designations appear in this book, and the publisher was aware of a trademark claim, the designations have been printed with initial capital letters or in all capitals.

The author and publisher have taken care in the preparation of this book, but make no expressed or implied warranty of any kind and assume no responsibility for errors or omissions. No liability is assumed for incidental or consequential damages in connection with or arising out of the use of the information or programs contained herein.

The publisher offers excellent discounts on this book when ordered in quantity for bulk purchases or special sales, which may include electronic versions and/or custom covers and content particular to your business, training goals, marketing focus, and branding interests. For more information, please contact:

U.S. Corporate and Government Sales
(800) 382-3419
corpsales@pearsontechgroup.com

For sales outside the United States please contact:

International Sales
international@pearson.com

Visit us on the Web: informit.com/ph

*Library of Congress Cataloging-in-Publication Data:*

Poniatowski, Marty.
  Foundations of green IT : consolidation, virtualization, efficiency, and ROI in the data center / Marty Poniatowski.
       p. cm.
    ISBN 978-0-13-704375-0 (pbk. : alk. paper)  1.  Information technology.  2.  Information technology—Environmental aspects.  3. Green technology.  I. Title.
    T58.5.P66 2009
    621.39028'6—dc22
                                    2009023071

ISBN-13: 978-0-137-04375-0
ISBN-10:     0-137-04375-9

Text printed in the United States on recycled paper at Courier in Stoughton, Massachusetts.
First printing August 2009

**Editor in Chief**
Karen Gettman

**Acquisitions Editor**
Jessica Goldstein

**Development Editor**
Chris Zahn

**Managing Editor**
Kristy Hart

**Senior Project Editor**
Lori Lyons

**Proofreader**
Sheri Cain

**Publishing Coordinator**
Romney French

**Cover Designer**
Alan Clements

**Senior Compositor**
Gloria Schurick

**Production Consultant**
Robert Mauhar

# Contents

**Foreword**    xiii

**Preface**    xv

What This Book Covers    xvii

About the Author    xxi

Acknowledgments  xxii

*The CDI Team    xxii*

*Mark Pohto: Microsoft    xxv*

*Permission for "Simple Power Savings and Other Green Tips"    xxvi*

**Introduction to Part I    2**

**Chapter 1  The Existing Server Environment: "The Old Way"    3**

Virtualization Considerations    3

Non-Virtualized Server Example    4

Power and Cooling    6

*HP Power and Cooling Calculator    8*

*Power and Cooling Estimate for Existing Servers    11*

*Explanation of Some Power and Cooling Factors    12*

*Virtualization Background    13*

Summary    17

**Chapter 2  Existing Server Environment Analysis with Capacity Planner    19**

Snapshot of Servers    20

Recommended Target Platform    22

Summary of Existing Servers    22

Processor Utilization Report    28

Detailed System Server Report    29

Summary    30

## Chapter 3  The Virtualized Server Environment    31

The New Server Environment    31

Assumptions    38

Blades Background    39

Performance Analysis After Virtualization    44

Summary    46

## Chapter 4  Server ROI Analysis    49

TCO for Existing and New Virtualized Environments    50

Summary    55

## Chapter 5  Virtual Server Implementation Plan    57

Blade Startup Implementation    58

Shared Storage Startup Implementation    59

VMware Startup Implementation    60

Data Replication Startup Implementation    62

VMware Site Recovery Manager Startup Implementation    63

Virtual Desktop With VMware View Startup Implementation    64

Summary    64

## Chapter 6  Desktop Virtualization    65

Desktop Virtualization Benefits Users and IT    66

Benefits of Desktop Virtualization    67

VMware View Components    68

Desktop Management    70

Desktop Virtualization Storage    72

Desktop Application Encapsulation    74

Desktop Access    75

Virtual Printing    75

Check In and Check Out of the Virtual Desktop    76

Desktop Virtualization TCO and ROI    78

Dedicated Workstation Blades    79

Benefits and Components of Workstation Blades    81

Summary    83

**Introduction to Part II    86**

**Chapter 7  The Existing Backup and Recovery Environment    87**
Existing Backup and Recovery Solution    87
Data De-Duplication    91
Archive    92
General Backup Considerations    94
    *Media    94*
    *Full Versus Incremental Backup    94*
    *Clone Versus Replication of Data    95*
    *Backup and Recovery Versus Disaster Recovery    95*
    *Distributed Backup Versus Centralized Backup    96*
Summary    97

**Chapter 8  Existing Backup and Recovery Analysis with Backup Assessment    99**
Snapshot of Backup Servers    100
Backup Client Capacity    103
Backup and Restore Job Summary    104
Recommendations for Improving the Environment    107
Summary    109

**Chapter 9  The Enhanced Backup and Recovery Solution    111**
New Disk Library Backup and Recovery Environment    112
Alternative New Backup and Recovery Environment    114
Disk Library Operation    117
Virtual Disk Library and Backup Software Implementation    125
Summary    129

**Chapter 10  Backup, Recovery, and Archive ROI Analysis    131**
TCO Summary for the New Environment    132
Five-Year Benefit Summary    133
Investment Summary    137
Return on Investment (ROI) Summary    137
Summary    140

## Chapter 11  Data Replication and Disk Technology Advancements    141

Data Replication Methods    141
   *Fabric-Based Replication    142*
   *Host-Based Replication    144*
   *Array-Based Replication    145*
Disk Technology Advancements    147
   *Disk Characteristics    148*
   *Disk Calculation Method    149*
   *Flash Disk Technology    150*
   *Total Cost of Ownership Advantages of Flash Disk    152*
   *Sample Flash Versus Fibre Channel Disk TCO Analysis    154*
Summary    156

## Introduction to Part III    158

## Chapter 12  The Existing Network Environment with Enhancements    159

Existing Network Environment Example    159
Upgrades to the Large and Small Existing Closets    161
Overview of Common Network Components    168
Cisco Operating System Overview    171
Cisco EnergyWise Technology    174
Summary    175

## Chapter 13  Existing Network Analysis with Discovery    177

Cisco Discovery Prerequisites Overview    178
Discovery Executive Summary    179
Discovery Detailed Reports    185
Software Life Cycle Legend    185
IOS Detailed Report: Software, Hardware, and Security    188
Summary    193

## Chapter 14  Voice over Internet Protocol (VoIP)    195

Telecommunications Overview    195
How Does VoIP Work?    196
How VoIP Is Different from a Traditional Phone System    199

VoIP, Green, and Cost Savings    203
   *Audio Conferencing    203*
   *Video over IP    204*
   *Data Center Consolidation    205*
   *Private Networking    208*
   *Maintenance Support Optimization    209*
   *Service Contract Optimization    210*
What's Next for VoIP?    210
Summary    211


**Introduction to Part IV    214**


**Chapter 15  SQL Server Consolidation to Achieve Green Results    215**
Opportunities    216
Initial Situation    217
Desired Situation    218
Solution Approach    218
Solution Implementation    225
Results    230
Summary    233
Resources    234


**Chapter 16  The Green Data Center    237**
Traditional Data Center    237
Rack and Air Flow History    240
High Density Racks    245
Green Data Center    248
Unstructured Data Cabling    249
Structured Data Cabling    250
Future of Data Cabling    250
Power Cabling    251
Summary    255

**Chapter 17  Cloud Computing     257**

Private Cloud Considerations     258
The Public Cloud     259
Sampling of Public Cloud Providers     262
Backup in the Cloud     266
Storage in the Cloud     269
Other Cloud Applications     270
Why Go to the Cloud?     271
Governance in the Cloud     272
Cautionary Note on Data Portability     273
Summary     273

**Chapter 18  Simple Power Savings and Other Green Tips     275**

Turn Off Your Desktop Computer     276
Some Interesting Facts     277
Some Tips for Saving Energy     277
Activate Desktop Computer Power Management to Save Energy     278
They're On Even When They're Off     282
Recycling Electronic Waste     283
Background on Electronic Waste     284
Green Printing     286
Summary     287

**Chapter 19  Managed Services: Remote Monitoring     289**

Executive Overview     290
Detailed Hardware Inventory     294
Detailed Software Inventory     298
Site Inventory     300
Site Health     303
Windows Server Health     305
Underlying Tool     307
Summary     308

**Index     309**

# Foreword

Data Centers are a significant consumer of power in the world today. The U.S. EPA estimates that 1.5% of the entire electricity consumption in the U.S. is attributable to data centers; a frequently overlooked statistic given all the uses of power in the country. The average data center is only 30% efficient, with 70% of the electricity lost due to inefficiencies of power and heat dissipation, along with powering cooling equipment.

Average per server power consumption is increasing, reflecting trends such as multicore processors, increases in memory, and packaging densities. This increase in server density is being driven by a shift in customer buying patterns from tower servers, that made up nearly all the systems sold in 1996, to rack-dense systems and mainstream adoption of blade servers today. This drive for density is a result of customers who need to add systems to support their business workloads and want to fit those systems into their current data center, versus having to buy or build a new one. The result is a 3x increase in server density at the rack level. In 1996, customers averaged 7 servers per rack, and by 2010, blade adoption will be at a level more like 20 servers per rack, with some customers having north of 60 blades in a rack. As a result, rack-level power consumption has increased eightfold.

One factor that is frequently overlooked in considering data center energy is that only half, and usually less than that, of the energy used in the data center goes toward servers and storage. The balance goes toward other uses, such as power conversion, networks, lighting, and of most importance, air conditioning. Fifty percent is for a carefully designed data center, with sealed flooring, minimum clutter under the floors, and equipment laid out for the most efficient cooling. If you get over 40%, you're well ahead of average.

Customers increasingly take a critical look at the energy footprint of the data center because they are concerned about the mounting electricity bill, or because they cannot deliver more electricity in the data center, or because of a corporate social-responsibility initiative, or because of all three.

No matter what the motivation, there is no more impactful technology for addressing the increasing power and cooling costs of modern IT infrastructures than virtualization. VMware enables data centers to decrease the electricity consumption in the data center by 70-80%. As a result, almost all IT organizations today are planning or conducting server virtualization projects. Proliferation of x86 servers is a nearly universal problem in data centers for several reasons. Today's applications are divided into many cooperating components or tiers. Prior to virtualization, each software tier ran on dedicated systems. Factor in application development, test, and staging needs, and the net is data center racks filled with servers running average CPU utilization in the 5-15% range with power and cooling capacity being stretched to their limits.

From the time VMware released its first server products, they were put to use immediately in server-consolidation projects by its customers, with impressive results. Now, with VMware vSphere 4.0, the 100% virtualized data center is here, capable of handling the most mission-critical workloads on virtual machines. It is common to find 30-40 virtual machines on a single multicore server. The net result is accomplishing the same workloads with an order of magnitude fewer servers to power, cool, and house. The encapsulation and separation of virtual machines from the underlying physical hardware with VMware delivers a flexible, dynamic environment with many additional operational efficiencies, including business continuity, rapid provisioning, automation, and standardized operating procedures.

In this book, Marty Poniatowski comprehensively discusses design considerations for the truly energy-efficient data center, achievable only through virtualization and the advanced data center-automation capabilities of VMware vSphere 4.0.

Scott Davis
Chief Data Center Architect
Office of the CTO
VMware, Inc.

# Preface

It's time to think about efficiency in Information Technology from a global standpoint. This means looking at all technologies in the data center and how they can be made more efficient, including the data centers themselves. This panoramic view is what I cover in *Foundations of Green IT: Consolidation, Virtualization, Efficiency, and ROI in the Data Center.*

Although all firms are looking at green and efficiency to varying degrees, what are the real compelling reasons to take on green-related work? I cover some interesting facts from a variety of groups that will shed some light on the reasons you must be considering improving efficiency in your IT environment.

IDC researched the following compelling reasons for consolidation virtualization:

- For every dollar spent on hardware, 50 cents is spent on power and cooling. This number has increased consistently over the last several years, and this is no doubt one of the primary drivers for virtualization and consolidation.

- The average data center is 52% utilized and 1/3 of data centers are approaching maximum floor space capacity.

- The average rack is 56% utilized and the 1/3 of data centers are approaching maximum rack space density.

The #1 challenge in the data center is power and cooling. The following is IDC's list of data center challenges. Take note of where "technology" resides in this list:

1. Power and cooling

2. Availability/redundancy/DR

3. Space/space planning/size limitations

4. Cost/budgets

5. Growth/change

6. Staffing/qualified staff

7. Maintenance

8. Security

9. Technology

10. Compete with offshoring/outsourcing

The following are some power and cooling-related facts:

• Power and cooling shortages cause server or storage downtime in 49% of data centers.

• According to American Power Conversion (APC), server and storage consume 50% of power and air conditioning consumes 34% of power.

• According to McKinsey, deploying virtualization saves 25-30% of power.

• According to the Department of Energy (DOE) data center electricity has doubled since 2000, costing about $4.1billion.

•

The #1 IT business goal is to reduce costs. The following list summarizes IDC's business goals:

1. Reduce costs

2. Improve customer satisfaction

3. Increase revenue

4. Improve quality/accuracy

5. Increase market share

6. Speed time to market

To those of us involved in IT the cost reduction objective is not a surprise. Every client with which I work is focused on reducing cost. At the time of this writing it is clear that a positive Return on Investment (ROI) is required to proceed with any new IT initiative.

All of these facts ring true based on my daily contact with clients grappling with all things "green" including reducing power and cooling, reducing floor space, planning and implementing consolidation and virtualization, and many such topics.

There is a true "green" benefit to all the efficiencies covered in this book. Greenhouse gas emissions (GHG,) related to carbon footprint, are greatly reduced when power and cooling are reduced as a result of improved when IT efficiency. It makes both business and environmental sense to implement mainstream IT efficiency in the areas I cover in this book.

I address the key topics related to "green" technology trends in this book and give you a plan in many key areas to embark on savings for your company.

## What This Book Covers

The following parts are covered in *Foundations of Green IT:*

**Part I: Server Consolidation.** Server consolidation with VMware and HP blades is mainstream to say the least. All my clients are either performing server consolidation or thinking about it. This part contains chapters on the following topics for an example client case study:

- Chapter 1 is an overview of the existing environment with server sprawl. The analysis includes a detailed power and cooling consumption overview of the environment that contains 134 existing servers.

- Chapter 2 is the VMware *Capacity Planner* analysis that includes information on the existing environment, including details on the existing servers, consolidating candidates, and recommended target-consolidation blade configurations.

- Chapter 3 is the new environment with all its additional efficiencies, including 134 servers consolidated to 12 blades, 1/10 the power and cooling, and a miniscule footprint compared to the original servers.

- Chapter 4 is a description of the Return on Investment (ROI) produced as part of *Capacity Planner.* This output has a LOT of detail, so I cover the high points of ROI. As you might expect, going from 134 to 12 servers has a compelling ROI associated with it.

- Chapter 5 is an overview of the implementation plan to make the proposed environment operational. The huge reduction in servers and physical-to-virtual implementation is not trivial and requires a detailed plan. Included is an overall solution plan that includes servers, shared storage (which is often a new component in a virtualized environment,) data replication, and other topics.

- Chapter 6 is an overview of virtual desktop solutions. There are various options for desktops, including a blade shared by many low-end users and dedicated workstation blades for high-end users, such as traders or architects. This area is becoming hot because of the high ROI typically associated with desktop virtualization and blade workstations.

**Part II: Backup, Recovery, and Archive (BURA).** Almost all backup environments on which I work have serious operational efficiencies. Most backup environments grow over time, which means that what was a good backup solution for a few clients has grown in to a marginal backup environment for a lot of clients. This part contains chapters on the following topics for an example client case study:

- Chapter 7 is an overview of the existing backup and recovery environment with many operational inefficiencies, including local tape drives on application servers for local, rather than centralized backup. Some background on technologies are included in this chapter, such as de-duplication, which can reduce backup capacity requirements by 90% or more! Archive background is also covered.

- Chapter 8 covers an EMC *Backup Assessment Using Quick Scripts* (called *Backup Assessment* in this book) that includes the details on the existing environment, including details on the longest backups, incomplete backups, failed restores, and other valuable backup information.

- Chapter 9 is the new backup environment with all its additional efficiencies, including disk libraries for backup rather than tape. Disk libraries look like tape drives to the backup software, but back up and restore in a fraction of the time of tape and employs de-duplication technology. An alternative environment using disk backup technology is ideally suited for a virtualized environment is presented as well.

- Chapter 9 is an overview of the implementation plan to make the proposed backup and recovery environment operational. Going from local tape drives to the disk library-based solution is complex and requires a comprehensive plan. This implementation plan gives you an idea of the key steps required as part of the plan.

- Chapter 10 is a description of the Return on Investment (ROI) produced along with the *Backup Assessment.* This output has a LOT of detail in it, so I cover the high points and assumptions used in the ROI. The numbers in this ROI are compelling and are based entirely on the input provided to the ROI tool. Even if these ROI numbers are reduced by 50%, they are still compelling and have resulted in my clients taking action on their outdated backup environments.

- Chapter 11 is an overview of replication technologies as well as advanced disk technologies. Replication is a key component in disaster recovery and high availability planning, so I cover these misunderstood technologies. Additional storage topics are discussed, including advancements in storage technology that have led to greatly reduced power consumption and massive green improvements. Disk technology is one of the most prominent areas of improvement.

**Part III: Networking.** Many networking environments have grown over time and are comprised of a lot of inefficient electronics. The operating systems running on the networking components have not been upgraded over time, and have security holes in them and other problems. This section covers evaluating an old networking environment and transforming it into a more efficient and modern solution and includes the following chapters:

- Chapter 12 is an overview of the existing network environment and background information on networking. The case study, on which the Cisco *Discovery* will be run in the next chapter, is a retail firm with a large distributed network. The background information covers various network concepts, such as an overview of network types, network terms, and other background-related topics that are important to understand before *Discovery* is run. Enhancements to this existing environment are presented, showing power and floor space savings while at the same time greatly enhancing the functionality of the environment. An overview of various green networking initiatives that can be deployed to save energy and power, such as telepresence, which reduces travel, and power monitoring of networking and other electronics.

- Chapter 13 is a detailed report on the *Discovery* output. The report includes a summary of devices based on operating system (*IOS* and *CatOS,*) and overview of security alerts that apply to networking electronics, where the networking components stand with respect to their lifecycle such as end-of-life, end-of-support, and other outputs from the analysis.

- Chapter 14 covers Voice over Internet Protocol (VoIP). This technology has many green overtones, which are presented in the chapter. This is a widely misunderstood technology.

**Part IV: General Green Topics.** The first three parts thoroughly covered server consolidation, backup, and networking, respectively. This part covers important, but different, green topics such as the following:

- Chapter 15 covers SQL Server consolidation techniques. Like server sprawl, many organizations have grown their SQL Server environments by continually adding servers and SQL Server instances. This chapter is based on the article *Green IT in Practice: SQL Server Consolidation in Microsoft IT* that appeared in the Microsoft publication written by Mark Pohto of Microsoft. This chapter is a fascinating case study of the techniques Microsoft IT uses to consolidate thousands of SQL Server instances.

- Chapter 16 covers Cloud computing, which means something different to everyone. I provide an overview of private cloud computing and a sampling of cloud solutions, including an HP print solution, that is mainstream as well as some emerging cloud applications that may play a role in your data center.

- Chapter 17 covers data center design techniques that play a big role in green computing. I focus on both proven techniques used by my firm to design and deploy data centers for our clients as well as emerging green techniques that are being considered for advanced data centers.

- Chapter 18 covers a product that continually monitors and reports on a small IT installation. Smaller businesses often don't have enough dedicated IT staff to monitor their environments so this is an ideal solution.

- Chapter 19 covers simple green techniques that can be implemented in the office and at home. This chapter is based on an APC Corp paper. These simple techniques are often overlooked in lieu of advanced techniques covered in earlier chapters, but they play an important role. Among the topics discussed in this chapter is power being consumed when devices are off and recycling e-waste.

Although everyone is thinking about the green data center, my experience, from having worked with hundreds of clients over the years, is that efficiency is usually addressed on a single-technology basis. This means that technology efficiencies are improved in a serial manner rather than looking at all the technologies in a holistic manner. I bring all the major technologies together in this book while using a lot of manufacturer analysis tools. The end result is a broad look at improving technology while using mainstream tools.

The key aspects of this book are the tools provided by manufacturer partners. These tools provide substantial detail on specific technologies and often include ROI information and recommendations on improvements to the environment. In several cases, I include an output from these assessment tools.

## About the Author

**Marty Poniatowski** is the Chief Technology Officer managing all pre-sales and consulting technical experts at Computer Design and Integration LLC. Marty leads the Professional Services Group that includes numerous practices that perform project-related consulting as well as staff augmentation. The pre-sales team of experts craft complex solutions for customers using the latest available technologies.

Marty is responsible not only for the teams he manages but also keeping abreast of all industry trends and technologies. *Foundations of Green IT: Consolidation, Virtualization, Efficiency, and ROI in the Data Center* was written in conjunction with many members of Marty's technical staff. This book covers all key technologies that CDI implements in client environments, including many key assessments that result in a quick ROI.

Prior to joining CDI, Marty was a Principal Solution Architect and a published author with Hewlett-Packard Company for 20 years in the New York area. He has worked with hundreds of Hewlett-Packard customers in many industries, including financial services, pharmaceutical, health care, media and entertainment, consulting services, Internet startups, and manufacturing.

Marty began his career as an Electrical Design Engineer on military computer systems at United Technologies Corporation. He performed numerous designs in this position, including his first chip-level design.

Before joining HP, Marty was the manager of a design group at startup Canaan Computer Corporation. Marty performed chip and board level computer design and managed the design group in this position.

Marty has been widely published in computer industry trade publications, including over 50 articles on various computer-related topics. He is also the author of 16 Prentice-Hall and one self-published book on computer-related topics.

Marty holds an M.S. in Information Systems from New York University (NYU) Polytechnic Institute (NY, NY), an M.S. in Management from the University of Bridgeport (Bridgeport, CT), and a B.S. in Electrical Engineering from Roger Williams University (Bristly, RI).

# Acknowledgments

So many people were involved in helping me with this book that it is impossible to list each and every one. I have, therefore, decided to formally thank those who wrote material for this book and those who took time to review it. I'm still not sure whether it takes more time to write something or review something that has been written to ensure that it is correct.

## The CDI Team

Many of my CDI colleagues contributed to chapters and sections of this book. This endeavor was company-wide, and I acknowledge some of the key contributors; however, many other CDI experts contributed in a variety of capacities. The following members of the CDI team were instrumental in producing this book:

- Michael St. Amour is a Solutions Architect at CDI, responsible for translating client business needs into efficient, reliable, and scalable technical solutions. Michael is certified in a host of technologies, including HP, EMC, VMware, Microsoft, and Cisco Systems. Prior to joining CDI,

Michael was a Systems Engineer and Solution Architect at Compaq and HP in the New York area. Earlier in his career, he held IT management positions in health care, financial, retail distribution, and transportation companies, managing the groups that designed, planned, implemented, and supported complex IT infrastructures. He also provided independent consulting expertise to over 80 companies across a wide range of industries. With both a business background and years of technical training and expertise, Michael brings a wealth of real-world understanding to his clients, understanding their concerns related to budgets, risk, regulations, scalability, reliability, and accountability.

- George Gosselin is CDI's Chief Network and Data Center Architect, responsible for working with clients to develop connectivity and security requirements. Using those requirements, George designs a LAN/WAN solution that meets the availability, scalability, performance, and budgetary requirement of his clients. In addition to designing networks, George has developed data center designs that include rack layouts, power distribution designs, airflow analysis, and modular structured cabling, allowing for data centers that are also highly scalable and ready to accommodate the rapid changes that occur in today's IT environments. While at CDI, George has developed solutions for hundreds of clients ranging from mid-size businesses to large global corporations found in Fortune 500. Prior to the current role as Chief Architect, George was the Director of networking and data center solutions, responsible for managing the CDI consulting staff surrounding these technologies. Before joining CDI, George held consulting and managerial positions with large enterprise corporations and IT consulting firms. With over 20 years of IT experience, George is an expert in defining client needs and developing solutions to satisfy those requirements.

- William Chin is a Technical Team Lead at CDI, specializing in virtualization technologies. He has over 12 years of experience working in the Information Technology field ranging from large-scale enterprise systems on mainframe, midrange, server and desktop systems. William's focus at CDI is on the intelligent and automated management of IT for its customers, specifically surrounding systems and applications management, configuration management, provisioning and virtualization of systems and applications. He is a graduate of New York University.

- Charles T. Brown III started his IT career with Ingersoll-Rand almost 30 years ago. Charlie began integrating the first generation of distributed networks from Novell and Microsoft with Centralized Systems, such as the

IBM System 36, 38 and AS400. After spending a few years with manufacturing firms and in the food-distribution industry as an independent consultant, Charlie developed a wide range of experience and skills focused on integrating multiple variants of UNIX systems, Windows-based networks, and the data they produce. Charlie then joined CDI, focusing on protecting data. He has also assisted numerous clients with forensic data analysis and recovery of backup data, and email retention and recovery for use in court litigation. He is now the Storage Solutions Architect for CDI and is involved in designing tomorrow's data protection solutions. Charlie earned his Bachelor of Arts Degree in Management 1983, and a Bachelor of Science Degree in Computer Science 1986, both from Moravian College, in Bethlehem, PA.

- Steven Klauz is a CDI consultant with skills in both traditional and IP telephony. Some of Steven's previous employment consists of Pfizer, Johnson & Johnson, Tiffany & Co, and Lord and Taylor. Steven's skill set consists of telecommunications and network engineering for IPT, switched and dedicated services, Contact Center ACD/CTI systems and solutions, Voice Messaging and Networking, Video conferencing system design and implementation, Domestic and International communications and services. He also has project management experience with IT infrastructure and networking systems worldwide, including projects varied from major construction initiatives to minor facility renovations, designing and establishing data centers, implementing warehouse and distribution centers, a television production studio and various CRM/Contact Center implementations.

- Michael Johnson is a Senior Solutions Architect with CDI. He has over 15 years of experience in Information Technology, including Microsoft, VMware, and a variety of storage systems. Michael has worked in the health care, manufacturing, and aviation industries before joining CDI. He is a graduate of the University of Southern Maine.

- David A. Weinstein began his IT career in 1989 in IT Operations with Telephone Credit Union in NH, while obtaining his B.S. in Computer Information Systems at New Hampshire College. Dave then relocated to the NYC area and joined Paragon Federal Credit Union as its Network Administrator, responsible for the design, installation, and management of all LAN and WAN networks. He then became the MIS Manager, responsible for the MIS Department. Over the next six years, Dave managed the MIS Department and was promoted to the VP of Information Systems and Technology. While working at Paragon Federal Credit

Union, Dave attended executive management training at the University of Wisconsin, Madison and completed his M.S. in Computer Science from Long Island University. In 1997, Dave accepted a position at Computer Design and Integration LLC (CDI) as a Technical Consultant. In 1999, Dave left CDI to work for Sun Microsystems, Inc. as a Systems Engineer. His responsibilities included, but were not limited to, solutions architecture, partner relationship management, and project management. In 2002, Dave returned to CDI as VP of Solutions Architecture. His current position at CDI is a Strategic Business Consultant, where his responsibilities and expertise continue in storage and server solutions architecture.

- Don Quoos is a Pre-Sales Solutions Architect at CDI. He has 20 years of experience in the Information Technology field with specific skills in systems engineering and sales. Before CDI, Don worked for Network Associates (Network General), Fluke Networks, Internet Security Systems, Cantor Fitzgerald, Kidder Peabody, and Unisys. His skill set consists of network engineering for Cisco-related products and CDI's IT Diagnosis Managed Services offering. Don is a graduate of DeVry Technical Institute.

- Kyle Mullin is a Technical Consultant at CDI with experience in systems development, application integration, and systems management of various Windows and Linux environments. He has hands-on experience in programming and scripting for C++, Java, Verilog HDL, and shell. He has hardware support experience on HP, IBM, Dell, and Gateway systems and servers. Prior to joining CDI, Kyle gained experience as an independent consultant by implementing Windows-based solutions for the medical and legal professions. He also ran his own internet game-server hosting company in 2003. Kyle is a graduate of The College of New Jersey with a Bachelor of Science in Computer Engineering.

- John Pettegrew is a Technical Consultant for CDI. John runs the help desk and customer support area of Managed Services and proactively monitors all clients. John attended New Jersey Institute of Technology (NJIT) and Bergen Community College.

## Mark Pohto: Microsoft

The SQL Server consolidation chapter is based on the article "Green IT in Practice: SQL Server Consolidation in Microsoft IT" that appeared in the Microsoft publication *The Architecture Journal* (www.architecturejournal.net) written by Mark. Special thanks go to Mark for collaborating on the formulation of the chapter and for providing permission for the use of the chapter.

Mark is a Senior Systems Engineer in Microsoft IT. Mark has worked in IT since 1987 and has a strong passion for leadership and database technologies. He joined Microsoft's Redmond Platform Services team in 1999. His diverse experience and education includes language training at the DoD Defense Language Institute, several years in the intelligence community, U.S. Army Officer training, and MIS training at Our Lady of the Lake University in San Antonio, Texas.

At Microsoft, he has worked as a senior DBA in the Database Operations Group and has managed the team responsible for application monitoring using Microsoft Operations Manager. He developed and published the automation tools used for database administration and has contributed to the books *SQL Server 2000 High Availability* and *Pro SQL Server 2005 High Availability* by Allan Hirt.

As the group manager for the Microsoft SQL Server Center of Excellence, Mark managed the team that developed SQL Server solutions, such as the Risk Assessment Program and Service Level Monitoring and the SQL Server Microsoft Certified Architect program.

He has taught architecture in programs for Exchange Server, Windows Server, and SQL Server. Mark recently returned to Microsoft IT to lead an IT-wide SQL Server consolidation project.

Jimmy May, Microsoft IT senior performance engineer, and Ward Pond, Microsoft Services technology architect, also contributed to the article on which the SQL Server consolidation chapter was based.

## Permission for "Simple Power Savings and Other Green Tips"

Chapter 18, "Simple Power Savings and Other Green Tips," is based on material that APC gave me permission to use in this book. Chris Mote of APC helped get permission for me to use the APC paper titled "Go Green, Save Green The Benefits of Eco-Friendly Computing."

# Part I
# Server Virtualization and Optimization

**Chapter 1: The Existing Server Environment: "The Old Way"**

**Chapter 2: Existing Server Environment Analysis with Capacity Planner**

**Chapter 3: The Virtualized Server Environment**

**Chapter 4: Server ROI Analysis**

**Chapter 5: Virtual Server Implementation Plan**

**Chapter 6: Desktop Virtualization**

# Introduction to Part I

Part I covers server virtualization by analyzing an existing non-virtualized environment to a virtualized environment. I cover the following topics in separate chapters going through the process of virtualizing an environment:

- Analysis of a non-virtualized environment which includes a power and cooling analysis of the existing environment and some background on virtualization.
- Example of a VMware *Capacity Planner* output and its findings
- Analysis of a proposed virtualized environment, including power and cooling improvements.
- An overview of an ROI analysis comparing the non-virtualized and virtualized environments.
- Implementation plan example to ensure the environment is properly implemented with minimal impact on the environment.
- Performance analysis with the Akorri BalancePoint tool.
- Virtual desktop and thin-client considerations, including alternatives.

In these chapters, you find a complete overview of the virtualization process and what you can expect when you embark on this process in your environment.

Although there are many options for virtualization, I cover VMware, which is by far the market leader and represents the vast majority of the projects in which I've been involved.

# Chapter 1

# The Existing Server Environment: "The Old Way"

This chapter covers several topics related to server virtualization, including the following:

- Some general considerations on virtualization
- An example of a non-virtualized environment that acts as the basis for the case study in this section
- A detailed power and cooling overview
- Background on virtualization

The next section covers virtualization considerations, including existing inefficiencies in most environments and what you can expect after virtualization.

## Virtualization Considerations

I've heard every imaginable anecdote about the ways in which countless Industry Standard Servers (ISS), also known as x86 servers, have proliferated in the data center. One customer described them as being like rabbits and multiplying daily. In the end, there are just too many inefficiencies having racks and racks of ISS, including the following:

- Too many ISS consume valuable floor and rack space.
- Each old server consumes as much as 1,000 watts of power as you'll see in the example.
- Each old server can produce as much as over 3,000 BTU/hr, as you'll see in the example.
- Deploying a new server for a new application requires procuring the server, installing the hardware, and then loading the image.
- The weight of many old and inefficient servers imposes requirements of excessive floor strength and careful positioning of equipment.
- Each server requires cabling for power, monitor, keyboard, mouse, networking, LAN, SAN, management, and possibly multiple cables for redundancy.

With these inefficiencies in mind, what can you expect from a virtualized environment? The following are some of the impacts you can expect from virtualization:

- Fewer physical servers to manage
- Fast deployment of new virtual servers, which does not require procuring a new server
- Greatly reduced power consumption with fewer servers
- Greatly reduced cooling requirements with fewer servers
- Greatly reduced floor and rack space and associated weight concerns

These and many other topics are covered in this chapter.

# Non-Virtualized Server Example

This section covers a modest sized client with a non-virtualized environment. Like most non-virtualized environments, this installation possesses a lot of the characteristics of "server sprawl," including the list presented earlier.

Figure 1-1 is a simplified depiction of the non-virtualized environment.

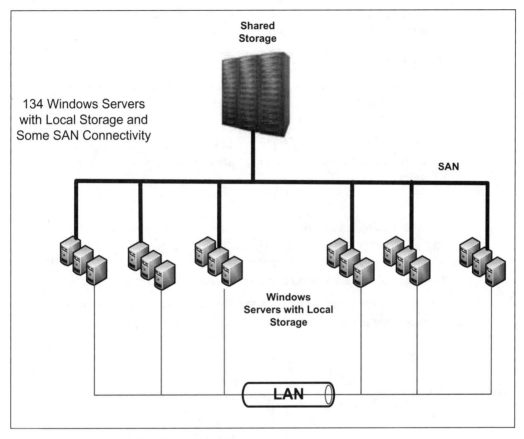

Figure 1-1    Non-Virtualized Environment

Although shared storage, shown in the figure, the vast majority of storage is directly connected or internal to individual servers. The good news is that the existing Storage Area Network (SAN) can be expanded when the server environment is virtualized.

Not all the servers shown in Figure 1-1 will be virtualized. Many applications are not considered good virtualization candidates for a variety of reasons when the virtualization analysis is performed, including the following:

- High processor and memory utilization, indicating the server may already be running efficiently and does not need to be virtualized.

- High I/O utilization on database applications, although many virtualization providers are working to change this perception and virtualize more applications that historically would have had I/O demands considered too high to virtualize.

- Unique dedicated I/O, such as fax boards.

- More than four network interface cards are active on the server.

- The server is used for physical tape backup.

- There are more than eight physical processors (at the time of this writing, eight processors are supported by some virtualization providers).

In this environment, as with most in which I've worked, the vast majority of servers can be virtualized, but there may be a few that for these, and other reasons, are best left unvirtualized. In some cases, however, after pass two takes place, these servers are sometimes virtualized as well.

I now perform some analysis on the existing environment to expose its inefficiencies compared to the virtualized design covered in Chapter 3.

# Power and Cooling

One of the most significant areas of savings when virtualizing is power and cooling, but getting specific numbers on existing and new servers can be elusive. HP has a tool for calculating the power of all servers. For the new servers I plan to deploy, power can be calculated to the watt. For the old non-HP servers to be replaced in this example, I use power estimate calculations of old HP servers and assume this is close to the power consumed by the old non-HP servers I am replacing. There are a lot of old one-and-two processor servers, so I calculate the power for both, such HP servers. Figure 1-2 is a screen shot from the HP Power Calculator, but there are a lot of servers in the tool, so it shows only the beginning of the list.

Revision 1.48

# Power Calculator Links

| | Power Calculator | Revision Number | Size | Revision Date |
|---|---|---|---|---|
| **Blade PC** | | | | |
| | BC1500-2500 | 0.09 | 3.01 MB | 8/23/2007 |
| **ProLiant DL Servers** | | | | |
| | DL140 | 0.02 | 124 KB | 12/15/2003 |
| | DL140G2 | 0.01 | 153 KB | 6/20/2005 |
| | DL140G3 | 0.10 | 244 KB | 10/04/2007 |
| | DL145 | 0.22 | 106 KB | 9/30/2004 |
| | DL145 G2 | 0.05 | 189 KB | 3/15/2006 |
| | DL145G3 | 0.02 | 185 KB | 2/12/2007 |
| | DL160G5 | 0.05 | 194 KB | 10/23/2008 |
| | DL160G5p | 0.01 | 237 KB | 11/13/2008 |
| | DL165 G5 | 0.04 | 229 KB | 11/20/2008 |
| | DL180 | 0.01 | 452 KB | 7/10/2007 |
| | DL180G5 | 0.05 | 229 KB | 10/23/2008 |
| | DL185G5 | 0.05 | 201 KB | 11/20/2008 |
| | DL320 | 0.5 | 105 KB | 5/21/2003 |
| | DL320 G2 | 0.4 | 142 KB | 9/04/2003 |
| | DL320 G3 | 0.01 | 188 KB | 6/01/2005 |
| | DL320 G4 | 0.01 | 294 KB | 12/05/2005 |

Figure 1-2    HP Power Calculator Showing Beginning of List

Because of the immense popularity of blades and high-end servers for consolidation, the HP Power Calculator tool also includes these products, which I use in an upcoming power analysis. This list of servers changes often, so I download the updated power calculator often. You can download the power calculator from the following URL:

**http://h30099.www3.hp.com/configurator/calc/Power%20Calculator%20Catalog.xls**

## HP Power and Cooling Calculator

The HP Power Calculator can estimate power for both old and new servers. Although I'm replacing non-HP servers, I can use the Power Calculator to give me an estimate of the power and cooling used by the old non-HP servers. I know the generation processor in the old servers and can "map" the old non-HP servers to old HP servers.

Figure 1-3 shows the Power Calculator output for the DL360, which has similar specifications to one of the existing installed servers.

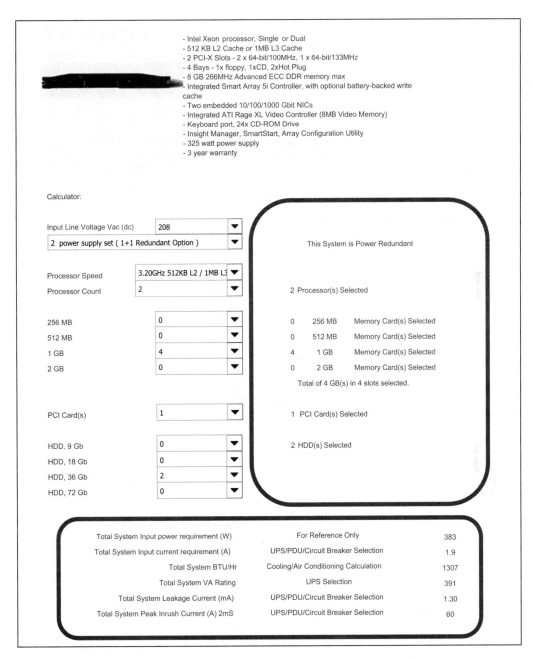

- Intel Xeon processor, Single or Dual
- 512 KB L2 Cache or 1MB L3 Cache
- 2 PCI-X Slots - 2 x 64-bit/100MHz, 1 x 64-bit/133MHz
- 4 Bays - 1x floppy, 1xCD, 2xHot Plug
- 8 GB 266MHz Advanced ECC DDR memory max
- Integrated Smart Array 5i Controller, with optional battery-backed write cache
- Two embedded 10/100/1000 Gbit NICs
- Integrated ATI Rage XL Video Controller (8MB Video Memory)
- Keyboard port, 24x CD-ROM Drive
- Insight Manager, SmartStart, Array Configuration Utility
- 325 watt power supply
- 3 year warranty

Calculator:

| | | |
|---|---|---|
| Input Line Voltage Vac (dc) | 208 | ▼ |
| 2 power supply set ( 1+1 Redundant Option ) | | ▼ |

This System is Power Redundant

| | | |
|---|---|---|
| Processor Speed | 3.20GHz 512KB L2 / 1MB L3 | ▼ |
| Processor Count | 2 | ▼ |

2 Processor(s) Selected

| | | |
|---|---|---|
| 256 MB | 0 | ▼ |
| 512 MB | 0 | ▼ |
| 1 GB | 4 | ▼ |
| 2 GB | 0 | ▼ |

| | | |
|---|---|---|
| 0 | 256 MB | Memory Card(s) Selected |
| 0 | 512 MB | Memory Card(s) Selected |
| 4 | 1 GB | Memory Card(s) Selected |
| 0 | 2 GB | Memory Card(s) Selected |

Total of 4 GB(s) in 4 slots selected.

| | | |
|---|---|---|
| PCI Card(s) | 1 | ▼ |

1 PCI Card(s) Selected

| | | |
|---|---|---|
| HDD, 9 Gb | 0 | ▼ |
| HDD, 18 Gb | 0 | ▼ |
| HDD, 36 Gb | 2 | ▼ |
| HDD, 72 Gb | 0 | ▼ |

2 HDD(s) Selected

| | | |
|---|---|---|
| Total System Input power requirement (W) | For Reference Only | 383 |
| Total System Input current requirement (A) | UPS/PDU/Circuit Breaker Selection | 1.9 |
| Total System BTU/Hr | Cooling/Air Conditioning Calculation | 1307 |
| Total System VA Rating | UPS Selection | 391 |
| Total System Leakage Current (mA) | UPS/PDU/Circuit Breaker Selection | 1.30 |
| Total System Peak Inrush Current (A) 2mS | UPS/PDU/Circuit Breaker Selection | 60 |

Figure 1-3    HP Power Calculator Output for DL360 G3 "Old Server"

This output shows all the key parameters I care about related to power, including 383 watts, 1.9 amps, and 1307 BTU/hr at 208 volts.

Figure 1-4 shows the Power Calculator output for the DL360 G4 for comparison purposes.

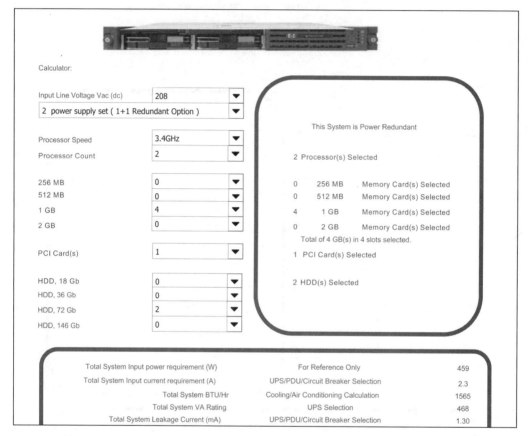

Figure 1-4    HP Power Calculator Output for DL360 G4 "Old Server"

This output shows all the key parameters I care about related to power, including 459 watts, 2.3 amps, and 1565 BTU/hr at 208 volts.

Using this technique I can come up with power and cooling estimates for all the old non-HP servers in the following section for all the servers that will be included in the virtualized environment.

## Power and Cooling Estimate for Existing Servers

Using the HP Power Calculator covered in the previous section, I produce power estimates for all the old non-HP servers. Table 1-1 shows the model and generation of old HP server that I'm using as an estimate for old non-HP servers.

**Table 1-1**   Power and Cooling Breakdown of 134 Old Servers

| Model and Generation | Qty | Watts | Total Watts | Amps | Total Amps | BTU/hr | BTU Total |
|---|---|---|---|---|---|---|---|
| DL360 G3 | 24 | 383 | 9192 | 1.9 | 45.6 | 1307 | 3168 |
| DL360 G4 | 36 | 459 | 16524 | 2.3 | 82.2 | 1565 | 56340 |
| DL360 G5 | 12 | 428 | 5136 | 2.2 | 26.4 | 1461 | 17532 |
| DL360 G5 | 28 | 505 | 14140 | 2.5 | 70 | 1723 | 48244 |
| DL380 G3 | 16 | 559 | 8944 | 2.7 | 43.2 | 1906 | 30496 |
| DL380 G4 | 10 | 459 | 4580 | 2.3 | 23 | 1563 | 15630 |
| DL380 G5 | 6 | 779 | 4674 | 3.8 | 22.8 | 2656 | 15936 |
| DL380 G2 | 2 | 1043 | 2086 | 5.1 | 10.2 | 3557 | 7114 |
| **Total** | **134** | | **65276** | | **324** | | **222660** |

There is a tremendous amount of useful information in Table 1-1 which was easy to calculate using the HP Power Calculator tool. Most of my customers have accumulated servers over time and have never taken the time to produce this easy calculation. These numbers are invaluable when it comes to determining the power and cooling required for your data center.

Chapter 3 covers the new design and its power and cooling requirements and provides the shocking results of the amount of power and cooling that can be saved in a consolidated environment.

## Explanation of Some Power and Cooling Factors

Although there is a lot of interest in power and cooling, not everyone understands watts and British Thermal Units (BTUs).

The amount of power a device turns into work is a watt. For electrical power, a watt is equal to roughly the amps times voltage. This power produces heat, which in turn requires cooling. This is the reason you want to minimize the amount of power electronics consume. The following equations determine watts and kilowatt hours:

**voltage (volts) x current (amps) = power (watts)**

**watts x time = kilowatt hour        (1,000 watts x 1 hour = 1kilowatt)**

There is a fixed cost associated with each kilowatt hour that is a key assumption when cost calculations are made in upcoming chapters. For the specific virtualization example in this chapter a cost of ten cents per kilowatt hour, which is generally considered low, is used.

To cool after heat is produced by power, the BTU determines the cooling capacity of a system. To determine the BTU required to cool, the following equation is used:

**BTU/hr = watts x 3.41**

If you know the watts consumed by a server, then BTUs are easy to calculate. Air-conditioning equipment is usually defined in terms of the ability of the equipment to cool tons of ice, as defined in the following equation:

**1 ton of cooling = 12,000 BTU/hr**

For more information on the HP Power Calculator and related topics see the following URLs:

HP Power Calculator Catalog
**http://h30099.www3.hp.com/configurator/powercalcs.asp**
or
 **www.hp.com/go/bladesystem/powercalculator**

HP UPS and PDU Sizer
**http://www.upssizer.com/**
All the material covered in this chapter related to power and Power Distribution Units (PDUs) is used in sizing, which is covered in this URL.

HP Rack and Power Products
**http://h18004.www1.hp.com/products/servers/platforms/rackandpower.html**
A key design factor when laying out servers and blades are the PDUs, which is covered in this URL.

HP Site Preparation Utility
**http://h30099.www3.hp.com/configurator/calc/Site%20Preparation%20Utility.XLS**

# Virtualization Background

The existing environment covered in this chapter will be consolidated with a virtualized environment. This section covers some background on virtualization, which acts as the foundation for the efficient environment covered in upcoming chapters.

Virtualization is a proven software technology that greatly reduces the number of servers required to run applications. Today's Industry Standard Servers (ISS), often called x86 or x64 servers, have become so powerful and fast that few single applications can fully utilize a server's resources. Virtualization allows you to create many virtual servers (machines) that run on a single physical ISS while sharing the resources of the physical server across the multiple virtual machines. The virtual machines can run different operating systems and host different applications while remaining completely independent of the operating systems and applications on the other virtual machines.

Several virtualization solutions are available. Some examples of the most commonly used are VMware, Citrix Xen, and Microsoft's Hyper-V. Because VMware is the most widely known and implemented, the virtualized solution presented in this book is based on VMware technology.

VMware ESX is the foundation for running numerous virtual machines on a singe server. ESX virtualizes the hardware resources of a physical server so those resources can be shared by numerous virtual machines. The server resources virtualized by ESX include the processor, memory, hard disk, and network controller. The result is a fully functional virtual machine that can run its own operating system and applications, just like a physical computer. Figure 1-5 shows a high-level depiction of ESX.

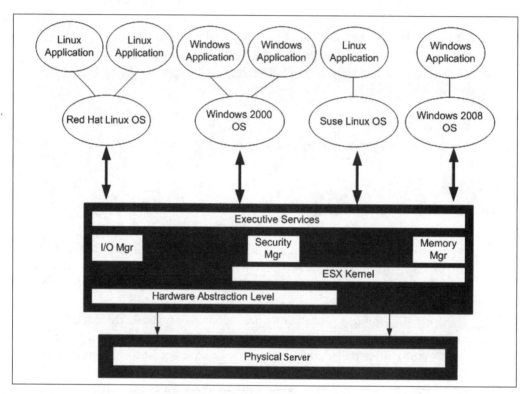

Figure 1-5     VMware Server Layout

VMware virtualization works by inserting a thin layer of software directly on a host operating system. This contains a virtual machine monitor or "hypervisor" that allocates hardware resources dynamically and transparently. Multiple operating systems run concurrently on a single physical server and share hardware resources with each other. By encapsulating an entire machine, including processor, memory, operating system, and network devices, a virtual machine is completely compatible with all standard server operating systems, applications, and device drivers. You can safely run several operating systems and applications at the same time on a single computer with each having access to the resources it needs when it needs them.

Figure 1-6 shows shared storage in a virtualized environment.

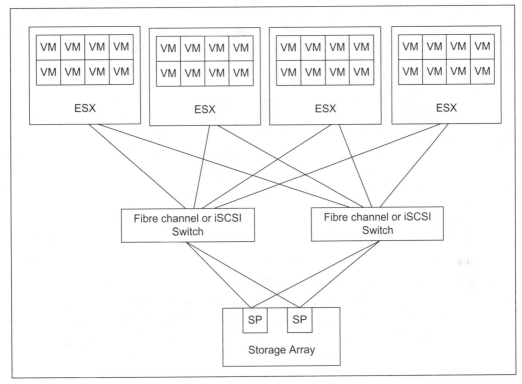

Figure 1-6    VMware Shared Storage

Figure 1-6 shows multiple physical servers running ESX at the top of the diagram. Each ESX host has eight virtual machines running in them. The middle of the figure shows two switches connected to the servers for redundancy purposes. The bottom of the figure shows the shared storage with two Storage Processors (SP) for redundancy. This shared storage setup facilities numerous advanced virtualization capabilities, including the movement of virtual machines from one server to another.

One common concern with virtualization in general is that you're now running a lot of applications on only physical server. Consider a case where one physical server is running ten virtual machines. Despite that server having all redundant hardware, it is still a single point of failure. If the server were to fail, so do all ten virtual machines. Although this may be acceptable for a development or acceptance environment, it would never suffice for true production servers.

VMware solves this problem with Virtual Infrastructure (VI). VI takes resource sharing to an expanded level by combining multiple ESX servers into clusters that allow virtual machines to move from one host to another to maximize resources and provide for high availability. At the core of VI is shared storage or a storage array. A storage array is a highly redundant, high performance array of disks that all ESX servers can access in a VI cluster. All virtual machine files reside on the shared storage and are accessible by all hosts in the cluster.

The glue that holds VI together is the Virtual Center (VC). VC is the management interface from which the VI cluster or clusters are managed. This application can run on its own virtual machine and is accessible through the VC client which can be installed on Windows desktop computers. It is also accessible through a browser interface, but has fewer features in this mode. All virtualization-related functions can be run in VC.

The VMware suite contains many products which are included in the solution covered in upcoming chapters. Here is a brief description of some of its products:

- **Site Recovery Manager (SRM)**   handles disaster recovery failover related to virtualization. SRM allows automatic failover to virtual machines that have been replicated to a remote location. Failover scenarios can be tested without impacting production systems. SRM helps eliminate complex manual steps required in most other disaster recovery systems.

- **Lab Manager** provides the ability to create and manage a library of commonly used VM configurations. Lab Manager is ideal for training, demo, and development situations where VMs are frequently provisioned and destroyed. Multi-machine deployments can be provisioned quickly because the library of commonly used machines are available to be deployed. Lab Manager allows you efficiently store and share multi-machine configurations across teams and locations.

- **Virtual Desktops with View** is the underlying technology that enables virtual desktops. You connect to a virtual desktop through thin clients or inexpensive PCs. There is a cost benefit to the low-end hardware and reduced administration because many clients run off the same server or blade. Provisioning new virtual desktops is faster and easier because of the centralized control. Users can be assigned to resource pools so they will log into desktops according to their individual or group profiles.

All these products are part of the virtualized environment covered in upcoming chapters.

# Summary

This chapter covered an existing environment and its many inefficiencies. This case study is similar to many non-virtualized environments that grew over time with many new servers being deployed as new applications came on line.

The next chapter covers the *Capacity Planner*, which analyzes the existing non-virtualized environment.

# CHAPTER 2

# Existing Server Environment Analysis with Capacity Planner

This chapter covers several topics related to analyzing an existing server environment to uncover inefficiencies and make recommendations on virtualizing the environment. VMware Capacity Planner is the primary tool used in this analysis along with custom analysis done by my firm, which is a VMware partner certified to run Capacity Planner, as part of the process.

Capacity Planner performs a thorough analysis of the environment and, when good virtualization candidates are discovered, produces a recommended consolidation template. Some servers are not considered good candidates for a variety of reasons, such as the following:

- The system has four or more active network interface cards (NICs).

- The system uses specialized peripherals not supported in virtual machines.

- The system is already running as a virtual machine.

This chapter covers some of the Capacity Planner output and how those recommendations were used to come up with a virtualized design for an example client.

## Snapshot of Servers

Capacity Planner performs an inventory of servers. For some of my customers, this is most revealing in the sense that they think they have some number of servers only to find out that they have many more servers than they thought. Table 2-1 summarizes the systems that were analyzed as part of the Capacity Planner process in an example customer environment.

**Table 2-1**   Summary of Existing Servers Analyzed From 158 to 154

| Name | Server Population | Number | Reason for Exclusion |
|------|-------------------|--------|----------------------|
| A | Original list provided by client | 158 | |
| B | No data | 0 | Capacity Planner was unable to connect to the server. |
| C | Invalid data | 0 | Capacity Planner identified questionable anomalies such as unusual processor speed. |
| D | Incomplete data | 4 | A complete sampling for the entire period was not obtained. |
| E | Total servers analyzed | 154 | |

Table 2-1 shows that of 158 original servers, 154 were analyzed by Capacity Planner. I found that the most common reason a server is excluded is because of an incomplete sampling of data, which means the server was shut down often or some other interruption caused a problem over the sampling period, which was true for four servers shown in the example.

The next step for Capacity Planner is to take the 154 servers and more thoroughly analyze them. Table 2-2 shows the analysis of the 154 servers.

**Table 2-2**  Summary of Existing Servers Analyzed from 154 to 134

| Name | Server Population | Number | Qualification Criteria |
|------|------------------|--------|------------------------|
| E | Total servers analyzed | 154 | All servers not disqualified due to sampling errors |
| F | Do not virtualize | 20 | Not supported or potentially poor VM performance |
| G1 | Maximum viable candidates | 134 | All remaining candidates |
| G2 | Minimum candidates | 90 | Conservative number of candidates based on analysis |

This analysis shows that between 134 and 90 servers could be virtualized. This client wants to take an aggressive virtualization approach, so 134 servers will be used in the subsequent planning for this virtualized environment.

Based on the analysis of 90 to 134 servers to be virtualized, the following summary of ESX hosts required was produced in Table 2-3.

**Table 2-3**  Summary of Existing Servers Analyzed

| Range | Number of Virtualization Candidates | Number of ESX Hosts Required | Average Processor Utilization for ESX Host | Average Memory Utilization for ESX Host |
|-------|-------------------------------------|------------------------------|---------------------------------------------|------------------------------------------|
| Minimum to maximum servers that can be consolidated | 90 to 134 | 5–12 | 11% | 25–67% |

Based on this information, the decision was made to virtualize all 134 servers that were considered good candidates. The processor utilization of 11%, although low, is much higher than the current utilization, as you'll see. When virtualization is implemented, utilization in the 60% range is common, making the hardware resources more efficiently utilized.

# Recommended Target Platform

Capacity Planner produced a recommended platform for the consolidation with the parameters shown in Table 2-4.

**Table 2-4**   Recommended Consolidation Target Platform

| Component | Number | Size, Speed, Type, Make, and Model |
|---|---|---|
| CPUs (this means cores, not processors) | 8 | 3.2GHz Quad Core |
| Random Access Memory (RAM) |  | 24GB |
| Network Interface Card (NIC) | 6 | HP NC364m Quad Port 1GBe (Two embedded 1 GB NICs plus one quad port 1 GB NIC) |
| Host Bus Adapter (HBA) | 2 | Qlogic QMH2462 |
| Local storage | 2 | 72GB SAS RAID 1 |

Several HP servers meet these requirements. To achieve maximum rack density and accommodate future growth, HP BladeSystem was selected as the target platform. Chapter 3 covers the target environment.

A lot of additional information was produced as part of the analysis, some of which is covered in the remaining sections. The next section covers the details of the servers that were analyzed as part of the Capacity Planner analysis.

# Summary of Existing Servers

Capacity Planner provides several charts and graphs summarizing the exiting environment. The figures in this section provide a technical profile of the existing environment, beginning with the CPU count (processors, in this case), shown in Figure 2-1.

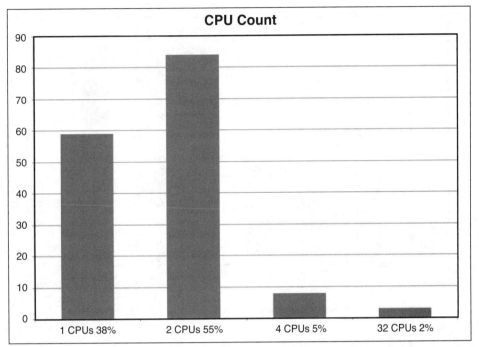

Figure 2-1    CPU (Processor) Count Showing Nearly All Servers Are 1 or 2 Core

Figure 2-1 shows that about 60 servers have one processor and more than 80 servers have two processors. The virtualization gains for these small servers is huge, because these are full servers with a large footprint, but they have only one or two cores. These are ideal consolidation candidates.

Figure 2-2 shows the frequency of the processors in the environment.

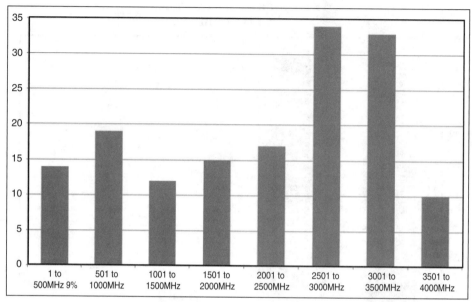

Figure 2-2    Processor Frequency Showing 50% of Servers Low

Figure 2-2 shows that low frequency processors, represented by the five leftmost bars in the chart, account for 50% of the processors in the environment. These are old, slow processors that are ideal consolidation candidates. So far, these low-density processors run at a low frequency for the most part. Figure 2-3 shows the utilization of these processors.

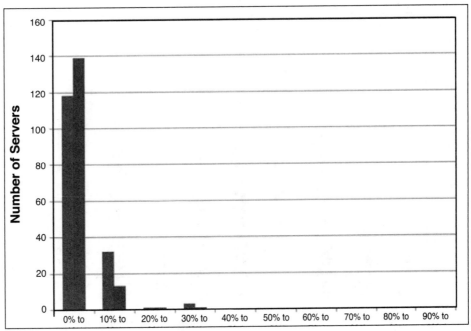

Figure 2-3    Processor Utilization Showing Nearly All Servers Below 10%

The "peak" is the leftmost bar and the "prime" hours utilization. Figure 2-3 shows almost all the servers are less than 10% utilized, which means the consolidation density will be high. Many servers can be consolidated on a single blade because of the low existing processor utilization. Next, consider the memory utilization of the servers, shown in Figure 2-4.

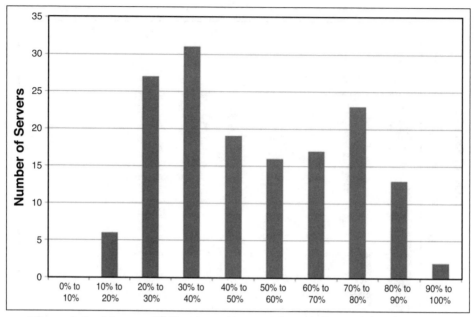

Figure 2-4    Memory Utilization Showing an Even Distribution

Figure 2-4 shows that, unlike the processor utilization and makeup, the memory utilization is higher on all servers. This means that although the servers can have a high consolidation ratio, the memory that will be devoted to each virtual machine can't be reduced nearly as aggressively. Servers and blades support high memory capacity, and I never cut back on memory to ensure every virtual machine has the memory it needs. The memory size per server is shown in Figure 2-5.

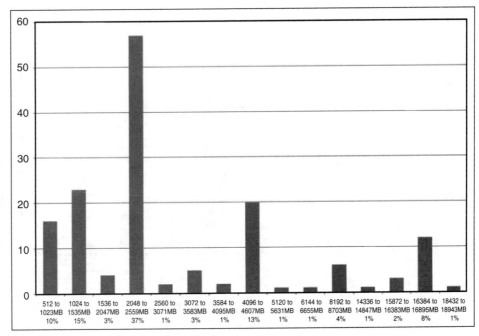

Figure 2-5    Memory Size Per Server

Figure 2-5 shows that more than 50% of the servers are in the 2-2.6 GB range of memory capacity, and this information needs to be considered when the memory recommendation is produced for virtual machines. Figure 2-6 shows the operating system breakdown in the environment.

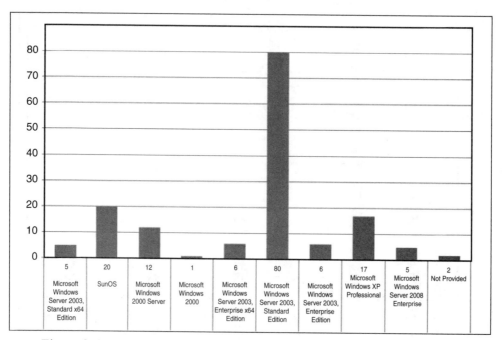

Figure 2-6    Operating System Breakdown of Servers

Figure 2-6 shows that a vast majority of servers are running a Microsoft operating system, and these servers will be consolidated. As described in the next section many of the servers, such as those running a Sun operating system, are not part of this consolidation.

This server-by-server report is invaluable to system administrators because all key information about the servers is provided. This alone is often enough justification to run Capacity Planner, because it produces such a detailed inventory. This data is also used in the power and cooling analysis done in Chapter 1 because the details of the server help produce the input to the HP Power Calculator.

## Processor Utilization Report

More than 100 servers were analyzed as part of this inventory, and one revealing statistic is to see how VMware compares the utilizations of this client environment to the overall industry utilization, as shown in Figure 2-7.

| Group | % CPU Utilization | CPU Queue | Disk Utilization | | Pages Per Second | Network BytesPer Second |
|---|---|---|---|---|---|---|
| | | | % Busy | Disk Queue | | |
| Industry Average | 5.33 | 0.69 | 7.06 | 0.68 | 36.04 | 65,394.65 |
| All Systems Group | 3.27 | 0.13 | 4.61 | 0.05 | 29.05 | 65,592.14 |

Figure 2-7    Client Results Versus Industry Average for Utilization

The following are explanations of the parameters in the figure:

- *Group.* The two rows shown under *Group* are a general industry average and then a summary of all the systems in the client environment that were evaluated.
- *% CPU Utilization.* Average percentage of CPU busy time for both groups.
- *CPU Queue.* These are the number of jobs waiting to be processed by the CPU.
- *Disk Utilization % Busy.* The percentage of elapsed time that the disk is busy servicing read or write requests.
- *Disk Utilization Disk Queue.* The average number of read and write requests queued for the disk.
- *Pages Per Second.* The pages read from or written to disk to resolve hard page faults. Hard page faults occur when a process requires code or data that is not in its working set or elsewhere in physical memory, and must be retrieved from disk.
- *Network Bytes Per Second.* The average number of bytes sent and received via the network per second.

## Detailed System Server Report

VMware Capacity Planner produces a detailed report on a system-by-system basis, giving the details of every server to which access was provided. This information is gathered using Windows Management Interface (WMI), Registry entries, or other techniques. Linux servers can also be analyzed by Capacity Planner, using tools such as **iostat**. Servers are categorized in a variety of ways. For this example, consolidation servers fell under the following categories:

- Potentially Obsolete Servers
- Servers with Insufficient Collection Data
- Servers Not to Be Virtualized Due to Business Requirements
- Servers Not to Be Virtualized Due to Specialized Hardware Requirements
- Servers for Possible Re-Purpose

The format of all these server lists is in the format shown in Figure 2-8.

| Hostname | Model | # of CPUs | CPU Speed (MHz) | Total RAM (MB) |
|----------|-------|-----------|-----------------|----------------|
| Server1 | HP ProLiant DL360 | 1 | 797 | 512 |
| Server2 | AT/AT COMPATIBLE | 1 | 996 | 512 |
| Sun1 | Sun Enterprise 220R (UltraSPARC-II 450MHz) | 1 | 450 | 2,048 |
| Sun2 | Sun Enterprise 220R (UltraSPARC-II 450MHz) | 1 | 450 | 2,048 |
| Sun3 | Sun Netra t1 (UltraSPARC-IIi 440MHz) | 1 | 440 | 1,024 |
| Sun4 | Sun Netra t1 (UltraSPARC-IIi 440MHz) | 1 | 440 | 1,024 |
| Sun 5 | Sun Netra t1 (UltraSPARC-IIi 440MHz) | 1 | 440 | 1,024 |

Figure 2-8    Potentially Obsolete Servers

All the lists of servers are in the format of this table. The characteristics of each server shown are clear in all the listings.

## Summary

This chapter covered the output of Capacity Planner and the tremendous amount of information it discovered about the existing server environment. The recommended target platform for virtualization provides a good start for designing the virtualized environment.

The next chapter covers the new design based on this detailed analysis.

# CHAPTER 3

# The Virtualized Server Environment

Based on the analysis performed on the existing server environment in the previous chapter, this chapter covers the virtualized solution. The Capacity Planner run in the previous chapter produced a tremendous amount of data about the environment, taking the guesswork out of the drawbacks to the existing environment. It results in a more efficient new solution. Based on the statistics, the ideal virtualized server solution can be crafted with predicted results.

This chapter covers the new solution based on the Capacity Planner and some of the technologies integral to the solution, including blade technology. The last section covers blades in general, which you'll want to review if you're not familiar with blades technology.

## The New Server Environment

Capacity Planner produced a set of general server recommendations. These recommendations can be implemented in the form of standalone servers or blade servers. An overview of blade servers is presented later in this chapter.

Capacity Planner recommended servers with roughly the configuration shown in Table 3-1.

**Table 3-1**   Recommended Consolidation Target Platform

| Component | Number | Size, Speed, Type, Make and Model |
|----------|--------|-----------------------------------|
| CPUs (this means cores not processors) | 8 | 3.2GHz Quad Core |
| Random Access Memory (RAM) | | 24GB |
| Network interface card (NIC) | 6 | HP NC364m Quad Port 1GBe |
| Host Bus Adapter (HBA) | 2 | Dual Channel Qlogic QMH2462 (Two embedded 1 GB NICs plus one quad port 1 GB NIC) |
| Local storage | 2 | 72GB SAS RAID 1 |

As discussed in Chapter 2, several HP servers meet these requirements. To achieve maximum rack density and accommodate future growth, HP BladeSystem was selected as the target platform.

The ideal solution was 12 blades with the following parameters:

- 12 HP BL460c Blade Servers each with 2 quad-core processors (eight core total per blade)
- 24GB memory (upgradeable to 32GB)
- 6 NIC ports per blade
- 1 dual-channel Fibre Channel (FC) Host Bus Adapter (HBA) per blade

Figure 3-1 shows the BladeSystem proposed along with shared storage replacing the 134 individual servers.

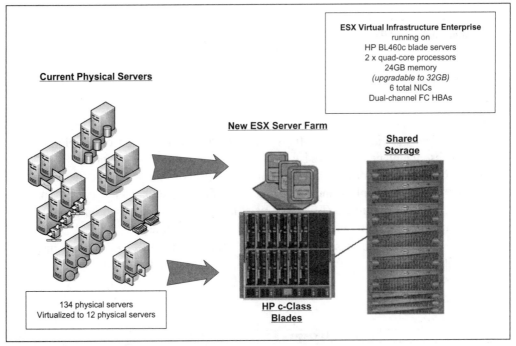

Figure 3-1 Virtualized Environment With Blade Solution

The savings the client will realize from reducing the 134 servers to 12 blades is immense, and the Return on Investment (ROI) is discussed in the next chapter.

The virtualized environment also requires shared storage, which partially existed before the virtualized design was crafted. The old shared storage was outdated, and the client determined that they needed new shared storage whether the virtualized environment was implemented or not.

To complete the savings estimate, I must calculate the power and cooling required to support the new environment. Table 3-2 covers the blade solution power and cooling.

**Table 3-2**  Power and Cooling Breakdown of the Blade Solution

| Model and Generation | Qty | Watts | Total Watts | Amps | Total Amps | BTU/hr | BTU Total |
|---|---|---|---|---|---|---|---|
| BL460c G5 | 12 | | 5873 | | 28.81 | | 20029 |

The individual *Watts*, *Amps,* and *BTU/hr* are missing from Table 3-2 because the blade enclosure has power associated with it based on the specifics of the configuration, including the number and type of blades, the number of power supplies and fans, and other factors, such as I/O cards. The totals shown in Table 3-2 were painstakingly determined based on the specific client requirements and the BladeSystem configuration.

Figure 3-2 shows the HP Power Calculator for the BL460c G5 in a c7000 enclosure with full Ethernet and SAN connectivity.

| Enclosure # 1 , 10 Fans , 6 PSU | | | | |
|---|---|---|---|---|
| Power Credentials | Idle | @100% Utilization | Circuit Sizing/HPTC | Unit(s) |
| Input Power | 3302 | 5080 | 5873 | Watt(s) |
| Input VA | 3369 | 5184 | 5993 | VA |
| BTU | 11260 | 17323 | 20029 | BTU(s) |
| Input Current | 16.2 | 24.92 | 28.81 | Amp(s) |
| Input Current Per Cord | 2.7 | 4.154 | 4.802 | Amp(s) |
| Airflow in CFM | 256 | 389 | 583 | |
| Airflow in CMM | 7.239 | 11.018 | 16.517 | |

Figure 3-2   HP Power Calculator for BL460c c7000 with Full I/O Capability

The power and cooling numbers for the blades compare favorably with the power and cooling from the 134 existing server solution, as shown in Table 3-3 and covered earlier.

**Table 3-3**   Power and Cooling Breakdown of 134 Old Servers

| Model and Generation | Qty | Watts | Total Watts | Amps | Total Amps | BTU/hr | BTU Total |
|---|---|---|---|---|---|---|---|
| DL360 G3 | 24 | 383 | 9192 | 1.9 | 45.6 | 1307 | 3168 |
| DL360 G4 | 36 | 459 | 16524 | 2.3 | 82.2 | 1565 | 56340 |
| DL360 G5 | 12 | 428 | 5136 | 2.2 | 26.4 | 1461 | 17532 |
| DL360 G5 | 28 | 505 | 14140 | 2.5 | 70 | 1723 | 48244 |
| DL380 G3 | 16 | 559 | 8944 | 2.7 | 43.2 | 1906 | 30496 |
| DL380 G4 | 10 | 459 | 4580 | 2.3 | 23 | 1563 | 15630 |
| DL380 G5 | 6 | 779 | 4674 | 3.8 | 22.8 | 2656 | 15936 |
| DL380 G2 | 2 | 1043 | 2086 | 5.1 | 10.2 | 3557 | 7114 |
| **Total** | **134** | | **65276** | | **324** | | **222660** |

I created power and cooling from both tables using the HP Power Calculator. The comparison between the existing and new virtualized solutions are compelling in terms of the power and cooling saved, shown in Table 3-4.

**Table 3-4**   Comparison of Existing and Virtualized Environments

| Total 134 Server Power | Total 12 Blades Power | Blades Power Requirement Compared to Existing Environment | Total 134 Server BTU | Total 12 Blades BTU | Blades Cooling Requirement Compared to Existing Environment |
|---|---|---|---|---|---|
| 65276 | 5873 | 9% of existing environment | 222660 | 20029 | 9% of existing environment |

A savings of 90% in both power and cooling for servers is compelling from an efficiency standpoint. Many other factor make up payback, such as floor space, but from purely a server standpoint, you can't do much better than that.

Because of the immense savings in power and cooling, this client decided to double the blades environment to accommodate the planned growth of roughly 100 servers over the next year. Figure 3-3 shows 12 blades in a rack, which replaces the existing server environment and will be doubled to support the additional 100 servers over the next year.

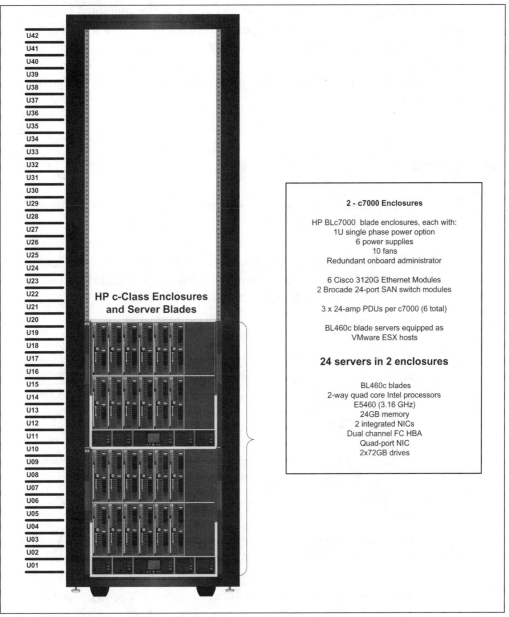

Figure 3-3    Virtualized Environment

Figure 3-3 shows how little space in the rack is consumed by the 24 blades. There is a substantial amount of space left for additional components. This huge savings in floor space is part of the ROI covered in Chapter 4 along with the many other savings realized by the blades-based virtualization solution.

Capacity Planner uses numerous assumptions, which are covered in the next section.

# Assumptions

Some key assumptions are produced in *Capacity Planner* in order for the new, virtualized environment to operate:

- All target VMware ESX host servers will be identical in configuration. Differences in configurations can impact sizing and may require modeling additional scenarios.

- All planned hosts will be located in two physical locations.

- All NIC ports in the target ESX hosts will be active. If not all ports are active, more ESX hosts may be required to distribute the potential network load to avoid network-based performance bottlenecks.

- The use of Gigabit NICs assumes a network using Gigabit speeds.

- Shared storage using a SAN will be available, which, in this specific client example, required an upgrade to the SAN.

- All target ESX hosts will have access to required storage, and storage limitations are not considered a gating factor.

- An additional server and database will be required for the Virtual Center management server.

- All workloads will utilize VMware virtual disks residing on a Virtual Machine File System (VMFS), and no virtual disks will map directly to SAN Logical Units (LUNs).

- Servers considered for reuse will have processor specifications to support VMotion compatibility. Non-identical hardware will limit the ability to use VMotion and restrict the ability to shift loads across multiple ESX hosts. VMotion allows you to move a virtual machine from one physical server to another with no impact to users.

- The target ESX hosts are reserved exclusively for server consolidation of the existing servers and server containment to support future provisioning requests.

- All target ESX hosts will be utilized to their maximum potential and workloads can be freely balanced across the target hosts with no network limitations.

These assumptions are key to designing the target solution. Select assumptions can be changed; however, this may result in a modified solution and affect the ROI.

The next section covers some rudimentary background in blades.

## Blades Background

A blade is a server in a format that allows it to be inserted into an enclosure housing numerous blades. The enclosure provides some common services, such as power, cooling, management, network, and SAN interconnects. The blade has its own resources, including processor(s,) memory, disks (optionally,) NICs, and other components. Each blade requires its own operating system, just like a rack-mounted or tower server, and is used in a way similar to any other physical server.

The blades used in the virtualized solution presented in this chapter are part of the HP c-Class BladeSystem. Some of the c-Class advantages include the following:

- Smaller physical format saves rack space in the data center. In the case of the HP c-Class c7000 enclosure, up to 16 half-height blades can be housed in 10U of rack space, including all power and interconnecting switches. A special-purpose blade that provides 32 independent server nodes in 10U of space is also available. Ethernet and SAN switch modules can be optionally added to the enclosure saving additional space compared to top-of-rack switch alternatives.

- Power and cooling are greatly reduced with blades. The results are higher power efficiency, dynamic power scaling, and a subsequent reduction in heat output. Air circulation is also optimized to efficiently exhaust the heat that is produced.

- HP's management suite allows management at the enclosure level and at the server blades. Shared and individual resources at the blades are all controlled and reported on through a common interface. Software deployment, patch management, and power management are some of the tools supported by HP's Integrated Control Environment (ICE) that's part of the BladeSystem. No separate connections to keyboard, video, and mouse are required, because Integrated Lights Out (iLO) allows full graphical remote control from any WAN-attached device with a browser.

- With common power, network, SAN, and management interfaces, cabling can be tremendously reduced. A fully provisioned rack-mount server could require 2 power cords, a keyboard, monitor, and mouse, up to 6 network connections, an iLO management connection, and 2 SAN connections. Those 14 cables mean 224 total connections for 16 conventional servers. In a c-Class blade environment, these needs could typically be met with 6 power cables, 2 iLO management connections, as few as 6 total network connections, and as few as 2 total SAN connections, resulting in a 14-to-1 reduction in cabling.

Figure 3-4 shows a front view of a c7000.

Figure 3-4    HP BladeSystem Front View

Figure 3-4 shows eight half-height and four full-height server blades and power supply modules, which are hot-pluggable from the front. An integrated touch-screen display allows easy access to status information and speeds up the initial configuration process.

Figure 3-5 shows a rear view of the c7000.

Figure 3-5    HP BladeSystem Rear View

Hot-pluggable fans plug in from the rear of the enclosure as well as single phase or 3-phase power. Management and connection to the iLO network interface is provided through one standard and an optional redundant Onboard Administrator Module.

Eight interconnect bays give flexibility to provide the required level of Ethernet, SAN, InfiniBand, and SAS storage connectivity. These can be simple pass-through modules (similar to patch panels) or full-function switch modules that reduce or eliminate the need for infrastructure or top-of-rack switches.

HP Virtual Connect modules give an option for Ethernet and SAN connectivity that allows all resources to be defined once at the start of the process, with dynamic provisioning of blades through the life of the enclosure.

All the interconnect modules are typically installed in pairs, and map to the physical NIC ports and mezzanine cards installed on each Blade server. Everything is tied together through a signal midplane and a power backplane.

The virtualized solution in this chapter consists of only server blades; however, storage blades, tape blades, and PCI expansion blades are also available.

Server blades are available in configurations from a single processor to 4 quad-core Intel or AMD processors in half-height and full-height formats. A special-purpose blade combines 2 independent server nodes in a single half-height blade carrier, allowing up to 32 servers in a single c7000 enclosure. Itanium processors are also supported in two current full-height and double-wide full-height Integrity Server Blade models.

Storage blades are available to provide either local direct-attached drives for an adjacent server blade or common access to other blades through iSCSI or NAS connectivity.

Tape blades give the ability to run tape backups within the same physical blade enclosure.

PCI expansion blades allow industry standard PCI-Express or PCI-X cards to be utilized by an adjacent server blade.

More information is available on c-Class blades at **http:// h18004.www1.hp.com/products/blades/components/c-class-components.html?jumpid=reg_R1002_USEN** at the time of this writing.

# Performance Analysis After Virtualization

After virtualization has been implemented, there are specialized tools to assist with performance analysis. After virtualization has been implemented, analysis is more complex because there are many virtual machines running on a single server. One such tool my firm has used on virtualized environments is Akorri BalancePoint. This performance-analysis tool for servers, storage systems, and applications is "virtualization aware" and ideally suited for use with VMware. Because of the virtualization of all the normally physical components of a data center—network, server and storage—it can be difficult to diagnose and resolve problems with traditional software tools. BalancePoint does the following in your virtualized environment:

- Displays a mapping of physical to virtual resources for each application running on a VM
- Measures the performance of physical and virtual elements
- Provides alerts and recommendations when problems are discovered
- Provides historical baselines of all virtual machines
- Identifies which virtual machines are overutilizing resources
- Provides detailed I/O data
- Provides comprehensive reporting

Even the most well-run data center is not immune to problems and bottlenecks. BalancePoint can provide invaluable troubleshooting capabilities. It facilitates deep analysis into the critical elements: operating systems, databases, servers, storage, virtualization systems, helping to accelerate the troubleshooting process. Figure 3-6 is a performance overview produced by BalancePoint.

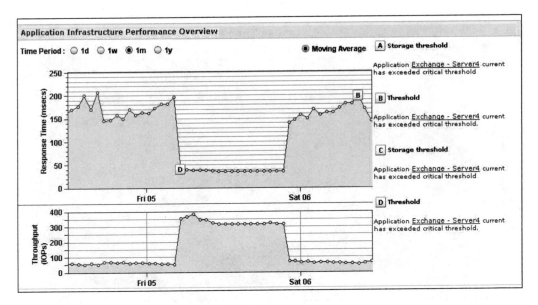

Figure 3-6    Performance Overview

The report shown in Figure 3-6 illustrates the response time and throughput of a Microsoft Exchange server with the underlying storage system. The thresholds can help alert potential bottlenecks. Response time is often the measure of whether an environment has been successfully virtualized, so this detailed analysis is immensely helpful.

Despite the gains in server utilization offered by virtualization, capacity planning is still a challenge. BalancePoint helps indicate where additional resources are available and where more virtual machines can be allocated without running into capacity or performance problems. Rather than waiting until problems are evident, BalancePoint can help an administrator strategically plan how virtual and physical resources are allocated. Virtualization is addictive, and with these useful outputs, you can clearly see where you can add additional virtual machines and still maintain the desired response times. Figure 3-7 shows the response time.

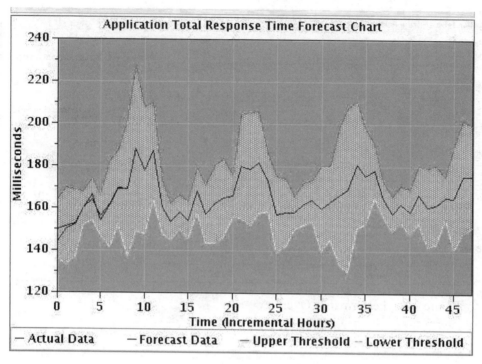

Figure 3-7     Response Time Forecast

Although the colors in Figure 3-7 are lost, you can see that actual and forecast data are provided The tool shows what you can expect to see when applications are added to the environment which, in some cases, may have an adverse impact on the applications currently running on the server.

It is easy to see how this tool can be invaluable for managing a virtual infrastructure. This, and similar software tools, can make the already impressive ROI that virtualization provides even more impressive with the ability to add forecast data to existing data.

## Summary

The benefits presented in this chapter make a compelling argument for server virtualization. The results presented are typical for server virtualization. The case study illustrates what can be expected in any server virtualization and is by no means extreme. Every such assessment I've run has resulted in a sever virtualization project because, with immense benefits presented in this chapter, it is difficult to decline taking on server virtualization.

The next chapter covers the Return on Investment (ROI) for the new environment.

# Chapter 4

## Server ROI Analysis

VMware Capacity Planner produces a lot of Total Cost of Ownership (TCO)-related information. This chapter presents both some of the high-level output produced and some of the more detailed information, which provides a breakdown of where the costs lie.

Because of the immense savings in power and cooling, the client decided to double the blades environment to accommodate the planned growth of roughly 100 servers over the next year. The TCO information in this chapter is based on 24 blades for the new virtualized design and 134 existing servers, plus 100 additional servers for planned expansion over the next year.

The diagram of the rack that appears later in this chapter shows both the blade enclosure to support the current environment as well as the enclosure to support the additional blades to accommodate growth over the upcoming year.

# TCO for Existing and New Virtualized Environments

The first estimate produced by VMware Capacity Planner is the TCO for the two solutions. Table 4-1 includes a high-level TCO comparison.

**Table 4-1**   TCO for 134 (plus 100 future) Existing Servers vs. 24 Blades

| Cost or Savings | Current Environment Cost Without Virtualization | Projected Cost with Virtualization | Savings Using Blades Solution |
|---|---|---|---|
| Direct Costs | $8,315,934 | $6,097,503 | $2,218,431 |
| Indirect Costs | $2,788,410 | $617,987 | $2,170,423 |
| TCO | $11,104,344 | $6,715,490 | $4,388,854 |

Capacity Planner produces this summary for a three-year period. The following assumptions are part of this analysis:

- Server consolidation of 134 total virtualization candidates will be consolidated onto 12 ESX hosts, with no hardware reuse. The assessment assumed all virtualization candidates can be migrated in the first year. The 12 ESX hosts in this case are the 12 blades.

- Server expansion of 100 total expected virtual machines will be provisioned on 12 ESX hosts, with no overlap with ESX hosts reserved for server consolidation. The alternative of not virtualizing assumes that all 100.5 servers that would have been provisioned as VMs would each require individual physical hardware. Again, the 12 ESX slots for this expansion are 12 blades.

Table 4-2 breaks down the TCO into more detail, including the specific VMware components.

**Table 4-2**   Further Breakdown of Three-Year TCO for Servers vs. Blades

| TCO for Components | Current 234 Server Environment | 24-Blade Virtualized Environment | Savings in Virtualized Environment |
|---|---|---|---|
| **VMware Infrastructure** | | | |
| TCO Direct | $5,675,603 | $5,147,431 | $528,172; 9.3% |
| TCO Indirect | $1,977,840 | $379,584v | $1,598,256; 80.8% |
| TCO (3-year) | $7,653,443 | $5,527,015 | $2,126,428; 27.8% |
| **VMware Lab Manager** | | | |
| TCO Direct | $2,124,234 | $611,968 | $1,512,266; 71.2% |
| TCO Indirect | $810,570 | $238,403 | $572,167; 70.6% |
| TCO (3-year) | $2,934,804 | $850,371 | $2,084,433; 71.0% |
| **VMware VDI** | | | |
| TCO (3-year) | $516,097 | $338,104 | $177,993; 34.5% |
| TCO | | | |
| TCO Direct | $8,315,934 | $6,097,503 | $2,218,431; 26.7% |
| TCO Indirect | $2,788,410 | $617,987 | $2,170,423; 77.8% |
| TCO (3-year) | $11,104,344 | $6,715,490 | $4,388,854; 39.5% |

This summary gives some of the details on TCO related specifically to VMware products. There are a lot of benefits to using these products, both direct and indirect. Not shown in Table 4-2 are the specific investments in VMware that are made over this three-year period. The total investment for this client was $754,000 over three years.

More revealing than just the virtualization components of the virtualized environment, however, is Figure 4-1, which shows the data center-related savings.

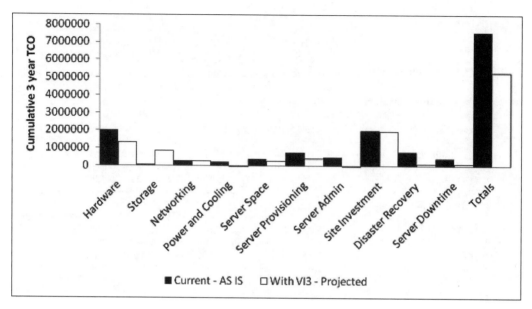

Figure 4-1    Data Center Three-Year TCO Comparison

The current environment entries are shown in black and the VMware Infrastructure 3 (VI3) is shown in white. Although some entries are too small to see, the overall benefit is clear. As you would expect, the *Hardware* column shows the server hardware over the years would cost much less in the virtualized environment shown on the right. This represents the cost of 24 total blades versus the 100 additional servers that would have to be procured to accommodate the planned growth over the next year.

The *Storage* column shows the investment that will have to be made in the virtualized environment. There is minimal investment required for additional storage in the *Current* environment. Although 100 servers will have to be procured to accommodate growth, there is not a commensurate storage investment required because the applications running require minimal storage. In the case of the virtualized environment, a new shared storage unit will have to be procured, which is an altogether new investment. Of all the data center-related investments that have to be made, this is the only one for which the virtualized solution costs are higher than the *Current* environment. This is true in every virtualization design on which I've worked, because non-virtualized environments do not have much shared storage, so this capital investment must be made as a prerequisite to implement virtualization.

Table 4-3 shows data center-related costs over five years using the virtualized approach.

**Table 4-3**  Data Center-Related Benefits From Virtualization

| Benefit Category | Year 1 | Year 2 | Year 3 | Year 4 | Year 5 | Total |
|---|---|---|---|---|---|---|
| Server Hardware | $186,436 | $233,045 | $291,306 | $364,133 | $455,166 | $1,530,086 |
| Server Storage | ($181,565) | ($241,481) | ($321,170) | ($427,157) | ($568,118) | ($1,739,491) |
| Server Networking | $7,931 | $9,914 | $12,392 | $15,490 | $19,363 | $65,090 |
| Server Power and Cooling | $63,772 | $79,715 | $99,644 | $124,555 | $155,693 | $523,379 |
| Server Space | $35,581 | $44,476 | $55,595 | $69,494 | $86,868 | $292,014 |
| Server Provisioning | $91,991 | $119,588 | $155,465 | $202,104 | $262,736 | $831,884 |
| Server Admin | $121,680 | $158,184 | $205,639 | $267,331 | $347,530 | $1,100,364 |
| Disaster-Recovery Site Investment | $18,185 | $18,185 | $18,185 | $18,185 | $18,185 | $90,925 |
| Server Disaster Recovery (Indirect) | $231,552 | $231,552 | $231,552 | $231,552 | $231,552 | $1,157,760 |
| Server Down-time (Indirect) | $301,200 | $301,200 | $301,200 | $301,200 | $301,200 | $1,506,000 |
| Total Financial Benefit | $876,763 | $954,378 | $1,049,808 | $1,166,887 | $1,310,175 | $5,358,011 |

In Table 4-3, the *Server Storage* row clearly shows that this is the only category for which there is not a significant positive payback immediately. The numbers in this table make for a compelling virtualization story for cost savings. Combined with the other efficiencies, it is difficult to make an argument for remaining un-virtualized.

In order to produce this table, there are 280 rows in the spreadsheet that contain assumptions. This means there is a lot of room to adjust the numbers in a variety of ways; however, using reasonably good assumptions, there is almost always a compelling reason to virtualize. I also recommend you review the assumptions, to see that they apply to your circumstances. Assumptions as simple as the cost of electricity, for example, vary widely. The assumption entry in the spreadsheet for this example uses a cost of ten cents per kilowatt hour (which is generally considered low at the time of this writing) that you may want to adjust.

A summary of the Return on Investment (ROI), Net Present Value (NPV), and Payback Period appear in Table 4-4.

**Table 4-4**   ROI, NPV, and Payback Period for the Virtualized Solution

| Category | Number |
|---|---|
| ROI | 388% |
| NPV Savings (three year, discount rate=9.5%) | $3,532,095 |
| Payback Period in Months | 6 |

These are the three key summaries supplied by Capacity Planner because they are so widely used. These parameters, however, are not widely understood, so I've included summaries of each.

Although technical experts are sometimes unfamiliar with these terms, the significant investment required to make virtualization operational makes it important to understand the basics of financial aspects of such a project. The following definitions of financial terms are often associated with major technology projects:

- **Return on Investment (ROI)** is the ratio of money gained or lost (realized or unrealized) on an investment relative to the amount of money invested. The amount of money gained or lost may be referred to as interest, profit/loss, gain/loss, or net income/loss. The money invested may be referred to as the asset, capital, principal, or the cost basis of the investment. ROI is usually expressed as a percentage rather than a fraction

- **Net Present Value (NPV)** is the present value of an investment's future net cash flows minus the initial investment. If positive, the investment should be considered (unless an even better investment exists); otherwise, it should probably be passed unless there are other compelling reasons for it.

- **Internal Rate of Return (IRR)** is a capital budgeting metric used by firms to decide whether they should make investments. It is an indicator of the efficiency or quality of an investment, as opposed to NPV, which indicates value or magnitude. The IRR is the annualized effective compounded return rate, which can be earned on the invested capital, such as the yield on the investment. Put another way, the IRR for an investment is the discount rate that makes the net present value of the investment's income stream total zero. A project is a good investment proposition if its IRR is greater than the rate of return that could be earned by alternate investments of equal risk (investing in other projects, buying bonds, even putting the money in a bank account). Thus, the IRR should be compared to any alternate costs of capital, including an appropriate risk premium. In general, if the IRR is greater than the project's cost of capital, or hurdle rate, the project will add value for the company.

- **Payback** is the amount of time it takes to break even on an investment. Because this method ignores the time value of money and cash flows after the payback period, it can provide only a partial picture of whether the investment is worthwhile.

## Summary

Although it is implied that going from more than 100 servers to a handful of blades would have a compelling ROI, it is helps to see the numbers broken out by category. Many of the numbers presented in this chapter may be too high for you in some categories but too low in others.

The next chapter covers a high-level implementation plan for server virtualization. It is the template used by my firm.

# Chapter 5

# Virtual Server Implementation Plan

When implementing a virtual environment, the key to success is a solid implementation plan. Almost every server in your data center could be affected by the transition to a virtual environment, so this is an area where you want to be sure adequate planning takes place.

My strong recommendation is to craft a formal project plan and formalize the implementation process as much as possible because there are typically many new components introduced in to a virtualized environment. I'm not presenting a formal project plan; however, I cover most of the high-level tasks to get the major components of this environment operational. The following high-level components are part of the implementation plan covered in this chapter:

- **Blades**. The existing environment uses standalone servers and not blades so the setup and management of blades represents a new platform.

- **VMware ESX cluster**. The ESX servers will be in a high availability cluster, which represents multiple new technologies in this environment.

- **VMware Lab Manager**. This product tests applications in a virtualized environment prior to deployment, known as "life cycle management," which is new to the environment.

- **Shared Storage**. New shared storage devices are to be implemented and will have to be managed long term.

- **Replication**. Storage replication between facilities, which is all new technology to this environment.

- **VMware Site Recovery Manager (SRM)**. Recovery with SRM needs to be designed, implemented, and tested.

All these high-level components and technologies are key to the operation of the new environment, and many are altogether new, so an implementation plan is important to ensure that a smooth transition is made from the old environment to the new one. Not shown in the list, but included in the implementation plan, is knowledge transfer on these and all other technologies.

Although I'm not presenting a project plan that would show the overlap of tasks, you can imagine that many parts of the implementation tasks covered can be done in parallel with one another. I cover the topics independently of one another, but there is typically a lot of overlap.

The upcoming sections cover various aspects of the implementation plan.

# Blade Startup Implementation

The first components to be implemented in the new environment are the blades-related infrastructure. There are tasks related to hardware installation, Storage Area Network (SAN), and blades management functionality in the following tasks:

- Perform blade hardware installation of the HP c-Class Blade Enclosure racking and power connectivity. This should be done by HP as part of hardware-installation services.

- Perform installation of the c-Class server blades and interconnect modules, which include Ethernet, Fibre Channel, and Infiniband as examples.

- Set up the blade enclosure and perform the initial configuration of the unit.

- Configure Cisco Ethernet switch module configuration.

- Perform Fibre Channel SAN switch module configuration.

- Configure redundant management modules in the blade enclosure(s).

- Establish Integrated Lights Out (iLO) connectivity in the blade enclosure, which provides the ability to manage and install blades.

- Perform knowledge transfer and compile documentation of the blade hardware and configuration steps performed to make the blade environment operational.


# Shared Storage Startup Implementation

Shared storage is often new to consolidated server environments. Traditionally, storage had been local to a server and the only shared storage were file systems on a local server to which several servers had access. In a virtualized environment, shared storage is a requirement and is often newly introduced to the environment. This section summarizes the tasks typically performed to implement shared storage, which in this example, is an EMC CX4-240:

### Phase 1: Planning

- Schedule site survey with EMC field services to ensure all prerequisites are met to support the storage environment.

- Work with the client to collect detailed storage configuration parameters in preparation for performing the configuration.

- Plan the CX RAID groups for the shared storage which, in this case, is one CX array.

- Create the Configuration Request Form (CCRF) and submit it for approval.

- Plan the Navisphere implementation.

- Plan the SnapView configuration and custom scripting for Clone or Snap sets.

### Phase 2: Implementation and Testing

- Coordinate installation of the CX storage array with EMC field services.

- Configure the CX array(s.)

- Install and configure the Fibre Channel switches.

- Install and configure NaviSphere and the associated agents.

- Create CX Redundant Array of Independent Disks (RAID) groups and Logical Units (LUNs).

- Connect hosts and CX Navisphere Array Agents (SPs).

- Create zones and zone sets for CX SPs and Host Bus Adapters (HBAs).

- Assign LUNs to hosts.

- Install, configure, and test SnapView software. This is part of the optional backup policy and does not apply in every environment.

### Phase 3: Create Documentation and Perform Knowledge Transfer

- Produce a detailed material list including serial numbers, support numbers, license keys, and code words.

- Compile a document with the steps performed to implement the SAN.

- Organize a review meeting to cover the completed implementation.

# VMware Startup Implementation

Virtualizing physical servers to virtual servers requires many steps. The experts in my firm do this work often and can converge on an environment and implement virtual machines quickly. It is important, however, that you as the client understand the tasks they're performing so you have a clear understanding of the setup of your virtual environment. This section covers the tasks performed to implement the virtualized environment.

### Phase 1: Planning and Design

- Organize a pre-implementation discussion to review virtualization objectives and begin implementation preparation.

- Plan the ESX Server, Virtual Center, and physical-to-virtual (P2V) implementation.

## Phase 2: Implementation and Testing

- Perform VMware ESX server installation and configuration.
- Review the virtual machine creation and management.
- Perform the Virtual Center installation, configuration, and provisioning.
- Review integration of servers into the new virtual infrastructure.
- Configure Virtual Center and ESX servers to participate in VMware clusters as architected.
- Create Virtual Machines and perform management of virtual machine resources.

## Phase 3: Physical-to-Virtual (P2V) Migration

- Review the migration and management of virtual machines.
- Perform the P2V migrations.

## Phase 4: Documentation and Knowledge Transfer

- Provide the ESX Server Build documentation.
- Provide the Virtual Center Build documentation.
- Perform VMware knowledge transfer.
- Perform a virtualization architecture and design review.
- Perform an ESX server installation review.
- Perform a Virtual Center installation review.
- Provide a server-provisioning process overview for virtual machines.
- Provide the templates and review standard build of virtual machines.
- Discuss and document the scheduling, backup options, monitoring, and performance reports.

# Data Replication Startup Implementation

Replication between two locations is often implemented with virtualization. The shared storage provides the perfect foundation to implement replication. Although replication is not a requirement to a virtualized environment, the introduction of shared storage creates the perfect opening to introduce replication. This section covers the tasks to implement EMC RecoverPoint replication, which includes four RecoverPoint appliances, two in each location:

- Meet with the customer to ensure that the environment and operational implementation requirements (hardware, software, and infrastructure) are met, and provide the customer with a list of required or beneficial updates.

- Perform all site-related planning for the appliances, including power and connectivity.

- Plan and design a RecoverPoint solution, which includes one or more of the following components:

  > Continuous remote replication
  > Fabric or array-based splitter drivers
  > Host-based fabric splitter drivers

- Install the Recover Point Appliances (RPAs).

- Configure RPAs in a cluster at the local site.

- Configure two RPAs in a cluster at the remote site.

- Install RecoverPoint client software on the servers.

- Perform all necessary zoning changes.

- Create all necessary volumes on storage arrays.

- Assign LUNs to one or more RPAs and servers.

- Configure the RecoverPoint replications, including consistency groups and replication jobs. (In a storage subsystem, a consistency group is a collection of LUNs against which operations must be performed together (consistently). Consistency groups are essential where I/O writes must be maintained in order—for example, databases. A consistency group may contain LUNs for both the data and logs for a particular database or set of databases to insure that they are synchronized. Otherwise, some transactions may be lost.

- Validate the implementation using the Test and Acceptance Plan.

- Perform knowledge transfer by conducting a basic product functional overview with the client covering the implemented RecoverPoint appliances.

# VMware Site Recovery Manager Startup Implementation

With data replicated between two facilities, the foundation for disaster recovery of the virtual environment is in place. This section covers the tasks required to implement VMware Site Recovery Manager (SRM) to quickly recover from one site to another:

- Perform on-site installation of VMware SRM to represent two sites: one primary and one recovery. The configuration and setup will be done at two locations. The two sites will function as one another's recovery site.

- Configure ESX hosts representing the primary and recovery sites.

- Configure two VirtualCenter servers representing primary and recovery site, each managing the respective ESX hosts.

- Configure two SRM servers representing the primary and recovery sites.

- Separate the SRM database and VirtualCenter database for primary and recovery sites.

- Configure Storage Replication Adapter (SRA) for compatible shared FC SAN with replication.

- Configure protection groups and recovery plans for primary and recovery sites.

- Test the recovery process for both recovery sites.

# Virtual Desktop with VMware View Startup Implementation

View is covered in a separate chapter, but I included the startup tasks in this chapter because VDI is often implemented, at least on a trial basis, along with server virtualization:

- Install and configure VMware ESX hosts for View.

- Install VMware Virtual Desktop Manager (VDM) connection broker on a physical server or virtual machine.

- Integrate VDM into the existing VirtualCenter and Microsoft Active Directory environments.

- Create a virtual desktop template to provision virtual machines in desktop pools with like functionality.

- Create and configure persistent and non-persistent VDM desktop pools.

- Entitle designated users and groups to VDM desktop pools.

- Configure client machines with the VMware VDM Client to connect to the broker.

# Summary

A solid implementation plan is the key to a successful project. Typically, some new technologies, such as shared storage, are introduced with server virtualization that must be planned if they're going to be successfully implemented. Production applications, in particular, must be carefully planned if migrations are going to take place with minimal disruption.

The next chapter covers desktop virtualization and blades workstations which have many green and administration benefits.

# CHAPTER 6

# Desktop Virtualization

A book on green IT couldn't be complete without a chapter on end-user computers. Desktops and laptops may seem like a small part of the IT infrastructure of a company, but because of the sheer numbers, the total effect on power, management complexity, risk to the business, and administrative overhead can be staggering. The cost of desktops and laptops has many components beyond the initial acquisition.

This chapter covers two completely different desktop solutions. First, desktop virtualization with VMware View is covered. This solution applies to the vast majority of users. High-end users who require dedicated computer and graphics resources are ideal candidates for workstation blades. Workers who require 3D graphics or run complex analytical software, such as engineers, architects, and financial traders, require this high-end solution—the HP c-Class blade workstation.

For the vast majority of users applying virtualization, you can achieve significant reductions in the following areas:

- Acquisition costs
- Deployment cost and time
- Time spent on moves, adds, and changes
- Space on the desk
- Power and associated cooling costs

- Data security risk
- Overhead related to software deployments and patch management
- Resources required for ongoing management

For years, various products have been available to automate software deployment, allow multiple users to share a single device, and provide access for remote users. This chapter covers desktop virtualization in general using VMware View as an application. View is VMware's latest generation solution to provide all these functions and several others.

## Desktop Virtualization Benefits Users and IT

Desktop virtualization benefits everyone involved, including desktop users and the IT group. The following are some of the needs of end users:

- Their own personalized desktop so they can work efficiently in their own way
- Access from anywhere for convenience and to provide business continuity and disaster recovery
- The ability to run Win32, legacy, or web applications without compatibility concerns

End users' needs for their desktop are much different than those of IT. IT needs:

- Tools and a structure that makes it easy to manage disparate desktop images
- The flexibility to manage a multitude of devices
- Secure, continuous access to desktops and applications
- The ability to manage and distribute Win32, legacy, and web applications
- Low management costs

In Chapter 1, I talked about VMware ESX server and its ability to host multiple server virtual machines (VMs.) VMware View is a natural extension of this capability into the desktop area, with each VM being a single user's desktop operating environment.

A desktop VM is much different than a server VM, and View leverages these differences to its advantage. For example, 500 Windows users in an environment with established standards will have a large percentage of the same operating system and application files. When the associated **C:** drives for those 500 users are virtualized, View Composer can manage the storage so that common files are only stored once rather than 500 times. The unique components for each user (including configuration files, custom applications, etc. are maintained for each user, but this is a fraction of the space that would be required to store the entire desktop image.

# Benefits of Desktop Virtualization

The benefits of desktop virtualization match the needs of IT in every area, including:

- **Lower cost**. Desktop computing costs are reduced through centralized deployment, administration, and resources. View also allows IT infrastructure to be removed from remote offices.
- **Better security**. All data and images are maintained within the corporate firewall. Built-in SSL encryption provides secure access to virtual desktops from unmanaged devices.
- **Greater management and control**. View Manager lets you manage all desktops centrally and provision desktops instantly to new users, departments, or offices.
- **Flexible provisioning**. Desktop capabilities are delivered to the user regardless of the type of hardware they have including thin client, physical PC, and so on.
- **Easier administration and policy setting**. Use a single management tool to provision desktops to new users or groups, complete with an intuitive administrative interface for setting desktop policies.
- **Reliable business continuity and disaster recovery**. VMware View is built on VMware Virtual Infrastructure and is able to leverage VMware Consolidated Backup (VCB) and VMotion, disaster

recovery solutions, and high availability capabilities to automate desktop backup and recovery and high availability of virtual desktops and applications.

- **Reduce energy costs and carbon footprint**. When used in conjunction with thin client devices which typically use 1/10th the power of a traditional PC, VMware View helps lower energy costs and reduce the carbon footprint by up to 80% ("Infrastructure Virtualization," Butler Group, September 2007).

## VMware View Components

This section uses VMware View as the basis for desktop virtualization. Figure 6-1 shows the components of View.

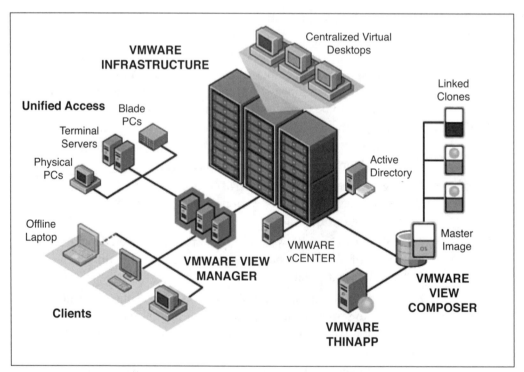

Figure 6-1   VMware View Components

View allows desktop computers to be encapsulated, isolated, and virtualized as VMs, much like it does for servers. These VMs are hosted on VMware Infrastructure (ESX servers) similar to server VMs. In fact, if you have an existing ESX server farm with available capacity, you can host desktop VMs along with your server VMs. Doing so reduces some of the management and licensing benefits of a separate environment, however.

In an enterprise with hundreds or thousands of desktops to manage, there are multiple benefits from creating a separate VMware Infrastructure to support VMware View and its associated components, including the following:

- **VMware licensing economies**. VMware has separate SKUs for View licenses, which give the flexibility to use as many physical ESX Servers as required.

- **Management isolation**. By placing virtual desktops in their own VMware Infrastructure, the desktop support team can have full control over and responsibility for their resources.

- **Resource control**. Shared storage, backup and DR considerations, network and WAN connectivity, and security can all be architected and managed according to the unique requirements of the virtual desktop environment.

I recommend that you place the servers that host virtual desktops into the VMware infrastructure, which provides several management, performance, and reliability benefits, including the following:

- Unified management
- Automated failover and recovery
- Dynamic load balancing of desktop-computing resources
- Consolidated backup

Figure 6-2 is a high-level depiction of the VMware infrastructure.

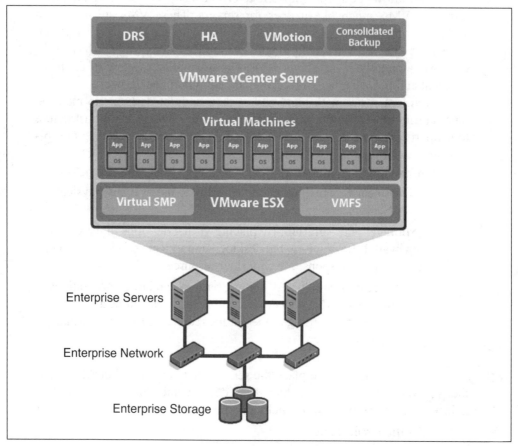

Figure 6-2    High-Level VMware Infrastructure

The next section covers View Manager, which is the console through which you perform desktop management.

## Desktop Management

View Manager is the desktop-management solution that gives you the tools to manage thousands of desktops from a single console. Deployments, upgrades, and patching are all handled centrally through this interface. Desktop and application virtualization decouples hardware, software, and operating systems, and eliminates the need for on-site desktop management and maintenance. Users can be connected through a variety of client devices, including thin clients with no moving parts and no unique personality until they load the virtual desktop image. If a hardware failure occurs with a thin client, the user can log in from another available station or one pulled off the shelf and plugged into replace their unit.

View Manager acts as a connection broker to users to allow them to securely access their virtual desktops hosted on VMware Infrastructure or on other supported platforms, including terminal servers, blade PCs, or remote physical PCs.

Figure 6-3 shows the different clients that can be part of virtualized desktops, which are under the control of View Manager. In addition, the virtualized desktops are on the ESX host, which results in a "nested" virtualized environment.

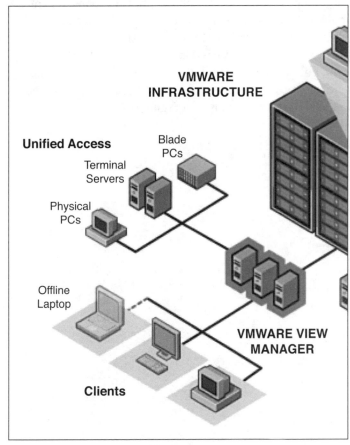

Figure 6-3    High-Level Client Layout

## Desktop Virtualization Storage

A desktop virtualization environment has unique storage needs. With most virtualization, a desktop or server is virtualized and encapsulated into a set of files associated with that physical unit. With traditional Virtual Desktop Infrastructure (VDI), each VM is an entire container, taking up a full disk volume. View Manager 3 enables "linked clones" that are based on a single Gold Master image. Linked clones use VMware snapshot technology.

There's a lot of value in just moving from traditional desktops to virtual, but recognizing that there are usually large groups of identical desktops allows creation of "gold master images" for those groups. The majority of the files (and associated disk space) in those master images or templates can then be shared. We can clone hundreds or thousands of desktops from those images to provide storage savings and to improve management.

Single instance storage is a great concept, but it does have some availability risks and potential performance risks associated with high read demand. To alleviate risk, View Composer is used. It starts with a single copy of the gold master image, but creates replicas to provide performance and overwrite protection, and then uses snapshots (linked clones) to personalize each user's image, as shown in Figure 6-4.

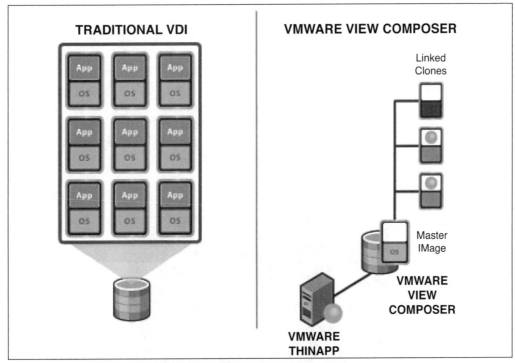

Figure 6-4    Linked Clones Versus Traditional Desktop Storage

The linked clone shown in Figure 6-4 is a copy of the original virtual machine that maintains a link to the virtual disks of the original VM to save storage. A linked clone has a separate identity, however, which means that it can be powered on, modified, suspended, etc, independent of the "master" VM from which it was cloned. Optionally, linked clones can have additional private disks that store unique user data.

All desktops that are linked to a master VM can be patched or updated by updating the master image, without affecting users' settings, data, or applications. This means that less storage is required while desktop management is greatly simplified.

## Desktop Application Encapsulation

In a virtual desktop environment, it would be ideal to decouple applications and user data from the operating system. This can be done by isolating and encapsulating applications into an EXE or. MSI file. The VMware application that accomplishes this is ThinApp, which is agentless. With no agent, it is simple to deploy, and it can be used in conjunction with other VMware View components or by itself. ThinApp encapsulates an application and all the components it needs to run and puts it in a container isolated from the OS and from other applications, as shown in Figure 6-5.

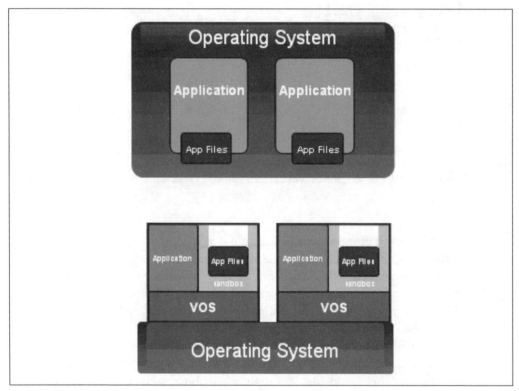

Figure 6-5    Encapsulated Applications

As you can see in the virtualized environment in the bottom of Figure 6-5, applications are encapsulated. With this approach, you can reuse VM templates for larger numbers of users, because the applications and user data can be served up from a central server rather than being part of the template. This results in a savings in storage and more control over each user's unique desktop. Because ThinApp is agentless, it can deploy to virtual or physical desktops and simplify upgrading and patching applications. ThinApp isolates the application from the OS, so it can run multiple versions of the same application side by side on the same client device.

# Desktop Access

A key to useful desktop virtualization is the ability to access your personalized, hosted desktop regardless of where it's located. In View, this capability is called Unified Access. With this functionality, a single user interface can gain secure access to multiple physical platforms, including the following:

- VMware virtual infrastructure
- Windows terminal server
- Blade PC
- Remote physical PC

Users are connected to the appropriate desktop environment, and connections can be audited and monitored to meet compliance and security requirements. Windows terminal servers can benefit from load balancing to improve performance.

# Virtual Printing

Printing in a virtual desktop environment often presents unique challenges. With View, the following capabilities exist:

- Driver-free printing, which consists of a server (on the Virtual Desktop) and a client (on the host) component.
- All printers are automatically available so a user can discover, connect, and print to any local or networked printer that's defined on the client device.

- Network utilization is reduced through print stream compression, allowing printing even over slower WAN connections.

Figure 6-6 depicts the Remote Desktop Protocol (RDP) and printing at a high-level.

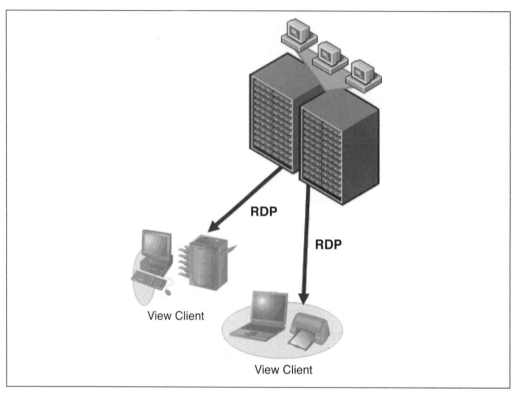

Figure 6-6    High-Level Remote Printing

## Check In and Check Out of the Virtual Desktop

Some devices are not constantly connected to the View infrastructure, but you may want these devices to have the same user features as the desktop. A user's virtual desktop may be "checked out" onto a physical device (laptop or a remote thin client), enabling the user to work when he is offline. Offline desktops can take advantage of local resources, which means that performance can be higher and latency can be minimized. Changes that a user makes to his configuration and all user data gets stored locally on the device until it's reconnected. Likewise, all changes made by the IT administrators that affect the virtual desktop image are queued up, awaiting its return. When the user "checks in" again, all changes are intelligently synchronized. This functionality in View is called Offline Desktop and is depicted in Figure 6-7.

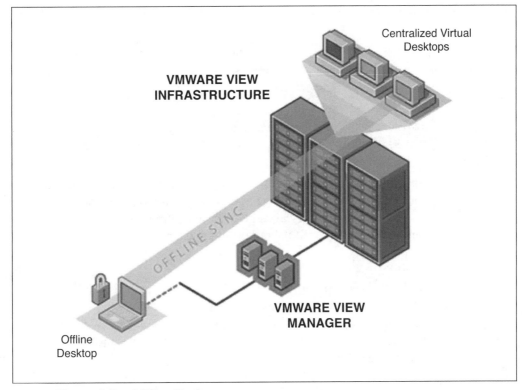

Figure 6-7    Offline Desktop

The Offline Desktop functionality is especially useful for mobile users and helps the IT management of mobile devices.

The next section discusses TCO and ROI as it relates to desktop virtualization.

# Desktop Virtualization TCO and ROI

A green endeavor must include a positive ROI in a short period of time. As with server consolidation, the desktop virtualization payback with View is calculated using Alinean. At the time of this writing, the following is the URL of the tool:

`www.vmware.com/go/calculator` redirects you to:

`https://roianalyst.alinean.com/ent_02/AutoLogin.do?d=593411470991915416`

The VMware TCO/ROI Calculator has an Analysis Option for Desktop Solutions that can help calculate the benefits of a move to VDI/View, the input to this tool is two tabs:

- **Profile.** Details of your organization, industry, location, and type of analysis. I chose the Desktop Solutions (using VMware View (formerly VDI) option for this analysis.

- **Questionnaire.** Here, quantities, costs, and other factors are entered. For Desktop Solutions, a large number of assumptions are predetermined based on industry averages. These assumptions can be viewed and edited to fit the unique circumstances of a particular organization.

A third tab (Desktop) appears after you enter the analysis type. After all parameters are entered, clicking this tab displays a detailed report of costs and savings. All input parameters and assumptions are shown.

The following is a quick three-year summary of what was produced for a client with 500 desktops:

- Power was reduced from 397,440KW to 179,820KW per year. This saves a total of 217,620KW per year. This assumes 12 hours of operation per day for the desktops.

- ROI of 87.8% is realized over three years. This includes all the investments in both the VMware virtualization tools and thin clients.

- NPV of $370,431 over three years and an IRR of 42.5% in 19 months is realized.

These numbers are based on a information provided to the TCO/ROI tool. The numbers can be adjusted in a variety of ways. The numbers assume, for instance, that a refresh of the existing desktops will be required in three years.

I always perform an exhaustive ROI/TCO analysis when planning desktop virtualization because, even if ultra-conservative numbers are used, the results are invariably compelling and result in substantial green benefits, which makes desktop virtualization a wonderful way to streamline desktop administration and save money and power. These factors combined make this an ideal green solution.

The next section covers blade workstations for high-end users.

## Dedicated Workstation Blades

Up to this point, I've covered desktop virtualization, which can provide some huge benefits in reduced costs, easier management, and power and cooling costs. Not all users fit the profile for virtualization, however, and in some industries, a large population needs another solution to meet their needs. Applications that require the computer, and graphics resources that only high-powered workstations can meet are candidates for a different solution. Workers that use complex 2D and 3D graphics software or that require multiple monitor support find that a virtualization using the Remote Desktop Protocol (RDP) protocol that provides access to it can't handle the processing, graphics support, and transmission requirements they need.

HP developed a communications protocol and a total solution to meet the needs of this unique segment. Financial firms with traders' workstations running complex analytical and graphics software packages with multiple monitors are an example of an environment that needs this type of solution. Engineers and architects running CAD and design software are another group that can benefit. Figure 6-8 shows the layout of a dedicated blade workstation.

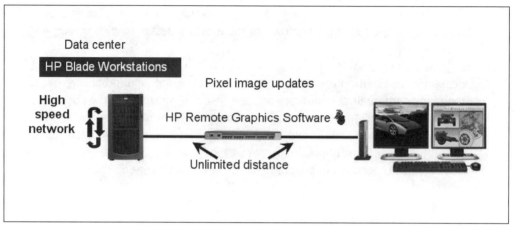

Figure 6-8    Simplified Blade Workstation Operation

As Figure 6-8 shows, Remote Graphics Software (RGS) connects the workstation blade, typically in a data center, to the thin client over any distance. RGS runs over TCP/IP.

The dedicated workstation blade is different than the virtualized desktop solution in many ways, including the following:

- Both solutions have thin client (or low-end desktop) units sitting on the user's desk, attached to monitor(s), keyboard, mouse, and network.

- View uses VMware ESX servers to host virtual desktops for multiple users. When a user logs in, she gets the same applications and appearance she did before virtualization. Upgrades and support are easier for the IT staff, and centralizing to a few physical servers saves power, cooling, space on the desk, and provides better control and data security.

- The HP blade workstation solution assigns a workstation-class blade to high-end users. A user can be assigned his own blade, or the blades can be in a pool, with users assigned the next available as they log in.

- HP's Session Allocation Manager (SAM) can control what resource—View virtualized desktop or Blade Workstation—is assigned based on the profile of the user logging in.

A key factor to consider when determining whether a blade workstation or a virtualized desktop is the right platform is on which platform the application is now running. If a standard desktop is getting the job done, and no more than two monitors are required, desktop virtualization is probably the right solution. If a high-end workstation is currently being used with complex graphics and over two monitors, then blade workstations are probably the right solution. My recommendation is that if you're unsure of which solution is right for you, then a limited scope Proof of Concept (POC) is in order. I've run many such POCs, and the process always makes clear which solution is right for the environment.

# Benefits and Components of Workstation Blades

Although the blade workstation solution is not for the majority of desktop users, it has many benefits for high-end users:

- **Centralized control**. Removing physical workstations from users' desks and centralizing them in the data center allows them to be administered more effectively and lets them be shared among multiple users in different locations, shifts, and time zones.
- **Reduced Move/Add/Change costs**. A user can sit at any desk and bring up their desktop on the thin client at which he's sitting.
- **Power and cooling savings**. The blade workstation has lower power consumption, including a smaller number of workstations shared among users, and power and heat are taken away from the desk and moved to the data center.
- **Better security**. Blade workstations and all data are housed in the secure data center. Only pixels are transmitted, and the stream is compressed and encrypted.
- **Greater management and control**. SAM lets you manage all workstations centrally and provision desktops instantly to new users, departments, or offices.
- **Business continuance and disaster control**. RGS allows users to access their workstations from other locations—from anywhere with WAN access. With pooling, if a blade workstation fails, the user can simply connect to the next available one.

These benefits are inherent in blade workstations and don't require a lot of customization to realize. It is important, however, to ensure your blade workstation design is solid because many components are involved, such as the workstation, thin client, network, management tools, and others.

Two key components of blade workstations are:

1. **RGS**. RGS is specially designed as a communication protocol to handle remote access and control of graphics-intense applications. It captures data as it goes to a graphics buffer, compresses and encrypts it, and sends only the pixel image updates across the wire to a receiving station. Because special high-power graphics card(s) are involved, the receiving device must have compatible graphics support, and may have multiple monitors connected to those graphics cards.

2. **Blade Workstation**. RGS will work with HP standalone workstation-class devices, but the true value of the solution is a space and power-efficient blade infrastructure using c-Class blade workstations. These blades are based on c-Class server blades, but with additional graphics cards and alternative operating system support. The blades use HP's c-Class infrastructure to house the blades, the power and cooling components, management interface, and network connectivity components.

Numerous blade workstations are available, which are a key consideration when designing your workstation blade solution.

In addition to the workstation blades, the thin client is also a key consideration. At the desk, the user is equipped with a thin client device and the appropriate monitor(s) and input devices (mouse, keyboard, and so on.) Other options are available, such as a low-power desktop, an available workstation, or any browser-equipped device on the WAN. Thin clients offer the best power savings in the smallest size.

The HP Session Allocation Manager (SAM) automatically provisions the blade workstation resources to your users. HP SAM provides the following capabilities with the blade workstation solution:

- Supports two types of resource assignments:
  1. **Static resources**. With static resources, a user and the user's client computer are connected to a predefined set of remote computing resources, even when the user changes location.

2. **Dynamic resources**. With dynamic resources, users are assigned remote computing resources from a pool of available computing resources.

- **Single log in**. Simplifies the user experience by allowing the user to log in just once, even if the user is connecting to multiple blade workstations. Furthermore, with a multi-monitor client computer, HP SAM automatically positions the user's windows on the monitors connected to the client computer based on pre-configured information.

- **Follow-me roaming**. Enables users to move to a different location, and automatically reconnect to the computing resources they used previously.

- **Automatic failover**. HP SAM can be configured so that if a blade workstation fails, another blade workstation is automatically assigned to the task performed by the failed unit. This feature works for both static and dynamic connections, maximizing the uptime of the blade workstation solution and the user's productivity.

- **Administration**. A a web interface that allows all parameters of HP SAM operation to be easily monitored and changed from a central location.

## Summary

Desktop virtualization is one of the few technologies that benefits users, administrators, and the financial members of your company. The ROI is clear for this technology and, as an administrator, you must be enthusiastic about this technology.

Part II covers backup and recovery advancements in an area where some of the oldest and inefficient technology remains in use and is overdue for an upgrade.

# Part II
# Backup and Recovery

**Chapter 7: The Existing Backup and Recovery Environment**

**Chapter 8: Existing Backup and Recovery Analysis with Backup Assessment**

**Chapter 9: The Enhanced Backup and Recovery Solution**

**Chapter 10: Backup, Recovery, and Archive ROI Analysis**

**Chapter 11: Data Replication and Disk Technology Advancements**

# Introduction to Part II

This part covers modernizing the backup and recovery environment by analyzing an existing backup and recovery solution and then covering the design and implementation of a new solution. There is also an archive component that is associated with backup and recovery, resulting in the umbrella term BackUp, Recovery, and Archive (BURA). I don't present an archive solution in the case study, but I do have a section in the chapter covering archive concepts in general.

This part covers the following topics, going through the process of evaluating the existing and proposed backup environments:

- Diagram and discussion of an inefficient backup and recovery environment with many more servers and tape devices than are required.
- Analysis of the existing backup environment, highlighting inefficiencies in the environment.
- Some general backup, recovery, and archive considerations before the assessment is performed.
- An example backup assessment run on the existing backup environment with the EMC tool *Backup Assessment Using Quick Scripts* (*Backup Assessment*).
- Analysis of the proposed streamlined backup environment, highlighting its many advantages, including greatly reduced backup and recovery time and power and cooling improvements.
- Implementation plan example to ensure the environment is properly implemented.
- An overview of an ROI analysis comparing the existing backup environment and the new streamlined environment.
- An overview of replication techniques, including array, disk, and fabric-based.
- Some advancements in disk technology. Although this is not specifically related to backup, recovery, and archive, some BURA solutions can benefit from these technologies.

The backup solution presented is advanced and does not require tape drives unlike the old backup environment, which was cobbled together over time with many clients with local tape drives connected to them.

# Chapter 7

## The Existing Backup and Recovery Environment

This chapter covers a case study of an existing backup environment. Like many backup implementations, the one covered in this chapter was first implemented when network speeds were slow, so local tape drives were required to be connected to each client.

Many general backup considerations are covered in this chapter, including de-duplication, archive, and many others.

## Existing Backup and Recovery Solution

This section covers the existing backup and recovery environment and its many inefficiencies, including the following:

- Backup server "sprawl" in which the environment has grown to 40 backup servers when many fewer servers are required
- Tape drives scattered throughout the environment
- Long backup window, which is unnecessarily long for the amount of data and number of clients that are part of the backup
- Consistent backup errors that are identified in the backup report

Figure 7-1 is a simplified depiction of the existing backup and recovery environment.

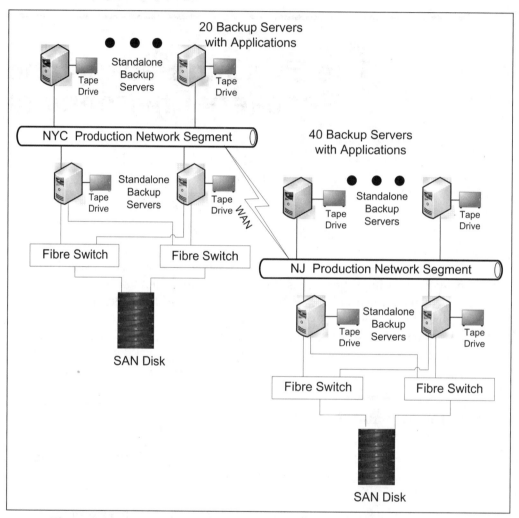

Figure 7-1    Existing Backup and Recovery Environment

Figure 7-1 shows a typical antiquated backup and recovery environment. Here are some parameters related to the figure:

- There are approximately 50 servers with local tape drives that do not back up any clients and handle only their own backup. (The next chapter covers the results of the assessment tool that produces details on the environment.)

- There is no centralized management of the backup environment.

- Most critical application servers act as their own backup server, meaning they have a dedicated tape drive connected to them.

- The two sites have nearly identical environments.

- There are both Windows-based and UNIX-based backup solutions in the environment supporting different applications.

- There is no de-duplication, so the backups are inefficient from a data standpoint, meaning the same data is backed up over and over again.

Many backup servers and tape drives are scattered throughout the environment. Not shown in Figure 7-1 are the many backup software and operational problems that exist. There is a tremendous opportunity to improve this backup and recovery environment at almost every level, including backup hardware, software, operational efficiency, backup and recovery time, and many others, which will be covered in when the new environment is presented.

The existing network shows a classic distributed backup environment. There is usually no single point of management or monitoring. Each application server runs its own copy of the backup software and uses its own management console. The only way to determine the status of the backup processes is to log on to each individual application server and check its status.

In this example, the backup operator has a combination of some 50 backup servers spread out over 2 physical locations. These backup servers are responsible for their own backup plus an additional 300 clients. More than 90% of the backup servers are completely isolated from each other in that they back up local data and don't communicate with other backup servers.

In addition to that, each site has its own implementation of a shared tape library attached to a Primary Backup Server and additional Media Server\Storage Node servers in operation.

There is also a mix of backup solutions. There is a Windows-based solution managed by the Windows group administrators, and there is a UNIX-based solution managed by UNIX administrators. Although they share access to the tape library, the six drives in the library are broken up into three for the UNIX backups and three for the Windows backups.

If the UNIX jobs are done but the Windows jobs continue to run, only the three tape drives devoted Windows are used by Windows. The three additional UNIX tape drives are not able to be used because of the library configuration.

The installation of the shared tape libraries is a step in the right direction. The power costs for running the additional 40 to 50 standalone tape drives is substantially higher than the shared tape libraries. There are many other disadvantages to the distributed tape libraries, including the organizational cost of purchasing tapes of different capacities that are required for the standalone tape drives, and the human resource cost of managing, transporting, loading, and unloading of this many tape drives manually.

In addition to these drawbacks, there are management-related issues, as well. The lack of a single point of management and monitoring for such a large backup environment makes any Service Level Agreement (SLA) for backup and recovery difficult to meet. Because there is no centrally located catalog of all enterprise backups available, in order to recover a requested file, the operator first needs to know which backup server he needs to access. The next step would be to run an inquiry on the catalog of that isolated server. Then, the tape would need to be located from a shelf, drawer, or off-site backup location. The tape would have to be manually placed into the direct attached tape drive of that backup server, and then the recovery could begin.

These problems can be solved with a centrally located catalog. A centrally located catalog allows for efficiencies that a distributed multi-catalog configuration can't accomplish. It provides a complete picture of the enterprise's backup failure and success rates. This means you can identify any client that is at risk because of incomplete or problem impacted backups.

Many of the existing backup programs provide for email notification, and you could argue that by using this form of monitoring and notification, you could resolve any problems that might arise. The saturation of emails that all system administrators receive today, and the white noise it creates in our Blackberry-driven IT world, has made this method of problem notification and resolution less reliable.

The upcoming sections describe some background information related to key backup topics before the assessment is covered in the next chapter.

# Data De-Duplication

Data de-duplication is a means by which data storage is reduced by eliminating redundant data. Data de-duplication is also known as "intelligent compression" or "single-instance storage," but I use data de-duplication in this overview.

With data de-duplication, only one unique instance of the data is retained on storage media. Redundant data is replaced with a pointer to the unique data copy. If 100 emails all contain the same 1MB attachment, for instance, 100MB would be consumed. With data de-duplication, however, only one instance of the attachment is stored; each subsequent instance is just referenced to the one saved copy. Rather than consuming 100MB, only 1MB of storage is consumed.

There are many efficiencies introduced with data de-duplication, resulting in considerably less storage space being consumed including reduced cost, power, and cooling. Recovery time is drastically reduced with much less storage being consumed.

With de-duplication, every block of data is examined by sophisticated algorithms to determine if the system is already storing it. If it is, that block is replaced with a pointer to the original copy. The result is a huge reduction in the amount of data stored.

Data de-duplication can generally operate at the file, block, and even the bit level. Block de-duplication looks within a file and saves unique iterations of each block. Each chunk of data is processed using a hash algorithm, such as MD5 or SHA-1. This process generates a unique number for each piece which is then stored in an index. If a file is updated, only the changed, data is saved. If only a few bytes of a document are changed, then only the changed blocks are saved, thereby greatly reducing the storage space required.

De-duplication assigns hash numbers to pieces of data. That number is compared with the index of other existing hash numbers. If that hash number is already in the index, the piece of data is considered a duplicate and does not need to be stored again. Otherwise, the new hash number is added to the index and the new data is stored. In rare cases, the hash algorithm may produce the same hash number for two different chunks of data. When a hash collision occurs, the system won't store the new data because it sees that its hash number already exists in the index, which can result in data loss. Metadata is also evaluated to identify data and prevent collisions.

De-duplication is the technology that made disk-to-disk backup and Virtual Tape Libraries (VTL) popular technologies. Now, most vendors offer it in both VTL and NAS presentations. This is technology with a compelling ROI that has only penetrated to a small percentage of the marketplace and will grow dramatically over the next few years.

De-duplication can be done at either the target or source. Source de-duplication minimizes the amount of data that is sent over the LAN or WAN reducing the amount of bandwidth required. This introduces even more efficiency in to the environment.

# Archive

By definition, archiving is the process of storing historic records. In terms of information technology, to archive is to transition infrequently accessed data and/or data that has been selected for long-term or even permanent retention from its existing storage location to another.

Archiving is a major component of any information lifecycle management (ILM) strategy. It is common to interchange the term archive with backup. Today's IT executives must deal with growing amounts of data, increased regulation, and compliance mandates and an ever expanding backup window.

An archiving solution, as opposed to a backup solution, is meant to hold static, unchanged data. As mentioned, storage tiering is becoming a more common business practice. Archiving is a major component of storage tiering. Once your organization classifies data, you establish policies that control the movement of the data through its lifecycle to the appropriate storage tiers.

As an example, your organization may have aged files that you need to retain for an extended period of time because of regulatory compliance. You would establish a policy using file archival software, along with write once read many (WORM) storage. Once the threshold within the policy has been met, the data would get transferred from its existing tier of storage to typically a less expensive, low performance, WORM storage for archival. Upon the data's expiration, the data is digitally shred and the WORM storage space is freed for use.

It is common with today's archiving hardware and software to maintain a single copy, or single instance, of each file in order to reduce duplicate copies of the data. One of the most popular archive solutions is content addressable storage (CAS) that EMC offers called Centera. EMC Centera is object-based WORM storage. It works in conjunction with an application server that either runs archive software or has an application that uses an application programming interface (API) that writes directly to the EMC Centera. EMC offers archive software for both file and email archiving. The products are called EMC DiskXtender and EMC SourceOne respectively. Many other third-party archival software products are available and hundreds of independent software vendors (ISV) have used the API to write to the EMC Centera.

With most archiving solutions, a software algorithm is placed between users, production disk, and archive disk. A typical archiving scenario is for an organization to establish a policy that transfers production data after it has reached a certain age, from its production tier of storage to its archival tier. Once the data is transferred, the archive software leaves a small tag or stub file behind on the production disk. It acts as a pointer to redirect the user to the archived file, which is now on a less expensive archive storage media.

In addition to allowing for the use of less expensive storage media to maintain older and infrequently accessed data, the archiving process allows an organization to reduce its total production disk usage. This, in turn, also greatly reduces the length of time for backups because the data that was archived is removed from the production backup job.

As an example, an organization had a production file server, which had a 1TB volume consisting of user directories. The volume was 98% utilized. An archive policy was applied to this volume that stated that data not accessed in the last 180 days should be transferred to archive. Once the policy was applied, the organization reduced its utilized capacity to just 25%, which reduced the amount of active production data and the length of time for the backup.

In summary, data archival is crucial and required by most regulated organizations. Many organizations are adopting a tiered storage model that includes data archival. Archival not only helps organizations maintain data integrity for compliance, but it also helps increase the efficient use of production storage, reduce backup windows, and helps improve production application performance. For these reasons, archival is increasing in popularity and is now a consideration for most organizations within a variety of industries.

# General Backup Considerations

This section covers some important backup topics, not all of which are related to the current or proposed backup environments covered in this book, but are important considerations about backup in general.

## Media

For the last 50 years, tape media has been used to hold data for the IT community. Media has gone through numerous technical improvements with massive gains in capacity and speed, but the underlying concept of a magnetically modified roll of chemically treated plastic tape remains in place. Over time, tape will degrade, and at some point, will begin to show I/O errors rendering that information inaccessible. This is a concern when compliance is a consideration because the integrity of the media must be in place for at least as long as compliance regulations require.

Tape has the additional limitation of being sequential in operation, which means data is written on the tape in a serial manner. Tape can never be considered online even if a tape is mounted in the tape drive; the process of streaming to the proper location on the tape can require a substantial amount of time because this is a mechanical process.

A preferred method of backup is disk storage. Disk storage is used in the proposed backup solution in this book. Disk has many advantages, such as being online and orders of magnitude faster than tape.

The current disk backup solution are intelligent storage arrays, which are fast, reliable, and dense. The flexibility and reliability these new arrays are more reliable than tape and do not suffer the major drawback of sequential reads and writes. Not only do intelligent storage arrays provide faster random access for both reads and writes, but they constantly scrub, analyze, and a monitor in a proactive way the disks and the data they contain.

You will see in the advanced backup solutions that disk technology is used as the recommended primary backup solution.

## Full Versus Incremental Backup

A full backup makes a copy of all the data on the storage devices pointed to by the backup process. If you run a full backup of 10TB over three consecutive days, you back up a total of 30TB of data on backup media. With an incremental backup, you back up only changed data after your first full backup. This results in substantially less than 30TB being backed up.

Incremental backups come in two forms: There is a differential type of incremental backup and there is the cumulative type of incremental backup. A differential will back up any changed files since the full and the last differential backup. A cumulative type of incremental backup will back up any changed files since the last cumulative backup and also back up any changed files since the last full backup.

Normally, the cumulative backup will use up more resources during backup; however, restoring required files will be much easier and quicker.

## Clone Versus Replication of Data

As it relates to backup and recovery, a clone is a duplicate copy of a backup image. That backup image can be either on a tape or a disk. The original backup image can then be copied to the same type of media—for instance, tape to tape, or disk to disk—as well as different types of media, such as tape to disk or disk to tape. The creation and management of a clone is handled by the backup software.

In the case of replication, you usually deal with the copying of a pre-defined LUN or area of disk storage from one LUN to another LUN. This process is usually carried out on an intelligence storage array and managed by a web-based console that has access to the storage array. Replication in most cases is best used for disaster recovery; however, many organizations feel that they can use replication to replace backup. Although arguments can be made for this position, true recovery capability requires the ability to recover files from yesterday, last week, last month, and last year. In order for replication to provide this capability, the organization may have to make a large investment in disk storage.

## Backup and Recovery Versus Disaster Recovery

As already discussed, there is a critical difference between what the organization uses for backup and recovery and what the same organization uses for disaster recovery.

Backup and recovery allows for restoring individual files and folders.

Disaster recovery requires a defined and acceptable Recovery Time Objective (RTO) and Recovery Point Objective (RPO). It will be limited by the total amount of disk made available and the number of snapshots required by the SLA.

The new backup and recovery environment proposed in an upcoming chapter has disk libraries, used as the backup and recovery foundation, in two different locations. The units are replicated, which means that in the event of a disaster in one location, the disk library in the other location can be used as the backup or restore device. This is by no means a complete disaster recovery plan, so be sure you analyze all aspects of disaster recovery in your environment.

## Distributed Backup Versus Centralized Backup

Early distributed forms of networking and storage required the need to install tape drives directly to the servers being backed up. Early network speeds also impacted the amount of data that could be transmitted in a given time window to perform a backup.When slow network speeds were the norm, it was a necessity in some cases to have local tape drives to backup clients because the slow network speeds would not support a centralized backup environment. This is true in the case study in which virtually all the clients have a local tape drive for backup.

In the distributed environment, the tape drives could only be accessed by a server directly attached to it. The tape resource was not able to be shared across multiple servers. With the advent of SAN fibre networks, storage resources could now be shared and would no longer be limited to a server with a direct attachment.

Although distributing the backup process may be an easy solution when first setting up backups, eventually the monitoring and management of the network as a whole will become difficult. There is no central reference point from which to monitor all the separate backup servers. Each backup server maintains its own catalog of data and tapes, and this information is not shared with any of the other backup servers in the organization's environment.

With the advent of 100MB and faster speeds, the network bandwidth growth has allowed for backups of clients from a few centrally controlled backup servers, media servers, and storage nodes.

For a centrally controlled backup solution, the primary backup server will maintain a shared database updated by the backup server, storage nodes, and the various clients they backup. This database can usually be accessed by a web-based console, and a complete picture of the status of the backup and recovery environment can be viewed.

The existing backup environment analyzed uses an overly distributed model in which almost all clients had local tape drives, making it impossible for all backup windows to be met and effective administration of the environment was difficult.

## Summary

Most clients with whom I work have antiquated backup environments that need to be modernized. There is sometimes, however, a reluctance to improve the backup environment because they have grown over time and there are a lot of unknown factors associated with them. It is considered onerous to take on this modernization.

The next chapter covers *Backup Assessment* and the many shortcomings of the existing backup environment.

# CHAPTER 8

# Existing Backup and Recovery Analysis with Backup Assessment

This chapter covers several topics related to analyzing the existing backup and recovery environment. This process uncovers many inefficiencies specific to the client environment under study, but also covers many problems inherent in outdated backup environments that grow incrementally over time until they're altogether inefficient. The EMC tool *Backup Assessment Using Quick Scripts* (Backup Assessment) output is the basis for the discussion in this chapter. (The tool used for the analysis is actually a spin-off of Backup Assessment but, for simplicity purposes, I use Backup Assessment throughout this book.) Backup Assessment performs a thorough analysis of the existing environment which, when carefully analyzed, provides tremendous insight in to the current environment and the areas where improvements can be made. My firm is certified by EMC to run Backup Assessment. Among the topics analyzed with Backup Assessment are the following, all of which are summarized for the assessment period:

- Backup server list, including backup software and the number of clients handled by each server
- List of media servers
- Summary of backup jobs
- Summary of restore jobs
- Diagram of the daily backup activity for each server

- List of the backups that take the longest amount of time
- Largest backup jobs by the number of files
- Fastest and slowest clients
- Largest clients
- Servers on which the highest failure rates took place
- Unreliable clients and their success rates
- Summary of the media pool
- mplementation plan using Virtual Tape Library (VTL) and de-duplication to improve the overall backup and recovery environment

These, and many other charts and graphs, are provided by the Backup Assessment output. I selected a subset of material in the Backup Assessment output for a specific client example and included them in this chapter.

In addition to the output about the specific client environment, there are high-level recommendations provided by Backup Assessment. I also include the Virtual Tape Library (VTL) capacity provided by Backup Assessment because a VTL is usually the upgrade to the existing environment that solves many of the inherent backup problems.

This chapter covers some of the Backup Assessment output and where the shortcomings are in the existing backup environment. The Backup Assessment was run for 30 days in this client example.

## Snapshot of Backup Servers

Backup Assessment produces an inventory of backup servers and important information about each server. Figure 8-1 shows backup server information for ten of the most actively used backup servers.

| Server | Backup Software | Version | # Clients | Backup in GB |
|--------|-----------------|---------|-----------|--------------|
| Server1 | Backup Exec | 11.0.5809.0 | 7 | 5,188.71 |
| Server2 | Backup Exec | 11.0.5809.0 | 4 | 1,802.19 |
| Server3 | Backup Exec | 11.0.5809.0 | 3 | 1,741.03 |
| Server4 | Backup Exec | 12.0.1269.0 | 17 | 37,821.50 |
| Server5 | Backup Exec | 12.0.1269.0 | 2 | 4,406.36 |
| Server6 | Backup Exec | 12.0.1269.0 | 1 | 167.23 |
| Server7 | Backup Exec | 12.0.1269.0 | 1 | 489.46 |
| Server8 | Backup Exec | 12.0.1269.0 | 1 | 484.80 |
| Server9 | Backup Exec | 12.0.1269.0 | 2 | 3,130.85 |
| Server10 | Backup Exec | 12.0.1269.0 | 29 | 14,844.64 |

Figure 8-1    Ten Most Active Backup Servers

These backup servers vary widely in the number of clients that are backed up by each and the amount of data backed up by each. One server backs up 29 clients and another backs up only 1. This indicates an environment that has grown by adding servers over the years as required, but no planning was performed related to balancing the number of clients handled by each backup server or the amount of data handled by each backup server. The dynamics of the environment later change and no adjustments are made to the backup environment, thereby making it inefficient.

Figure 8-2 shows a backup job summary for the Backup Assessment.

| Server | Clients | # Jobs | Success Rate (%) | # Clients > 8 Hours | Backed Up (GB) | # Files |
|--------|---------|--------|------------------|---------------------|----------------|---------|
| Server1 | 7 | 865 | 100.00 | 1 | 5,188.71 | 11,419,006 |
| Server2 | 4 | 424 | 100.00 | 0 | 1,802.19 | 7,519,850 |
| Server3 | 3 | 380 | 100.00 | 0 | 1,741.03 | 3,419,572 |
| Server4 | 17 | 1,660 | 96.69 | 0 | 37,821.50 | 30,410,055 |
| Server5 | 2 | 135 | 92.59 | 0 | 4,406.36 | 49,306,062 |
| Server6 | 1 | 105 | 90.48 | 0 | 167.23 | 581,429 |
| Server7 | 1 | 89 | 100.00 | 0 | 489.46 | 4,004,192 |
| Server8 | 1 | 90 | 100.00 | 0 | 484.80 | 1,310,850 |
| Server9 | 2 | 240 | 98.33 | 1 | 3,130.85 | 6,047,950 |
| Server10 | 29 | 3,409 | 96.83 | 2 | 14,844.64 | 26,992,777 |
| Server11a | 5 | 132 | 100.00 | 0 | 535.51 | 2,713,325 |

Figure 8-2    Backup Job Summary

Figure 8-2 shows the summary of backup activity during the 30-day monitored period. The number of clients shown is the number of clients for which at least one backup job was attempted. There are some clients for which the backup exceeded eight hours, which is well outside the backup window and needs to be addressed. The job summary shows many glaring inefficiencies, including an imbalance between backup servers, including the following:

- Number of clients assigned to a backup server ranging from 1 to 29
- Number of jobs run on a backup server ranging from 89 to 3409
- Amount of data backed up by a server ranging from 167GB to 37821GB

A red flag in the Figure 8-2 is the number of clients for which the backup took more than eight hours and the success rate of less than 100%. The low success rate could be for a variety of reasons, including a tape that was full and not changed.

A failed backup job can translate in to a failed recovery. A failure to recover critical files following a disaster could result in data inconsistency or or loss. This could lead to lost revenue, fines, or other problems.

Figure 8-3 shows the hours of backup for the servers in the environment.

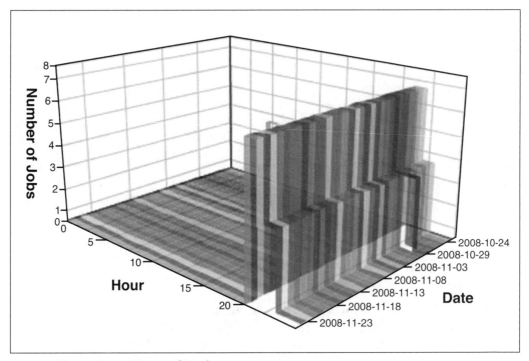

Figure 8-3    Hours of Backup

Figure 8-3 shows that for the 30-day period over which the Backup Assessment was run, almost all backup jobs were initiated from roughly 6:00 to 10:00 PM every evening, which is a common time to initiate backup jobs. This is the time during which jobs were initiated, not the time during which the backups completed.

## Backup Client Capacity

An important factor in evaluating the backup environment is for which clients the largest backups are taking place and for which clients the largest number of files are being backed up. These characteristics help you understand the existing environment and to design a new solution.

Figure 8-4 shows the clients for which the largest daily backups take place.

| Server | Host | Peak Daily Capacity (GB) | Avg MB/sec | Fastest Single Job (MB/sec) | Success Rate (%) | Percent of Total Capacity | Type | Avg Daily Duration (Hours) |
|---|---|---|---|---|---|---|---|---|
| Server1 | Server1 | 1,367.73 | 27.92 | 73.40 | 93.28 | 6.08 | Server | 1.50 |
| Server2 | Server2 | 1,148.19 | 54.51 | 133.23 | 97.62 | 44.00 | Server | 5.46 |
| Server3 | Server3 | 749.55 | 21.57 | 37.26 | 83.82 | 5.22 | Server | 1.09 |
| Server4 | Client1 | 639.58 | 38.17 | 62.19 | 100.00 | 3.39 | Client | 6.12 |
| Server5 | Server5 | 438.75 | 8.07 | 16.99 | 97.92 | 4.73 | Server | 3.66 |
| Server6 | Client2 | 245.99 | 7.53 | 10.59 | 96.79 | 1.42 | Client | 1.30 |
| Server7 | Client3 | 236.89 | 10.02 | 10.94 | 100.00 | 1.69 | Client | 1.16 |
| Server8 | Client4 | 224.67 | 10.72 | 11.16 | 96.67 | 3.77 | Client | 2.42 |
| Server9 | Client5 | 149.36 | 18.17 | 65.31 | 100.00 | 2.12 | Client | 0.80 |
| Server10 | Client6 | 108.88 | 10.26 | 10.67 | 94.62 | 3.32 | Client | 2.21 |
| Server11 | Client7 | 101.71 | 7.12 | 8.97 | 100.00 | 1.66 | Client | 1.61 |
| Server12 | Client8 | 94.76 | 11.16 | 11.28 | 96.88 | 0.97 | Client | 0.60 |

Figure 8-4    Largest Client Backups

The list of largest backup clients indicates that several backups take place for the backup server and not a client. This list goes on for several pages but for illustrative purposes, I included only the first few clients on the list.

Backup Assessment also produced a list of clients for which the largest number of files were backed up.

This information is used in producing recommendations for the improved backup environment.


# Backup and Restore Job Summary

The backup environment overview in the previous section revealed many configuration problems with respect to the overall layout of the backup servers, the relationship between the backup servers and number of clients, and other potential problems. These problems may manifest themselves in long backups and restores with many potential problems, such as a failures (low success rate) for some of the backups. The upcoming diagrams in this section confirm that many such problems exist.

Figure 8-5 shows that some of the jobs took an exceptionally long time to run.

| Duration (Hours) | Capacity (GB) | MB/sec |
|---|---|---|
| 30.87 | 246.00 | 2.27 |
| 14.90 | 119.76 | 2.29 |
| 10.24 | 727.60 | 20.21 |
| 6.05 | 230.74 | 10.84 |
| 6.04 | 22.10 | 1.04 |
| 6.00 | 229.68 | 10.88 |
| 5.96 | 21.56 | 1.03 |
| 5.95 | 228.93 | 10.94 |
| 5.94 | 227.75 | 10.91 |
| 5.93 | 226.46 | 10.87 |
| 5.87 | 21.06 | 1.02 |
| 5.85 | 20.54 | 1.00 |
| 5.62 | 20.07 | 1.02 |

Figure 8-5   Longest Running Backup Jobs

A lot of additional information was provided for each job, such as the server name, but I included only a few columns of information.

These backup jobs run far beyond the time it should take to back up the amount of data that is part of the job. The first backup, which runs for more than 30 hours, clearly won't complete if that job is initiated at the same time every day. The resources being consumed to run these long backup jobs require an extensive amount of backup server networking and memory resources to be consumed just to support the backup. A restore typically takes much longer than the time for backup, so it is possible that a restore would not take place for some of these jobs.

Equally concerning is the queue time for some jobs, as shown in Figure 8-6.

| Time Queued (GMT) | Hours Queued |
|---|---|
| 2008-11-15 19:00 | 46.65 |
| 2008-11-15 19:00 | 46.64 |
| 2008-11-15 19:00 | 46.63 |
| 2008-11-15 19:00 | 31.73 |
| 2008-11-13 11:00 | 10.63 |
| 2008-11-13 11:00 | 10.62 |
| 2008-11-13 11:00 | 10.62 |
| 2008-11-15 03:00 | 10.41 |
| 2008-11-15 03:00 | 10.41 |
| 2008-11-06 11:00 | 10.06 |
| 2008-11-06 11:00 | 10.06 |
| 2008-11-06 11:00 | 10.05 |
| 2008-11-08 03:00 | 9.95 |
| 2008-11-08 03:00 | 9.95 |

Figure 8-6    Longest Queue Jobs

A lot of additional information was provided for jobs with a long queue such as the job name, host media, and so on, but I focus on *Hours Queued*.

These queued jobs are waiting for some resource, such as a tape drive, to become free so that the job can be initiated. This is great information because it allows these problems to be identified and corrected.

If the time to complete backup jobs is long, it stands to reason that restores will also take a long time to complete. Figure 8-7 shows a summary of recent restore jobs for the environment.

| Server | Clients | # Restore Jobs | Success Rate (%) | Restored (GB) | # Files |
|--------|---------|----------------|------------------|---------------|---------|
| Server3 | 1 | 1 | 100.00 | 1.25 | 384 |
| Server5 | 2 | 15 | 73.33 | 227.30 | 4,285 |
| Server9 | 1 | 2 | 100.00 | 0.02 | 54 |

Figure 8-7    Restore Job Summary

The success rate of the second restore job is below 75%, indicating that there was contention, possibly for the tape drive, that caused the success rate to be low.

There isn't much about the current backup and restore environment that gives me confidence that all backups are taking place and that, if required, a restore of any of the information in the environment could take place. The following section summarizes what Backup Assessment produces as recommendations for the new backup and restore environment covered in the next chapter.

# Recommendations for Improving the Environment

There are some fundamental problems with the existing backup environment. However, they can be easily solved with new and streamlined technology. Using Virtual Tape Libraries (VTLs) in the existing environment, the following benefits are realized:

- Increased parallelism of backups by employing a disk library, called a VTL, in the in the analysis document. With VTL, you can create hundreds of virtual tape drives within dozens of VTL, thereby supporting a large number of backup servers and clients.
- Increased throughput of backups because many can be performed simultaneously without slow tapes involved.
- Rapid recovery can be performed because the disks of VTL are always online, unlike slow tapes for which media retrieval must take place.
- Data de-duplication built in to the VTL greatly reduces the amount of data included in the backup.

- Data can be copied to tape after the initial backup takes place to VTL at a more "leisurely" pace so the tapes can be shipped offsite.
- As an alternative to tape, data can be replicated to a remote VTL using encryption.

These recommendations are based on statistics gathered during the Backup Assessment process. The Backup Assessment uncovered a substantial amount of "low change rate data" meaning the same data is being backed up in full and incremental backups. The following are the statistics associated with this data:

**Full backup analysis** (numerous full backup only per week)

- There was a peak of 12,528GB per week backed up in a full backup schedule. This typically has a high degree of redundancy, meaning the same data is being backed up over and over again that would benefit greatly from de-duplication.
- If this full backup data had a 10% change rate, which is a high change rate, de-duplication would reduce the weekly full backup to roughly 1.253 GB.

**Full and then incremental backups** (one full and numerous incremental backups per week)

- There was a peak of 4,848GB per week backed up in a full and then incremental backup schedule (at least one full and at least one incremental).
- The daily incremental change rate of this data is approximately 2%.
- Of this data, there was a peak of 2,581GB/week of full backups, which would be greatly reduced through de-duplication.
- By de-duplicating the full backups, a peak of 2,267GB per week of incremental data exists, which could also be de-duplicated.

With de-duplication, both the full and full/incremental would be drastically reduced. This reduction, combined with VTL, would immensely improve the efficiency of this backup environment.

# Summary

Backup Assessment provides a lot of valuable information about the short-comings of the existing backup solution. There are serious problems in this environment, some of which may violate compliance rules. They need to be corrected in order to ensure that data backup completes and recoveries can take place.

The next chapter covers the new backup environment that is much more operationally efficient than the existing environment.

# CHAPTER 9

## The Enhanced Backup and Recovery Solution

Based on the analysis performed on the existing backup and recovery environment in Chapter 8, this chapter covers the new backup and recovery solution. The Backup Assessment Using Quick Scripts (Backup Assessment) run in the previous chapter produced a tremendous amount of data about the existing backup and recovery environment, taking the guesswork out of the drawbacks to the existing environment and results in a more efficient new solution. (The tool used for the analysis is actually a spin-off of Backup Assessment but for simplicity purposes, I use Backup Assessment throughout this book.) Based on the statistics, the ideal backup and recovery solution can be crafted with predicted results.

This chapter covers the new solution based on the Backup Assessment and some of the technologies integral to the solution, including de-duplication and a replicated disk library. The EMC disk library in this solution has a legacy with many names, including Virtual Tape Library (VTL), Enterprise Disk Library (EDL), DL3D (which you see in the upcoming screen shots), and many others. I use disk library, but you may see these names used in output documents from various tools and online when researching disk libraries.

Although the recommended solution is based on the disk libraries, this chapter covers a backup and recovery solution ideally suited for virtualized environments, called Avamar Data Store. The section about the Avamar-based solution covers its capabilities related to source-based de-duplication, which greatly reduces network bandwidth required and has other advantages.

## New Disk Library Backup and Recovery Environment

The new backup and recovery solution employs a lot of advanced technologies that replace the old and inefficient backup environment. The old environment did not handle the backup needs of the client and, in the case of some application servers, did not complete backup and recovery consistently. The old environment, for example, had many local tape drives connected directly to application servers. The review of the Backup Assessment output and the ROI analysis both made clear that the old solution, like many I see during the analysis process, was not getting the job done.

The new solution employs a disk library that backs up applications like a tape library. This virtual tape functionality of the disk library does more than "fool" the backup software into thinking it is a tape, and not a disk, library. By emulating a lot of tape functionality, backup software does not have to be changed, so backup administrators can operate the disk library in the same way they operate a tape library. In addition, tape drives connected to the disk library can be written directly to tape. Many backup programs are supported by the disk library, so the operational change to employ the disk library is minimal while realizing the immense benefits of de-duplication and other technologies.

Figure 9-1 shows the new backup environment.

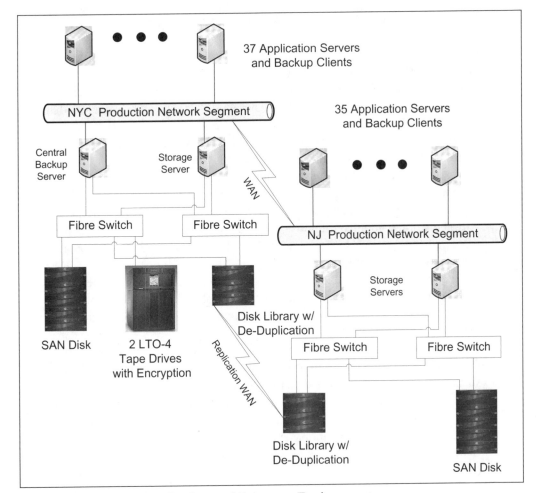

Figure 9-1   New Backup and Recovery Environment

Figure 9-1 shows that the two locations, NYC and NJ, each have a disk library local to them. Each location has a series of clients across the top of the figure that back up locally to their disk library. In the old solution, there were roughly 50 local tape drives locally connected to the clients where local backup took place.

The next level down in Figure 9-1 shows that each location has storage servers, also called storage nodes. The "Storage Nodes" shown in both NY and NJ receive data from all clients to be backed up and sent to the disk library. The data is then replicated from NYC to NJ and vice versa from disk library to disk library. This bidirectional replication takes place after the backup is complete. The backup takes place to the local disk library during backup hours, typically beginning around 8:00PM, and is completed before business hours. When business hours begin, the bidirectional replication takes place between the disk libraries in NY and NJ.

In addition, the NYC location has a central backup server, which is a NetWorker server, that contains metadata on all backups and recoveries that have taken place. It controls the backup process in both the NYC and NJ locations. This node contains the catalog database, which is metadata related to all backups. The NetWorker server contains the backup schedule and initiates the backup process. The 40 application servers shown in each location have a NetWorker backup client agent on them that communicates with the storage node to facilitate backup and recovery. The client communicates with the storage node continuously during this backup process by obtaining the data from the SAN and passing it on to the storage node, where it is then written to the disk library.

The production data is stored on storage connected to the SAN. Numerous production servers run various applications in both locations. There is no change in the operation of the data storage for applications with the change in the backup solution.

The tape library is shown in Figure 9-1 because tapes may need to be shipped to a secure location in some cases. The disk library data is replicated so the backup data is in two different locations. For this reason, the client does not need physical tape backup to ensure the data is shipped offsite. There are, however, some compliance requirements that may include tape shipment offsite. The tape library shown also includes encryption capability. In addition, the tape library may be required to read old tapes.

## Alternative New Backup and Recovery Environment

Some advanced backup technology ideally suited to virtualization, but works with non-virtualized environments as well, could be part of the backup and recovery solution rather than only disk libraries covered in the previous section. The more advanced solution includes Avamar Data Store, which performs source-based de-duplication in a virtualized environment. The de-duplication takes place before data is transferred to the Avamar Data Store. In the original solution, the disk library performed target-based de-duplication, which means the data was transferred to the disk library where de-duplication takes place. The following are overviews of target and source-based de-duplication:

- Target based de-duplication takes the backup stream from backup clients, moves the data through the network LAN and WAN, then through the fiber channel pathways to the target device, such as the disk library. Once on the target, the data is then reduced based on common data block chunks when the data is received in the data stream (in-band) or after the backup stream has been completely received at a later time (out-of-band). This solution allows for de-duplication to be incorporated into existing backup environments with no retraining or modification of the backup process.

- Source-based de-duplication solves the problem differently in that the de-duplication process takes place before any data is transferred through the LAN or WAN infrastructure. Using software algorithms located on the client, the application monitors all new disk writes executed by the client and analyzes it for commonality of data chunks. Once the delta, or changed pieces of data, are identified, categorized, and globally compared with other prior client backups, only the unique, new chunks of data are transferred over the network. After initial seeding of the source-based data store, these deltas are typically reduced by more than 90%.

This source-based de-duplication is essential in a virtualized environment. Physical resource issues are created by attempting to back up 20 or more virtual machines on a single ESX server with a limited number of networking ports. Backups may not complete within the backup window under these circumstances. In an example where there are four networking ports, each of the 20 virtual machines consider those 4 physical ports their own and use them for the backup. All the virtual machines are hitting those four ports simultaneously during a standard backup. By using source-based de-duplication, you can limit the data that will hit those four physical ports by more than 90%. This removes the limiting factor of throughput in the ESX server to achieve a successful backup within the backup window.

Virtualization is not required for source-based de-duplication and non-virtualized blades or servers can take advantage of this benefit in the form of greatly reduced LAN and WAN traffic.

The disk libraries are not required if the Avamar Data Store units are used as the backup and restore solution; however, I included both solutions in the alternative solution to show that both solutions can co-exist.

The individual virtual machines run the Avamar client that enables them to perform source-based de-duplication backups. The disk library looks like a tape library to the backup software, but the Avamar Data Store uses a specialized backup interface that manages all aspects of the backup and restore processes.

Figure 9-2 shows the alternative backup environment.

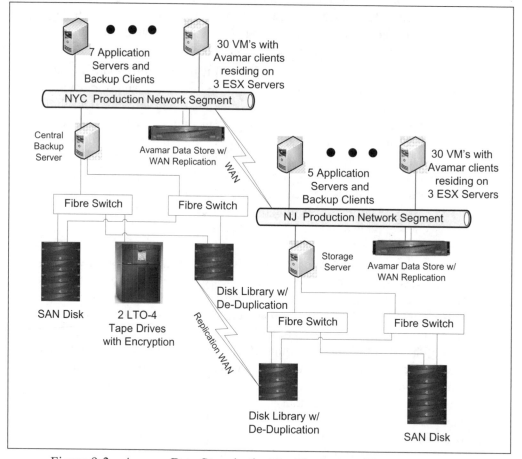

Figure 9-2   Avamar Data Store in the New Backup and Recovery Environment

Figure 9-2 shows that the two locations, NYC and NJ. Each location has an Avamar Data Store and disk library local to them. Each location has a series of clients across the top of the figure that back up locally. In the old solution, there were roughly 50 local tape drives locally connected to the clients where local backup took place.

The next section covers the operation of the disk library, which was the key to the first proposed backup solution.

## Disk Library Operation

In this section, I configure the disk library (know by many other names and shown as DL3D in the figures, including creating a virtual tape library and virtual tape drives, and establish a connection to a backup server over Fibre Channel using worldwide names. I then initiate a backup from the backup server using a virtual tape drive and show the result of the backup and deduplication on the disk library.

Figure 9-3 shows the home page of the Management Console of the disk library.

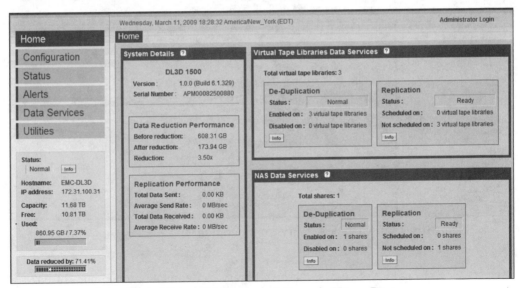

Figure 9-3    Disk Library Management Console Home Page

Some points of interest in Figure 9-3 are:

- All backups to the disk library from clients were 608.3GB, and the disk library space consumed was 173.94GB. This represents a de-duplication of 71.41%. At the end of this section, you see that these numbers slightly go up when I back up an additional client.

- Under *Virtual Tape Libraries Data Services,* de-duplication is enabled on three virtual tape libraries. I configure an additional virtual tape library shortly. *Replication* is *Ready,* but not enabled.

- *NAS Data Services* refers to disk library disk area that is used for backup to the disk library as a file system as opposed to a tape library. This is an alternative to writing to a virtual tape.

Figure 9-4 shows the details of the three virtual tape libraries that currently exist on the disk library.

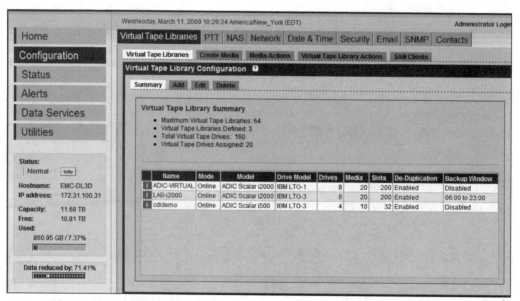

Figure 9-4    Virtual Tape Library Configuration

As Figure 9-4 shows, the disk library can emulate a maximum of 64 unique tape libraries. There is a maximum of 160 tape drives spread across the tape libraries. The disk library in this example is the smallest available from EMC at the time of this writing, so the virtual tape library and virtual tape capacities are the minimum numbers you'll see for any disk library. The three tape libraries have model numbers associated with them to emulate the devices shown in the figure. Figure 9-5 shows the process of adding a fourth tape library.

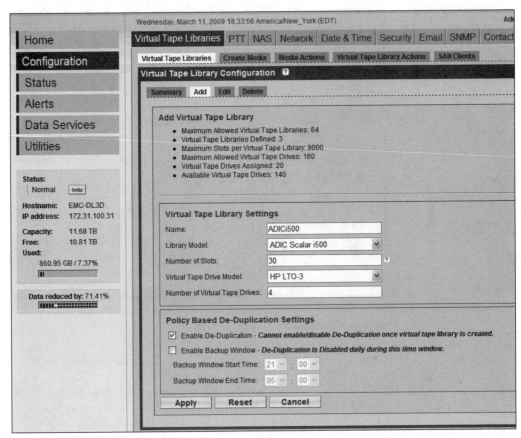

Figure 9-5    Adding a Virtual Tape Library

The virtual tape library being added in Figure 9-5 is an ADIC i500 with 30 slots to hold HP LTO-3 tapes. De-duplication is enabled on this virtual tape drive.

Figure 9-6 shows creating virtual media, which are tape definitions.

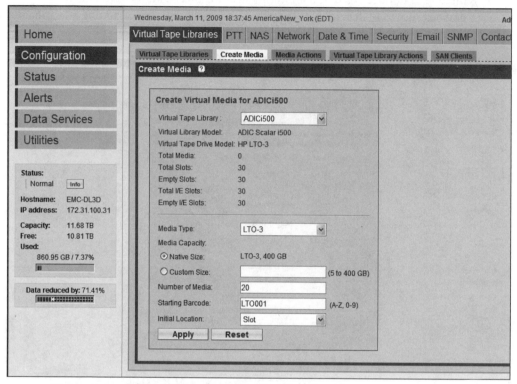

Figure 9-6    Creating Virtual Media Tape Drives

In Figure 9-6 I selected a tape media type of LTO-3 that will go in to the ADIC i500 tape library. I have now created the virtual tape library and the 20 tapes that will go into the library. The tapes have barcode range LTO001-LTO020.

Figure 9-7 shows the process of connecting the backup server to the virtual tape library I just created.

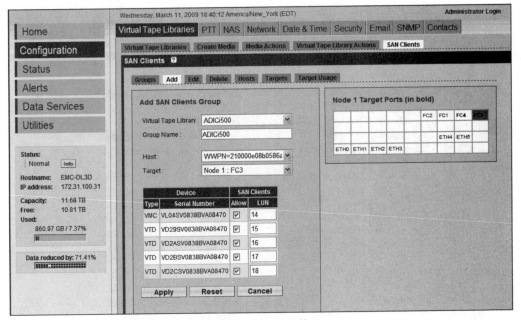

Figure 9-7    Connecting the Virtual Tape Library

Under *Add SAN Clients Group* are the following key areas to fill in to connect the backup server to the virtual tape library:

- The *Host* is the backup server with the worldwide name shown in the figure. The *Target* is the disk library Node 1:FC3.
- The table of *Device* and *SAN Clients* shows a Type of *VMC*, which is the disk library, and Type *VTD,* which is the virtual tape drive.
- On the right of the figure are all the *Target Ports* available on the disk library. There are four Fibre Channel ports and six Ethernet connections on the disk library.

Figure 9-8 shows the devices connected the Windows backup server.

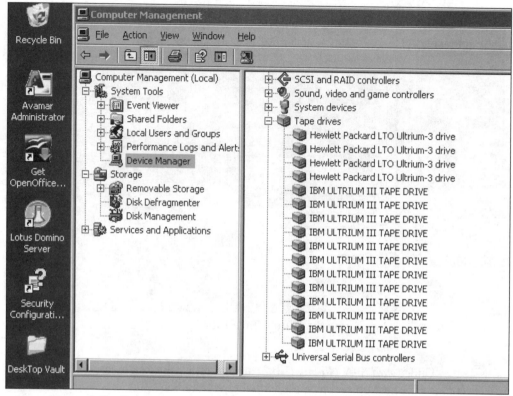

Figure 9-8    Devices on Windows Backup Server

Figure 9-8 shows several tape drives available for backup. The four HP LTO-3 tape drives are part of the VTL created earlier.

Figure 9-9 shows initiating a NetWorker backup job.

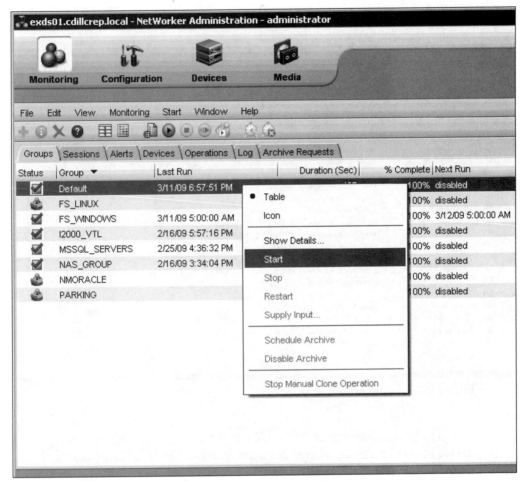

Figure 9-9    Initiating a NetWorker Backup Job

The backup job shown in Figure 9-9 will back up the client group *Default* to the VTD I have specified.

Figure 9-10 shows some of the specifics related to this backup job.

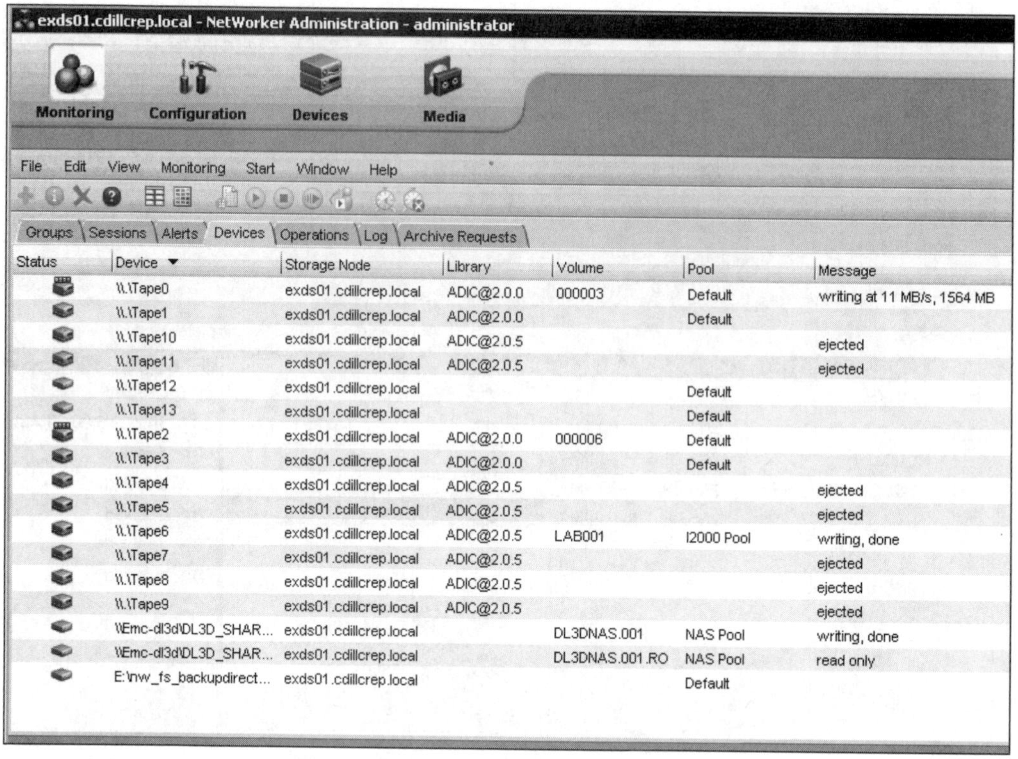

Figure 9-10    Backup Job Information

The backup job uses an ADIC VTL and VTD \\*Tape0*. This virtual tape device looks like a physical tape device in Windows and the NetWorker program.

Figure 9-11 shows the results of the backup on the disk library.

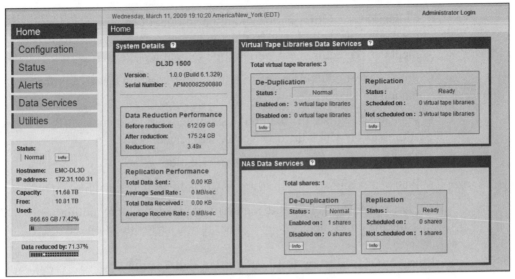

Figure 9-11    Backup Results on the Disk Library

Figure 9-11 summarizes the backup results for all backups run to the disk library, including the small backup of group *Default* (shown in the earlier figures). The total data backed up before any de-duplication was 612.09GB but the de-duplicated space required to hold this data on the disk library was only 175.24GB. This represents a data reduction of 71.37%.

The next section covers the implementation plan I follow when implementing a disk library for backup and recovery.

## Virtual Disk Library and Backup Software Implementation

This section covers the planning and implementation of the disk library and backup software. In this case, EMC Networker is the software deployed; however, the disk library supports many other enterprise backup programs. The following three phases cover disk library-related work:

## Phase 1: Disk Library Planning

- Collect detailed information about the amount of backup size needed on the disk library, backup window Service Level Agreement (SLA) requirement, and desired retention policy.

- Plan the desired tape library and drive configuration based on information collected.

- Plan and designate the required backup network segment and IP addresses on which the disk library will reside.

- Plan for call-home requirement configuration.

- Plan and designate the disk library Console Management Server

- Plan and design for off-site requirement via cloning or vaulting using the embedded storage node or media server functionality.

## Phase 2: Disk Library Implementation and Testing

- Configure the disk library environment based on the required tape library and drive requirement.

- Implement zones on all required backup servers and the disk libraries to see all configured virtual tape library and drives.

- Configure all needed SAN clients.

- Assign planned drives and robotics controller to the planned backup server.

- Assign planned drives to the designated media server or storage node.

- Verify the ability to see all assigned tape library and drives on designated servers.

- Load all required tape drives licenses depending on the backup software used.

- Integrate the disk library into the backup environment solution.

- Implement and Integrate the disk library design for offsite requirement.

## Phase 3: Documentation and Perform Knowledge Transfer

- Produce a detailed material list, including serial numbers and support numbers.

- Compile a document with the steps performed to implement the disk library.

- Organize a review meeting to cover the completed implementation.

The next three phases cover NetWorker-related implementation.

## Phase 4: NetWorker Planning

- Collect details about the backup size that needs to be protected, gather information about backup window SLA requirement, and desired retention policy.

- Plan the desired tape library and drive configuration based on information collected.

- Plan and designate the required backup network segment and IP addresses that will be used in the configuration.

- Plan, design, and designate the required platform on which the NetWorker server will run.

- Plan, design, and designate the required platform and the number of NetWorker storage nodes required to meet the backup window and SLA requirement. (Best practice at the time of this writing is to have one storage node for a 2TB data environment.)

- Plan, design, and designate the required platform and the number of dedicated NetWorker storage nodes required. (Best practice is to have a dedicated storage node once the data on a server is above 500GB.)

- Provide the minimum technical requirement for installation on the NetWorker server, the NetWorker storage node, the NetWorker dedicated storage node, and the NetWorker clients.

- Provide the minimum technical requirement for installation on NetWorker application module.

- Verify that all required licenses are available before any installation and configuration is scheduled.

- Plan and design for VMware backup environment either via VCB backup or VMware Guest backup.

- Plan, design, and designate the backup policy, schedule, and retention policy.

- Plan and design the offsite requirement.


## Phase 5: Implementation and Testing

- Configure the disk library environment based on the required tape library and drive requirement.

- Setup all required zones on backup server and the disk library to see all configured tape library and drives.

- Configure all needed SAN clients.

- Assign planned drives and robotics controller to the backup server.

- Assign planned drives to the planned media server or storage node.

- Verify the ability to see all assigned virtual and physical tape libraries and drives on designated servers.

- Load all required tape drive licenses depending on the backup software used.

- Install and configure NetWorker Server and apply all required patches.

- Install and configure NetWorker Storage Node Server and apply all required patches.

- Install and configure NetWorker Dedicated Storage Server and apply all required patches.

- Install and configure NetWorker clients and apply all required patches.

- Install and configure NetWorker Application modules and apply all required patches.

- Install and configure NetWorker VCB proxy host and apply all required patches for all VMware clients.

- Test backup and restore functionality for all installed and configured server and clients.

- Implement and integrate the disk library into the backup environment solution.

- Implement and integrate the offsite design.


**Phase 6: Documentation and Knowledge Transfer**

- Implement and integrate the offsite design.

- Produce a detailed material list, including serial numbers and support numbers.

- Compile a document with the steps performed to implement the disk library.

- Organize a review meeting to cover the completed implementation.


## Summary

The advanced backup solution presented in this chapter, based on disk library technology, is much more operationally efficient and advanced than the old backup solution based on local tape drives.

The next chapter shows that there is a compelling ROI associated with the new backup solution.

# Chapter 10

# Backup, Recovery, and Archive ROI Analysis

As a result of the Backup Assessment Using Quick Scripts (Backup Assessment), a lot of TCO-related information is produced. This chapter presents both some of the high-level output produced and some of the more detailed information, which provides a breakdown of where the costs lie.

The existing Backup, Recovery, and Archive (BURA) environment studied in this chapter is highly inefficient and the proposed solution is a complete makeover of the existing environment. The financial benefits presented in this chapter are the result of a completely redesigned BURA implementation.

The TCO information in this chapter is based on replacing an antiquated tape backup environment with a backup to disk solution. Chapter 9 covers the details of the new solution.

The following is a quick review of the proposed environment:

- Disk library with de-duplication.

- The de-duplication ratio for unstructured data is 6.0 to 1, database data is 24.0 to 1, and email data is 24.0 to 1.

- The disk library contents will be archived to a second location obviating the need for tape backup.

The next section gives an overview of the TCO for this solution.

# TCO Summary for the New Environment

Before going in to the details of the TCO there are three summaries produced for BURA TCO that I present in this section. The first is cumulative
benefits, summarized in Table 10-1.

**Table 10-1**   Top Cumulative Benefits of the BURA Project

| Benefit Category | Dollar Amount |
|---|---|
| Tape and Library Savings | $2,406,000 |
| Media Savings | $67,186 |
| SAN Port Savings | $258,500 |
| Administration Costs Savings | $785,728 |
| Productivity Impact From Improved Backup Time | Excluded in this analysis |
| Backup Ratio Savings | $35,447 |
| Offsite Tape Storage Savings | 157,500 |
| **Total IT Reductions** | **$3,711,161** |
| Productivity Impact From Improved Recovery Time | $885,491 |
| Revenue Impact From Improved Backup Time | Excluded in this analysis |
| Productivity Gain From Improved Tape Reliability | $296,195 |
| **Total Business Strategic Advantage** | **$1,181,686** |
| **Total Benefits (Direct plus Indirect)** | **$4,892,846** |

These three categories result in a savings of almost $5M total. The
next section, covering the five-year benefit summary, breaks out these two
categories of IT reduction and strategic advantages in to more detail but

numbers of this magnitude are common for backup, recovery, and archive solutions.

Table 10-2 shows key reductions and an opportunity that result from this improved environment.

**Table 10-2**   Cost Savings and Opportunity

| Category | Dollar Amount |
|---|---|
| Reduced IT Capital Costs | $2,925,433 |
| Reduced IT Operating Costs | $785,728 |
| Improved Revenue Opportunities | $1,181,686 |

## Five-Year Benefit Summary

The numbers presented in the previous section amount to almost $5M in savings. Numbers of this magnitude require more explanation because, in many cases, my clients just don't believe it! Table 10-3 provides a detailed breakdown of the benefits of this BURA solution.

**Table 10-3**   BURA Five-Year Benefit Summary

| Benefit Category | Year 1 | Year 2 | Year 3 | Year 4 | Year 5 | Total |
|---|---|---|---|---|---|---|
| **Total Benefits** | **$856,685** | **$889,907** | **$1,015,290** | **$1,071,245** | **$1,059,719** | **$4,892,847** |
| | | | | | | |
| **IT Cost Reductions** | | | | | | |
| Tape and Library Savings | $492,560 | $384,960 | $492,360 | $534,760 | $502,160 | $2,406,800 |
| Administrative Cost Savings | $115,010 | $157,948 | $164,265 | $170,836 | $177,669 | $785,728 |

| Benefit Category | Year 1 | Year 2 | Year 3 | Year 4 | Year 5 | Total |
|---|---|---|---|---|---|---|
| SAN Port Savings | $0 | $55,500 | $63,000 | $65,500 | $74,500 | $258,500 |
| Offsite Tape Storage Cost Savings | $31,500 | $31,500 | $31,500 | $31,500 | $31,500 | $157,500 |
| Media Savings | $11,895 | $10,599 | $12,495 | $14,733 | $17,464 | $67,186 |
| Backup Ratio Savings | $22,550 | $3,440 | $3,328 | $3,098 | $3,031 | $35,477 |
| **Total IT Cost Reductions** | **$673,515** | **$643,947** | **$766,948** | **$820,427** | **$806,324** | **$3,711,161** |
| | | | | | | |
| **Business Strategic Advantages** | | | | | | |
| Improved Recovery Time Savings (Revenue Impact) | $139,814 | $186,419 | $186,419 | $186,419 | $186,419 | $885,491 |
| Improved Tape Reliability (Revenue Impact) | $43,355 | $59,541 | $61,923 | $64,400 | $66,976 | $296,195 |
| **Total Business Strategic Advantage** | **$183,170** | **$245,960** | **$248,342** | **$250,819** | **$253,395** | **$1,181,686** |

Here is an explanation of the categories in this table:

- **Tape and Library Savings**. The disk library solution obviates the need for large tape libraries and tape drives for the growth anticipated in this client environment. A growth rate of 25% per year in data capacity was anticipated for this client, which would result in a the procurement over five years of large tape capacity. This number also includes support on the tape libraries. This number assumes an additional 12 tape drives per year. If the disk grows by a set amount, the tape and library will grow...

- **Administrative Costs**. The libraries that would be maintained over a five year period require administrative costs on site to support backup and recovery. These libraries are high-maintenance devices that require a lot of hands-on support. The maintenance required on the disk library solution is substantially lower than a physical tape library. The backup to disk solution takes roughly 40% the effort to manage and maintain as the tape library-based solution, which means a 60% savings which is $115,010 in the first year. (The first quarter is not included in this savings, so it's lower than the other years.) There are two categories of administrators in the backup world. The senior administrator handles the backup software and the junior administrator does primarily tape-handling work. There are fewer administrators involved in the disk library solution in general.

- **SAN Port Savings**. This savings reflects the difference in SAN ports between going with the proposed disk library solution versus a tape-based solution. The tape-based solution requires 66 SAN ports to implement, and the disk library solution requires only 30 SAN ports to implement, resulting in a savings of 36 SAN ports at $2,500 each. The savings in the first year is $165,000. The tool used assumes two targets and one initiator or two tape drives per initiator. One more SAN port is added per tape drive. Using de-duplication greatly reduces this port count.

- **Offsite Tape Storage Costs**. This solution is disk library-based with one disk library replicating to another disk library in another location. The offsite tape storage savings amount to $31,500 per year, which includes the following:

  - A daily courier costs 260 days per year for $19,500

  - Monthly offsite facility costs of $12,000 per year.

  - These costs, like all figures in the ROI, can be modified, but they are the actual costs this client incurs in their environment.

- **Media Savings**. This is simply the capacity of the disk library converted to tapes and the realized savings:

  VTL SPACE
  TAPE CAPACITY
  TAPE COST

- **Backup Ratio Savings**. This savings is the result of reducing the frequency of full backups. The savings in this case is for file backup only because the database backups remains the same. The savings in this category are purely tape savings, which in the first year, are substantially higher than in subsequent years. In the first year, about 451 tapes are saved and, in the second year, 86 tape cartridges are saved.

- **Retention also plays a part in this savings**. Revisiting this issue also encourages people to rethink retention. Although it is not the case, in this example, some clients save a full backup per week for a full year. When this is revisited, some clients reconsider retention and reduce the number of full backups retained over the course of the year. The backups to disk are now 10 per year versus the 28 full backups in a year. Incremental backups take place to disk.

- **Improved Recovery Time Savings (Revenue Impact.)** This is related to additional operational uptime associated with faster application recoveries. This means that, in the existing recovery environment, an application can be down for a long period of time. In the new disk library environment, recoveries take place more quickly. If a billing application, for instance, had to be recovered, the new environment would allow much faster time for billing experts to again be productive, thereby having a direct savings impact to the client. Any revenue-generating application that is down will cost you revenue until it is recovered. There may also be a penalty clause in an SLA for an outsource firm in which this plays a large part.

- **Improved Tape Reliability (Revenue Impact.)** This is altogether a reliability-related category. Tapes are inherently less reliable than disk. If a recovery fails because of a bad tape resulting in lost data, the impact in the institution is expensive and, in some cases, unrecoverable. The assumption is that some recoveries will fail. This is different than the Improved Recovery Time Savings, which assumes a successful but much faster recovery. This category assumes that some recoveries will fail and the cost of the failures.

# Investment Summary

There is not an insignificant investment required for this advanced solution. The benefits presented in the previous section are immense and far offset the investment, but an analysis of the investment is required. Table 10-4 summarizes the five-year investment.

**Table 10-4**  BURA Five-Year Investment Summary

| Investment Summary | Initial | Year 1 | Year 2 | Year 3 | Year 4 | Year 5 | Total |
|---|---|---|---|---|---|---|---|
| Disk Library With De-Dup | $610,000 | $0 | $91,200 | $85,760 | $82,944 | $80,282 | $950,186 |
| Additional Prof Services | $10,000 | $10,000 | $10,000 | $10,000 | $10,000 | $10,000 | $60,000 |
| Setup and Installation | $4,000 | $0 | $0 | $0 | $0 | $0 | $4,000 |
| **Total Operating Investment** | $624,000 | $10,000 | $101,200 | $95,760 | $92,944 | $90,282 | $1,014,186 |

Amazingly, the benefits of this technology far outweigh the total investment of roughly $1M.

The next section covers the Return on Investment, comparing the benefits of this advanced technology versus the total investment.

# Return on Investment (ROI) Summary

A summary of the Return on Investment (ROI), Net Present Value (NPV), Internal Rate of Return (IRR), and Payback Period appear in Table 10-5.

**Table 10-5**   ROI, NPV, and Payback Period for the Virtualized Solution

| Category | Number |
|---|---|
| Risk Adjusted Return on Investment (ROI) | 382% |
| Net Present Value (NPV) Savings (Three year, discount rate=9.5%) | $2,803,677 |
| Internal Rate of Return (IRR) | 134% |
| Payback Period | 6.0 months |

These are the four key summaries supplied by the Backup Assessment ROI tool. The ROI tool supplies a table that gives the details of these numbers as well, which I did not include, but they are part of the summary supplied to the client as part of the analysis.

The six-month payback period is appealing and the graph in Figure 10-1 shows the break-even graph for this solution.

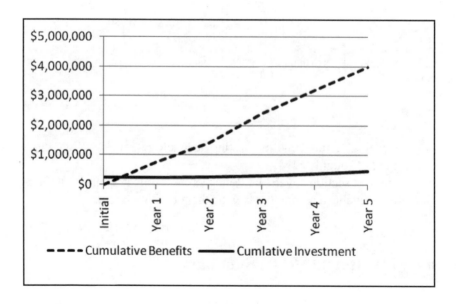

Figure 10-1   Payback Period of Six Months

Figure 10-1 shows that there is an initial investment and a modest follow-on investment over the years, but the payback is dramatic over time.

Although technical experts are sometimes unfamiliar with these terms, the significant investment required to make this disk library solution operational makes it important to understand the basic financial aspects of such a project. The following are some definitions of financial terms often associated with major technology projects:

- **Return on Investment (ROI)** is the ratio of money gained or lost (realized or unrealized) on an investment relative to the amount of money invested. The amount of money gained or lost may be referred to as interest, profit/loss, gain/loss, or net income/loss. The money invested may be referred to as the asset, capital, principal, or the cost basis of the investment. ROI is usually expressed as a percentage rather than a fraction.

- **Net Present Value (NPV)** The present value of an investment's future net cash flows minus the initial investment. If positive, the investment should be considered (unless an even better investment exists); otherwise, it should probably be passed up unless there are other compelling reasons for the investment.

- **Internal Rate of Return (IRR)** is a capital budgeting metric used by firms to decide whether they should make investments. It indicates the efficiency or quality of an investment, as opposed to NPV, which indicates value or magnitude. The IRR is the annualized effective compounded return rate, which can be earned on the invested capital, such as the yield on the investment. Put another way, IRR for an investment is the discount rate that makes the NPV of the investment's income stream total to zero. A project is a good investment proposition if its IRR is greater than the rate of return that could be earned by alternate investments of equal risk (investing in other projects, buying bonds, even putting the money in a bank account). Thus, the IRR should be compared to any alternate costs of capital, including an appropriate risk premium. In general, if the IRR is greater than the project's cost of capital, or hurdle rate, the project will add value for the company.

- **Payback** is the amount of time taken to break even on an investment. Because this method ignores the time value of money and cash flows after the payback period, it provides only a partial picture of whether the investment is worthwhile.

# Summary

The ROI numbers presented in this chapter are compelling. The six-month payback period is typical when an antiquated local-tape-drive environment is replaced with an advanced disk library-based solution. When the ROI supports the improved backup environment, all the factors are in place for a successful project.

The next chapter covers data replication techniques and advanced disk technologies.

# CHAPTER 11

# Data Replication and Disk Technology Advancements

This chapter covers some storage-related topics that do not fall under the category of backup and recovery, but are important to the operation of storage.

The first section covers several techniques for replicating data between locations. Replicated data is important to the operation of a business to ensure application availability. The three replication techniques covered are fabric, host, and array-based. An overview of how the replication technique works, what is required to make it work, its benefits, a diagram of the technology, and other topics are covered.

The second section covers advancements of disk technology in general, which is directly related to green IT in power, cooling, and floor space savings, as well as higher performance.

## Data Replication Methods

Because of the need for business continuity and application availability, data replication between data center locations has increased in popularity. There are three main methods for data replication. The selection of the proper type is based on a number of factors. Some factors are the support of heterogeneous environments, reduced costs, business recovery specifications, like

Recovery Point Objectives (RPO) and Recovery Time Objectives (RTO), network bandwidth limitations, and so on.

The three main methods of data replication are fabric-based, host-based, and array-based. Each method has its own benefits and characteristics. The following sections illustrate the hardware and software components, the differences, the benefits, and the requirements of each.

## Fabric-Based Replication

Fabric-based replication provides support for concurrent local and remote replication of the same volumes, heterogeneous hosts, and storage arrays. This is a block-level asynchronous replication method. One of the most popular fabric-based replication products is EMC's Recoverpoint technology.

In addition to the servers, storage, LAN/WAN, and SAN components, fabric-based replication also requires special appliances that perform the actual replication of the data. They are integrated within the fabric as an out-of-band mechanism facilitating and managing the data movement. These appliances are configured in redundant pairs for high availability and scalability and are sized to support the amount of data to be replicated.

As mentioned earlier, one of the main differences when using fabric-based replication is the use of appliances that are integrated with the fabric. EMC Recoverpoint offers continuous data protection (CDP) for Logical Units (LUNs) on the same SAN, continuous remote replication (CRR) between LUNs across two SANs, and a combination of concurrent local and remote (CLR) replication across two SANs. Local continuous data protection and remote asynchronous replication are handled at the block level. EMC Recoverpoint is asynchronous only.

Data changes are journaled locally to maximize the number of recovery points for crash consistency. Bookmarks and consistency groups are used to provide application consistent replication. All application tiers (database, application server, and web) can be grouped to provide application state consistency so that all related components are in sync when recovered at that point in time. Dependent write order consistency is managed both locally and remotely.

The data replication is performed with a combination of intelligent SAN switch technology and EMC Recoverpoint appliances and software. The data is replicated via a splitter that is resident within the fabric. As data is written to the array, the transactions are replicated and written to a local journal and then transported to another set of appliances located at the remote site, where the data is compressed and transferred to a remote journal and then written to the remote array.

One of the benefits of fabric-based replication is that all the overhead of the replication process is handled within the intelligent fabric and not on either the host or array. This alleviates any concern for production performance issues and minimizes the impact on production I/O performance and CPU load. EMC Recoverpoint is integrated with intelligent fabric from Cisco and Brocade. Other splitter methods exist as well.

Fabric-based replication supports heterogeneous storage and hosts. This is also a benefit. You could have storage from one hardware manufacturer and storage from a different one at the remote location. This provides additional flexibility within the storage architecture. Because this is an out-of-band solution, the data that is replicated is transferred outside of the production data path. The replicated data is compressed and sent across the network, reducing bandwidth requirements and improving efficiencies and performance. Fabric-based replication also provides application consistency in addition to crash consistency. Figure 11-1 shows a high-level depiction of fabric-based replication.

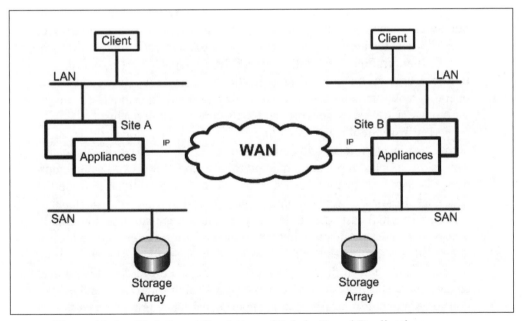

Figure 11-1    High-Level Depiction of Fabric-Based Replication

The appliances, along with intelligent SAN switch fabric, make up the hardware architecture. In addition to the hardware, there is a software component that is licensed based on replicated capacity.

## Host-Based Replication

Host-based replication provides support for heterogeneous hosts and storage arrays. This is a block level asynchronous replication method. There are many different host-based replication products, such as EMC Replistor for Windows, Symantec Volume Replicator for UNIX and Windows, and Data Domain. One of the more popular host-based replication products for Microsoft Windows environments is EMC's Replistor technology. Other host-based replication products exist that are specific to certain relational database management platforms, such as Oracle, Microsoft SQL, and Sybase. There are also some native tools or mechanisms that are included in some application server products. Such products are integrated with applications such as Microsoft Exchange, messaging, application server, and middle-ware applications.

The hardware component of host-based replication is the server technology on which the replication software runs. No special storage array or SAN fabric hardware is required. This type of replication is done via host-to-host communication over an IP network. Most popular host-based replication software runs on either Microsoft Windows or various Linux and UNIX operating environments. Host-based replication is not dependent on any of the storage, LAN/WAN network, and SAN network components.

Host-based replication offers near real-time replication between hosts across two or more locations, provided there is a high-speed link in place. This is the simplest replication method to implement; however, as the number of host-to-host relationships increase, so does the effort to manage the processes. Host-based replication is typically used in small environments or on a departmental basis. It provides asynchronous replication and is usually transparent to the application, but not to the operating system on the host. It does create some overhead on the host system because the host is performing the data replication to the remote location. This overhead depends on data change rates. The hosts do not have to be identical in some cases and neither does the storage. It typically won't support consistency groups like a fabric-based replication method.

One of the benefits of host-based replication is that it supports heterogeneous storage and hosts. You could have storage from one hardware manufacturer and storage from a different one at the remote location. This provides additional flexibility within the storage architecture. Host-based replication is easier to deploy and is reasonably inexpensive as compared to either fabric or array-based replication methods. A high-level representation of typical host-based replication architecture is illustrated in Figure 11-2.

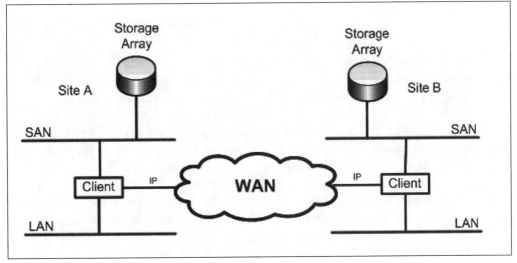

Figure 11-2    High-Level Depiction of Host-Based Replication

The client or hosts, with associated storage internal or external, along with an IP network, are the primary components required for host-based replication. In addition to the hardware, a software component is licensed based on host and operating environment.

## Array-Based Replication

Array-based replication provides support for heterogeneous hosts, but not heterogeneous storage. The storage is usually similar in make, model, and/or product family. Supportability may vary between manufacturers. This is a block-level synchronous or asynchronous replication method. There are different array-based replication products, such as EMC Mirrorview for EMC CLARiiON arrays, EMC SRDF (Symmetrix Remote Data Facility) for EMC

DMX arrays, HP Continuous Access for HP EVA (Enterprise Virtual Array) arrays and HP XP arrays, IBM XRC (Extended Remote Copy), and IBM PPRC (Peer-to-Peer Remote Copy). Other array-based replication software products are available, such as replication between network attached storage (NAS) appliances (for example, EMC Celerra Replicator.) Another array-based replication technology is the mechanism used between archival content addressable object-based storage, such as EMC Centera and the disk library technology covered earlier.

The hardware component of array-based replication is the storage technology on which the replication software runs. Similar storage array technology is required. This type of replication is done via array-to-array communication over an IP network. In some cases, Fibre Channel (FC) to IP bridging or routing is required. In the case where the storage array may have integrated IP ports, the additional FC to IP bridging may not be necessary. The integrated IP ports may be used for site-to-site replication. Array-based replication is dependent on the storage, but is not dependent on the hosts, LAN/WAN network, and/or SAN network components.

Array-based replication offers near real-time replication between arrays across two or more locations. Array-based replication provides either synchronous or asynchronous replication, depending on the distance between sites, and is usually transparent to the application because the overhead is processed by the storage processors in the array. This overhead is dependent on data change rates. Array-based replication is host and operating system agnostic. Typically, array-based replication is more expensive and complex to manage. It is also constrained by vendor lock-in due to proprietary storage array specifications.

One the benefits of array-based replication is that it supports heterogeneous hosts and SAN fabrics. All of the replication overhead is serviced by the on-board cache and controllers within the arrays, which alleviates any resource contention on the hosts. Hosts are not required at the remote site for replication to take place. Another benefit is that you only need one site to control replication that supports multiple hosts. A high-level representation of typical array-based replication architecture is illustrated in Figure 11-3.

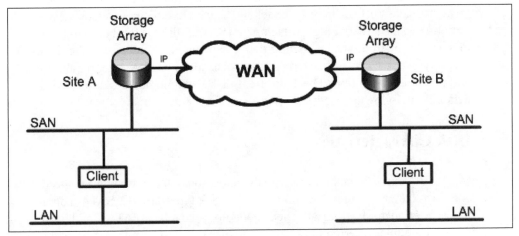

Figure 11-3    High-Level Depiction of Array-Based Replication

The storage array is the primary component required for array-based replication. In addition to the hardware, a software component is licensed based on either the class of the storage array or is capacity based.

In summary, the selection of the proper replication method varies between organizations. In some cases, a combination of methodologies is implemented. All the different replication methods have their own characteristics and benefits. The proper method would be chosen based on specific requirements defined by the organization to support their business continuity and data replication needs. All methods offer a flexible replication service that can be implemented and managed in different fashions and selected based on the organization's Recovery Time Objectives (RTO) and Recovery Point Objectives (RPO).

# Disk Technology Advancements

Many disk technology advancements are taking place that have power, cooling, and cost implications making this a prominent green topic. Most organizations, for instance, have adopted some form of storage tiering. By definition, storage tiering is the process of performing a classification and categorization of your data by assigning an associated value or importance to the organization and then storing it on the appropriate disk technology.

An organization, for instance, may place its mission-critical, high-performance data on fast Fibre Channel (FC) disk technologies versus slower Serial Advanced Technology Attachment (SATA) disks. Many decision factors are considered when selecting the proper disk technology for the data. These typically consist of criteria such as disk speed needed, size, reliability, and power consumption. These different disk technologies are described in detail in the following section.

## Disk Characteristics

Many different disk technologies are available today that vary in size, speed, and form factor. Some of the more popular disk types are FC, SATA, sometimes referred to as fibre attached technology adapted (FATA), and flash disks (sometimes referred to as solid state disks (SSD.)) Another disk type is serial attached SCSI (SAS), which are typically a smaller form factor.

All these technologies are all available in different sizes. The sizes or disk densities increase on a somewhat regular basis. At the time of this writing, FC disks are available in either 146 gigabyte (GB), 300GB, and 450GB sizes. SATA or FATA disks are currently available in larger sizes, such as 750GB and 1 terabyte (TB) sizes. Some of the flash disks or SSD drives are available in 73GB or 400GB sizes.

Many organizations will classify their data and store it on the appropriate disk type based on its classification. For example, an organization may classify its mission-critical applications on Tier 1 storage, such as FC or flash disks. It may then select SATA for its Tier 2 applications and tape technology for Tier 3, etc. These selections and storage tiering definitions vary between organizations.

Depending on the disk type, the disk speed will vary. Generally speaking, a flash disk provides approximately 2,500 IOPS (maximum number of I/O per second), and a 15,000 RPM FC disk provides approximately 180 IOPS (maximum number of I/O per second).Whereas a 10,000 RPM FC disk provides approximately 140 IOPS, and a 7,200 RPM SATAII disk operates at approximately 75 IOPS.

Most organizations will select a certain disk type based on performance, capacity, availability, and/or power consumption. For example, an organization may select FC disk or even flash disks to satisfy high performance, high availability applications that require fast I/O performance and reliability. Others may opt for larger, slower SATA disks for archival, backup, and/or slower applications. The next section explains one method to calculate the number of disks needed in a disk group.

## Disk Calculation Method

One of the ways to determine how many disks are required within a disk group is to mathematically calculate it based on the required IOPS for the application. This is typically performed for estimation purposes as a starting point. Redundant Array of Inexpensive Disks (RAID) is a key factor in determining disk type. I do not cover RAID background, and I assume you have RAID knowledge. If not, the Internet has a wealth of information on RAID. Depending on the RAID type selected, typically RAID 5 or RAID 1+0, the following algorithms are used:

**For RAID 5:**
**RAID Adjusted IOPS = Read IOPS + (Write IOPs * 4)**

**For RAID 1+0:**
**RAID Adjusted IOPS = Read IOPs + (Write IOPs * 2)**

The way that this calculation is performed begins with knowing the maximum number of IOPS needed for the application that you are providing storage for, along with the desired RAID type, and the percentage of reads and writes. The IOPS required by the application need to be adjusted to include the overhead of the RAID type selected. Because of the fact that RAID 5 has a higher write penalty, the total writes has to be increased to account for the overhead. For example, if an organization has a database application that requires 1,000 IOPS, it wants to use RAID 5, and the database transactions consist of 40% reads and 60% writes, then the sample calculation would be as follows:

**RAID Adjusted IOPS = 400 + (600 * 4)**
**RAID Adjusted IOPS = 400 + 2,400**
**RAID Adjusted IOPS = 2,800**

After the RAID Adjusted IOPS are calculated, then based on the disk type selected and its respective IOPS, the total number of disks can be estimated. Assuming that the organization would like to use 15,000 RPM FC disks for its database and that a 15,000 RPM FC disk can provide 180 IOPS per disk, then the following calculation determines the number of disks needed in the disk group:

> **RAID Adjusted IOPS = 2,800**
>
> **One 15,000 RPM FC disk = 180 IOPS**
>
> **2,800 / 180 = Minimum of 16 Disks (15.5)**

The result of this exercise will vary and should only be used to estimate the number of disks needed in the disk group. Results will vary and adjustments to the disk quantities may be needed.

Storage array disk configurations are based on these estimations and other real-world results. As application I/O performance requirements increase, the need for faster disk technologies increases. Flash disk technology addresses the need for high IOPS requirements, lower power consumption, and efficiency.

# Flash Disk Technology

With the recent re-introduction of flash disk technology, also known as solid state disk, many organizations seeking high I/O performance for their mission-critical applications are considering the deployment of flash disks. Many storage manufacturers understand the value of flash disk technology. As an example, EMC Corporation introduced flash disk technology into their enterprise storage product line. The EMC flash disks are not the same as the flash-based solid state disks found in some consumer products, such as laptops. The EMC flash disks have been optimized for data writes and have a dual Fibre Channel interface for availability. They use a technique that ensures that all cells in the flash memory are used evenly to minimize the risk of "wear out," common to less advanced flash disk.

The EMC flash disks also protect the data with full round-trip error correction code (ECC) data integrity protection and de-stage battery backup. The EMC flash disk has excess capacity in every disk, as memory cells are used aggressively, the data is dynamically moved to less frequently used cells. They are designed for much higher I/O performance than the consumer flash, with a much lower failure rate.

Some of the reasons organizations are considering flash disk technology are for high performance databases, high volume transaction processing, and disk consolidation. Applications such as electronic trading, real-time data feed, or any high performance online transaction processing (OLTP) application requiring the fastest possible retrieval and storage of data are considering flash disks.

Flash disks perform best with random read misses (RRM). They can deliver single millisecond application performance response times. Because of the high IOPS of each flash disk, typically around 2,500 IOPS per disk, organizations can gain the same performance with fewer disks, as shown in Figure 11-4.

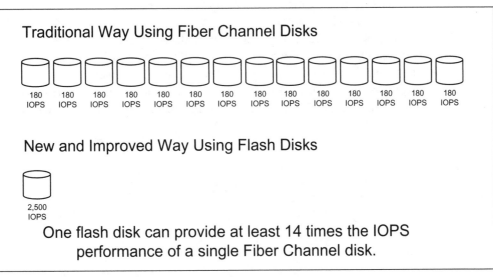

Figure 11-4    FC Versus Flash Disk to Achieve 2,500 IOPS

Some other benefits of using flash disks are that they don't require "spin up" to start, they provide fast random access for reads because of the fact that they don't have moving parts (disk read/write head), they provide relatively consistent read performance, they don't create noise, and they perform in a wider range of operating temperatures. There is a compelling total cost of ownership as well.

## Total Cost of Ownership Advantages of Flash Disk

Flash disks can provide high performance for latency-sensitive applications. Flash disks contain no moving parts, which eliminates rotational latency and reduces power consumption. According to recent studies performed by EMC Corporation, flash disks offer memory cache type performance, providing up to 10 times improvement in response time over the fastest FC disk today. In some cases, each flash disk can deliver IOPS of up to 30 15,000 RPM FC disks, requiring less floor space and even noise level reductions. The utilization of flash disk reduces up-front hardware costs because fewer disks are required to obtain the desired level of IOPS. This also potentially lowers operating costs, such as maintenance, power, and cooling, because of the lower number of disks required.

According to EMC Corporation, flash disks require up to 98% less energy per IOPS than traditional disk drives. When the power comparison is made between flash disk technology and fibre channel, power consumption can be reduced by as much as 97.7%. Figure 11-5 shows the comparison of power consumption per TB between flash disk technology and Fibre Channel.

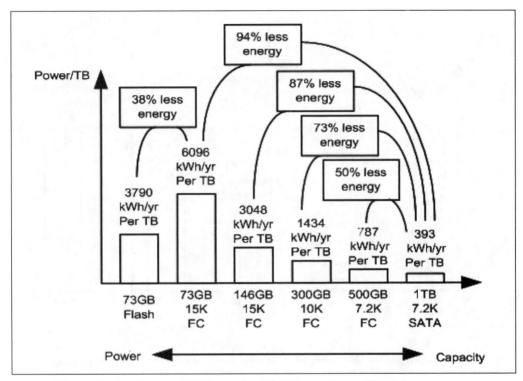

Figure 11-5    Energy Efficiency by Disk Type: Power/Capacity

Figure 11-6 illustrates the power consumption per IOPS. This provides a more compelling story. Because of the higher IOPS per flash disk, multiple Fibre Channel disks could be replaced (based on IOPS) with fewer flash disks. This provides a significant energy cost savings.

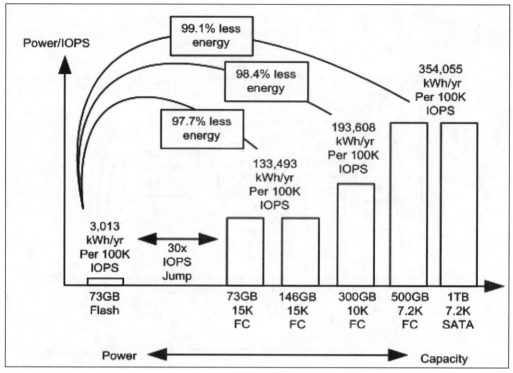

Figure 11-6    Energy Efficiency by Disk Type: Power/IOPS

## Sample Flash Versus Fibre Channel Disk TCO Analysis

To illustrate the potential cost savings of using flash disk technology over Fibre Channel disk, a sample Total Cost of Ownership (TCO) analysis is provided in Figure 11-7. As an example, if an organization had an application that required 1TB of capacity in a RAID 5 configuration that required 20,000 IOPS and was comparing the use of 73GB flash disk versus 146GB Fibre Channel disk, the following results would be provided using the EMC TCO analysis tool.

| TCO RESULTS (CALCULATED) | | | | |
|---|---|---|---|---|
| **TCO** | | **Flash** | **HDD** | **Difference** |
| | Drives | $236,250.00 | $316,880.00 | $80,360.00 |
| | Infrastructure | $11,800.00 | $99,700.00 | $87,900.00 |
| | Hardware Maintenance | $0.00 | $0.00 | $0.00 |
| | Power | $2,265.35 | $40,437.15 | $38,171.80 |
| | Space | $4,320.00 | $34,560.00 | $30,240.00 |
| | Response Time | $0.00 | $0.00 | $0.00 |
| | Total | $254,635.35 | $491,577.15 | $236,941.80 |
| **Total TCO Savings** | | $236,941.80 | | TCO Savings |
| **Percentage** | | 48% | | |
| **Other Notable Metrics** | | **Flash** | **HDD** | **Improvement** |
| | Drives {w/spares} | 21 | 233 | 91% |
| | Resp Time {ms} | 1 | 7 | 85% |
| | Watts {total} | 332 | 5918 | 94% |
| | Watts/TBu | 332 | 5918 | 94% |
| | Watts/kIOPS | 13 | 292 | 95% |
| | $/IOP | $10 | $24 | 58% |
| | $/GB | $255 | $492 | 48% |

Figure 11-7    EMC TCO for Flash Versus FC

The major points to highlight are the reduction in the number of disks required to satisfy both the IOPS performance requirements and the potential estimated cost reduction in power, disks, infrastructure, and space. The costs used are estimated and the results will vary. This is purely a sample exercise and should not be used to size a configuration

In summary, a variety of disk technologies are available and a combination of these technologies is commonly used. Storage tiering is becoming more popular as organizations classify their data and increase the efficient use of their storage environment. This provides them with the ability to store their data on the proper class of storage. The number of disks needed in a disk group can be estimated via a mathematical calculation. These estimates can help configure the disk layout. After the calculation is complete, selection of the proper disk technology can be performed. Depending on the application characteristics and requirements, a disk technologies can be chosen, such as FC, SATA, SAS, or flash disk. Flash disk technology is increasing in popularity. Because of their high performance, flash disks can provide more IOPS with less physical disks. Costs can be potentially reduced because fewer disks are needed to provide the equivalent or better IO performance. For many compelling reasons, flash disk technology is being seriously considered.

# Summary

The data-replication techniques covered in this chapter show the key options to ensure your data is in more than one location.

Disk technology has advanced quickly, just as processor technology has advanced. Flash technology, for instance, may prove to be a widely implemented technology with both green and technological advantages.

The next section covers some key networking technologies.

# Part III
# Networking

**Chapter 12: The Existing Network Environment with Enhancements**

**Chapter 13: Existing Network Analysis with Discovery**

**Chapter 14: Voice over Internet Protocol (VoIP)**

# Introduction to Part III

This part covers a sample network environment. This is a modest network environment and, like many networks, grew in phases over time and has a lot of outdated equipment and embedded operating systems. I cover the following topics in this part, going through the process of documenting the networking environment:

- Analysis of the existing network environment, which includes a lot of old, outdated equipment. Some equipment is at risk in the sense that it is too old to be supported.
- Proposed enhancements of the environment at the closet level to show how new technology can be inserted in to the environment to get immediate savings and reliability.
- Some background information on common network components.
- Background information on the Cisco operating systems and the Discovery tool that provide the fundamental knowledge to make sense of the Cisco Discovery output.
- List of prerequisites required before the Discovery can be run.
- Example of a Cisco Discovery output and its findings for the modest environment covering equipment that is in varying degrees of support.
- A Voice over IP (VoIP) chapter that covers the background of this technology that possesses many green characteristics.

The Cisco Discovery process is integral to evaluating the networking environment in much the same way the VMware Capacity Planner tool analyzed a non-virtualized environment and EMC Backup Assessment Using Quick Scripts (Backup Assessment) analyzed a backup environment.

# Chapter 12

## The Existing Network Environment with Enhancements

This chapter covers an existing network environment and the replacement of old networking electronics to modernize the environment. The replacement of the old networking electronics has both technological and green advantages in the environment.

The case study presented in this chapter is a typical antiquated network environment that can easily be updated to be more efficient.

## Existing Network Environment Example

This section covers a case study network environment that my firm analyzed and upgraded. Like most network environments, this network grew in a piece-meal fashion by adding networking electronics, such as switches, in small increments. The network is operational, but this network is at risk because of end of engineering and end of life on some of the electronics.

Figure 12-1 is a simplified depiction of the existing network components in the example environment.

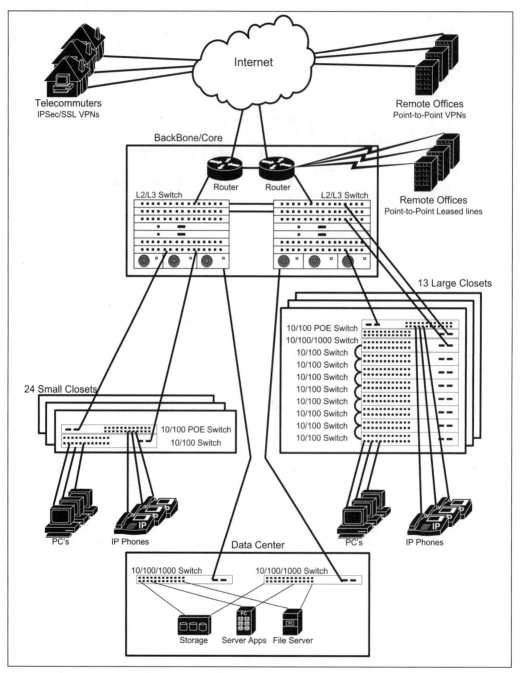

Figure 12-1     Existing Network Environment

Figure 12-1 shows the existing components in the network at a high level. The case study shown in the figure is that of a hospital. This section concentrates on the data or wiring closets and focuses on the existing setup in the closets and the proposed upgrade to them. The example network has 37 wiring closets at the main headquarters. Each wiring closet has at least one switch and usually some sort of Uninterruptable Power Supply (UPS) along with wiring leading out to user desks and back to the network core. Small data closets usually support no more than 50 end users. Larger data closets contain numerous switches and support possibly hundreds of end users.

I focus on the 24 small and 13 large closets as part of the upgrade because the old electronics in these closets are off support in many cases and are technologically obsolete in general.

Every desktop has a copper connection, such as CAT5 or CAT6, to the nearest closet. In the interest of keeping the runs from client to closet short, there are multiple closets per floor.

The small closets are typically found in areas where there are fewer client connections, such as floors where a lot of beds are located and there is not a dense user base. The large closets are in areas where there are more client connections required, such as office areas. The small closets are sometimes not even closets; they are just a couple of shelves in a location where a small amount of space is available for the networking components to rest.

There are two fiber connections from the switch in the closet to the switch that is part of the core.

## Upgrades to the Large and Small Existing Closets

This section drills down to the large and small closets presented in the previous section as part of the overall environment. There were a total of 24 small and 13 large closets with obsolete equipment that desperately needed to be upgraded. The focus on upgrading the closets reflects what I see in a lot of my customer base that has old equipment, in some cases from a manufacturer where support of the equipment is suspect, and the many advantages that this technology insertion brings to the environment.

Figure 12-2 shows the old networking electronics in a large closet.

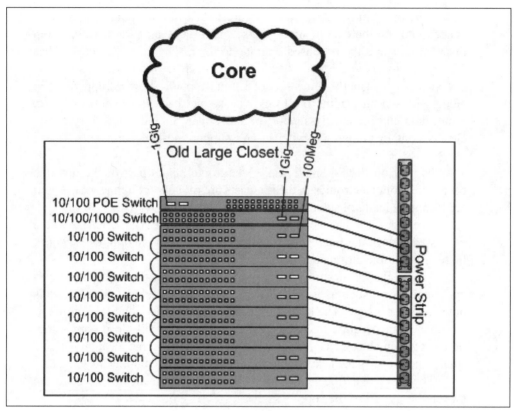

Figure 12-2    Existing Network Electronics in Large Closet

Figure 12-2 shows the existing components in the network at a high level. There are a total of 10 switches shown in this figure to support the many workstations and phones connected to the closet. In this environment, roughly 150 total end point devices, which include workstations, phones, and wireless access points, are connected to the large closet. The following are some facts related to the old closet:

• Three different switch models are deployed in a large closet, including the following:

    • 10/100 Mb switch

    • 10/100 Power Over Ethernet (POE) switch

    • 10/100/1000 Mb switch

- No redundancy is built into the switches, including the fact that each has only a single processor and power supply.

- There is a single uplink per switch type in the closet and, in Figure 12-2, there are a total of three uplinks, one for each switch type.

Figure 12-3 shows the new switch proposed for the large closet.

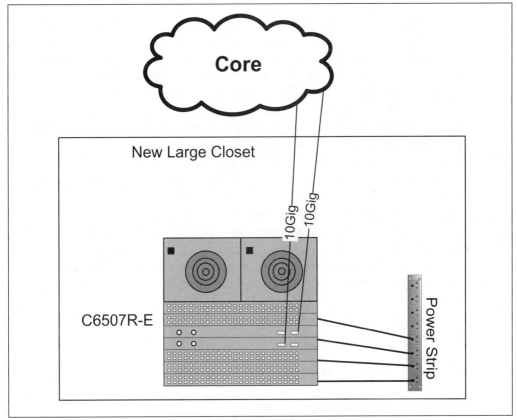

Figure 12-3    New Network Electronics in Large Closet

The following is a summary of the new Cisco device replacing the ten old switches in a large closet:

- One slot-based chassis supports all of the functionality the old three switch types and more.

- The chassis supports five slots for 48 port 10/100/1000Mb POE modules.

- The switch supports dual processors and power supplies, which means if one processor or power supply fails, the switch remains operational.

- The chassis has dual uplinks, which can be up to 10Gb, to ensure if there is a problem with one uplink, it will remain operational.

With the large closet scenario, a single multi-slot chassis-based switch can be used to replace ten individual switches. This solution has all the benefits of the small closet, but also allows greater fault tolerance with a second power supply and a second processor. The multi-slot chassis also allows you to populate the chassis with different cards as requirements change.

This solution uses a converged platform, which means that any port can be used for any purpose, including POE or standard Ethernet. In the large closet example, three old switches are replaced with one converged switch that can have POE or 10/100/1000Mb on every port.

Another benefit of a converged platform allows greater port usage. In the example, many old closets had switches that are not fully populated, which means many ports were unused.

With the new solution, all the ports in both the large and small closet can be used for either POE or standard Ethernet. No ports are wasted.

Converged switches are often more expensive because of the increased functionality, but by having increased port usage, the "port cost" brings the initial expense closer together.

Table 12-1 shows how the new closet solution saves power and space by moving to the converged switch platform.

**Table 12-1**   Large Closet Environment Comparisons

| Hardware | Ports | Rack Units (RU) | Maximum Power in Watts | BTU/hr |
|---|---|---|---|---|
| Old 10/100Mb Switch | 192 | 12 | 1120 | 3822 |
| Old POE | 24 | 1 | 115 | 392 |
| Old 10/100/1000Mb Switch | 24 | 1 | 135 | 460 |
| **Old Equipment Total** | **240** | **14** | **1370** | **4674** |

| Hardware | Ports | Rack Units (RU) | Maximum Power in Watts | BTU/hr |
|---|---|---|---|---|
| New Cisco C4507R-E w/ 5 WS-4648-RJ45V+E | 240 | 11 | 1142 | 3897 |
| **New vs. Old Difference** | **0** | **-3** | **-228** | **-777** |

Table 12-1 shows some significant rack, power, and cooling savings in the large closets. These numbers multiplied over 13 large closets result in compelling annual savings.

Similar advancements take place in the small closets. Figure 12-4 shows the old networking electronics in a small closet.

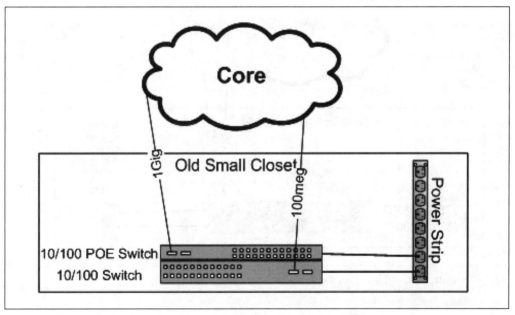

Figure 12-4    Existing Network Electronics in Small Closet

Figure 12-4 shows the existing components in the network at a high level. The following are some comments about each component:

- Two different switch models are deployed in a small closet, including the following:

  - 24-port 10/100Mb switch

  - 24-port 10/100 POE switch

- No redundancy is built into the switches, including the fact that each has only a single processor and power supply.

- There is a single uplink per switch type.

Figure 12-5 shows the new component proposed for the small closet.

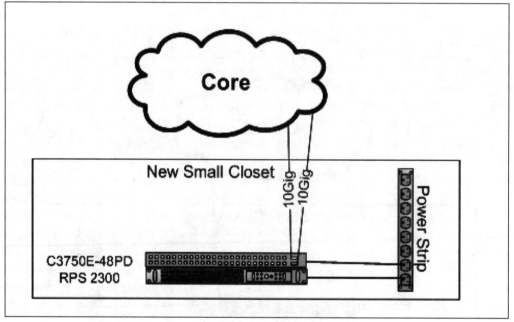

Figure 12-5   New Network Electronics in Small Closet

The following is a summary of the new Cisco switch replacing the two old devices in a small closet:

- There is a single switch in the small closet rather than two.
- The converged switch is a 48-port device with 10/100/1000Mb and POE on every port.
- This switch, unlike the large closet device, is not a slot-based chassis.
- The switch supports dual power supplies, which means if one power supply fails, the switch remains operational.
- The chassis has dual uplinks, which can be up to 10Gb, to ensure if there is a problem with one uplink, it remains operational.

The new hardware in this example draws less power due to new, more efficient power supplies and a single chassis. It also takes up less space, has increased bandwidth capacity, and optional redundant power supplies, which are part of the solution. Other benefits include less thermal output and greater POE wattage, shown in Table 12-2.

**Table 12-2** Small Closet Environment Comparisons

| Hardware | Ports | Rack Units (RU) | Maximum Power in Watts | BTU/hr |
|---|---|---|---|---|
| Old 10/100Mb Switch | 24 | 1.5 | 140 | 478 |
| Old POE | 24 | 1 | 115 | 392 |
| **Old Equipment Total** | **48** | **2.5** | **255** | **870** |
| New Cisco C3750E-48PD-SF | 48 | 1 (2 with 2 redundant power supply) | 152 | 516 |
| **New vs. Old Difference** | **0** | **-1.5 or -.5** | **-103** | **-354** |

The savings in Table 12-2 is for one of the 24 small closets, so the power savings of 103W and other advantages get realized for all the 24 small closets.

Replacing old switches result in significant power and cooling savings and have the added benefit of reliability as well, in the form of dual uplinks, redundant power supplies, and other advantages. In some cases, just having supported networking electronics, rather than old, antiquated devices is a compelling reason to make the upgrade to new components. Regardless of the reason, there is surely a green advantage to the upgrades.

Table 12-3 estimates the overall savings from all the closet upgrades.

**Table 12-3**   Estimate of Overall Savings

| Category | Number of Switches | Rack Units (RU) and Inches | Maximum Power in Watts | BTU/hr |
|---|---|---|---|---|
| Old Environment | 114 | 228 RU 399 inches | 21,505 | 73,378 |
| New Environment | 37 | 167 RU 292 inches | 10,910 | 37,226 |
| **Total Savings** | **77 switches** | **67 RU 106.75 inches** | **10,595** | **36,152** |

The next section covers some common network components, some of which were part of the example covered in this description.

# Overview of Common Network Components

There are some network components commonly found in network environments. Before covering the components, I start with some basic and helpful network terms. The components listed cover only the type of component and its definition; I omitted product numbers:

**Network terms**: T-3 is a dedicated connection supporting data rates of about 43 Mbps. A T-3 line actually consists of 672 individual channels, each of which supports 64Kbps.

T-3 lines are used mainly by Internet service providers (ISPs) connecting to the Internet backbone and for the backbone itself. T-3 lines are sometimes referred to as DS3 lines.

Asynchronous Transfer Mode (ATM) is a network technology based on transferring data in cells or packets of a fixed size. The cell used with ATM is relatively small compared to units used with older technologies. The small, constant cell size allows ATM equipment to transmit video, audio, and computer data over the same network, and assure that no single type of data hogs the line.

Digital subscriber line (DSL) refers collectively to all types of digital subscriber lines, the two main categories being ADSL and SDSL. Two other types of xDSL technologies are high-data-rate DSL (HDSL) and very high DSL (VDSL).

DSL technologies use sophisticated modulation schemes to pack data onto copper wires. They are sometimes referred to as last-mile technologies, because they are used only for connections from a telephone switching station to a home or office, not between switching stations.

Open System Interconnection (OSI) is an International Organization for Standardization (ISO) for worldwide communications that defines a networking framework for implementing protocols in seven layers. Control is passed from one layer to the next, starting at the application layer in one station and proceeding to the bottom layer, over the channel to the next station and back up the hierarchy.

Synchronous Optical Network (SONET) is a standard for connecting fibre-optic transmission systems. SONET was proposed by Bellcore in the middle 1980s and is now a standard.

SONET defines interface standards at the physical layer of the OSI seven-layer model. The standard defines a hierarchy of interface rates that allow data streams at different rates to be multiplexed. With the implementation of SONET, communication carriers throughout the world can interconnect their existing digital carrier and fibre-optic systems.

**Network router:** A network device that forwards packets from one network to another. Based on internal routing tables, routers read each incoming packet and determine how to forward it. The destination address in the packets determines to which line, or interface, outgoing packets are directed. In large-scale enterprise routers, the current traffic load, congestion, line costs, and other factors determine to which line packets are forwarded.

Most routers in the world sit in homes and small offices and do nothing more than direct web, e-mail, and other Internet transactions from the local network to the cable or DSL modem, which is connected to the ISP and Internet. Sitting at the edge of the network, they often contain a built-in firewall for security, and the firewall serves all users in the network without requiring that the personal firewall in each computer be turned on and configured.

In large network environments, however, routers also separate local area networks (LANs) into subnetworks, or subnets, to balance traffic within workgroups and filter traffic for security purposes and policy management.

Within a large enterprise, routers serve as an Internet backbone that connects all internal networks which are typically connected via Ethernet. Within the global Internet, routers do all the packet switching between the backbones and are typically connected via T-3, Asynchronous Transfer Mode (ATM) or SONET links.

**Voice over Internet Protocol (VoIP) phone:** A telephone set designed specifically for use in a VoIP system by converting standard telephone audio into a digital format that can be transmitted over the Internet, and by converting incoming digital phone signals from the Internet to standard telephone audio. A VoIP phone allows the user to take advantage of VoIP technology without involving a personal computer, although an Internet connection is required.

Physically, a VoIP phone set resembles a traditional hard wired or cordless telephone set. It employs the familiar ear and mouth arrangement with an earphone (or earpiece) for listening to incoming audio, and a microphone (or mouthpiece) for transmitting audio. Some VoIP phone sets offer enhanced quality audio, comparable to that on compact disc. A few VoIP phone sets allow for the transmission and reception of image data during calls, so they can be considered video telephones.

Chapter 14 is devoted to VoIP.

**Cisco Unified Call Manager:** An enterprise-class IP telephony call-processing system that provides traditional telephony features advanced capabilities, such as mobility, presence, preference, and conferencing services. This product does the following:

- Simplifies voice systems by replacing old PBX (private branch exchange) and key systems with unified communications

- Enables mobility with software that has embedded unified mobility capabilities so mobile workers can connect from different locations

- Collaborates in a variety of ways, including starting an IM session, initiating a phone calls, and establishing a video-conferencing call

**PSTN and Internet:** The Public Switched Telephone Network (PSTN) is the network of the world's public circuit-switched telephone networks, in much the same way that the Internet is the network of the world's public

IP-based packet-switched networks. Originally a network of fixed-line ana-log telephone systems, the PSTN is now almost entirely digital and now includes mobile and fixed telephones.

**Local area network** (LAN) is a group of computers and associated devices that share a common communications line or wireless link. Typically, con-nected devices share the resources of a single processor or server within a small geographic area (for example, within an office building). Usually, the server has applications and data storage that are shared in common by multi-ple computer users. A local area network may serve as few as two or three users (for example, in a home network) or as many as thousands of users (for example, on a corporate network).

These terms are for informational purposes only, but they may help you if you're unfamiliar with some of them.

The next section covers Cisco IOS version numbers and related topics.

# Cisco Operating System Overview

To understand the *Discovery* presented in the next chapter, this chapter pre-sents some background information on the Cisco operating systems. A lot of this information comes from **http://en.wikipedia.org/wiki/Cisco_IOS**, which provides a clear description of the operating system and related infor-mation.

Cisco IOS (originally Internetwork Operating System) is the software used on most Cisco Systems routers and all current Cisco network switches at the time of this writing. Older switches ran CatOS and, as you'll see in the Discovery output, many of the devices in the case study run CatOS.

Cisco IOS uses a version structure with three numbers and some let-ters, in the general form *a.b(c.d)e* described in the following list:

- a is the major version number.
- b is the minor version number.
- c is the release number, which begins at one and increments as new releases in the same a.b train are released.
- d (omitted from general releases) is the interim build number.

- e (zero, one or two letters) is the release train identifier, such as none (which designates the mainline), T (for technology), E (for enterprise), S (for service provider), XA as a special functionality train, XB as a different special functionality train, etc.

For example, release 12.3(1) is the first mainline Cisco IOS release of version 12.3. 12.3(2) is the next release, and so on. 12.3(1)T is the first release of the T train, 12.3(2)T the next, and so on. Interim builds are candidates for the next release, and are frequently made available by Cisco support as a faster way to provide fixes for bugs before the next release is available. For example, 12.3(1.2)T is the second interim build after release 12.3(1)T.

Some additional factors related to releases include the following:

- **Rebuilds**. Often, a rebuild is compiled to fix a single specific problem or vulnerability for a given IOS version. For example, 12.1(8)E14 is a Rebuild, the 14 denoting the 14th rebuild of 12.1(8)E. Rebuilds are produced to either quickly repair a defect or to satisfy customers who do not want to upgrade to a later major revision because they may be running critical infrastructure on their devices, and hence prefer to minimize change and risk.

- **Interim releases**. Are usually produced on a weekly basis and form a roll-up of current development effort. The Cisco advisory web site may list more than one possible interim to fix an associated issue (the reason for this is unknown to the general public).

- **Maintenance release.** Rigorously tested releases that are made available and include enhancements and bug fixes. Cisco recommends upgrading to Maintenance releases where possible, over Interim and Rebuild releases.

Of particular interest when discussing releases are *trains*. Cisco IOS releases are split into several trains, each containing a different set of features. Trains roughly map to markets or groups of customers for which the Cisco products are targeted. The following bullets describe some example trains:

- The mainline train is the most stable release the company can offer, and its feature set never expands during its lifetime. Updates are released only to address bugs in the product. The previous technology train becomes the source for the current mainline train. As an example, the 12.1T train becomes the basis for the 12.2 mainline. Therefore, to determine the features available in a particular mainline release, look at the previous T train release.

- The T (Technology) train gets new features and bug fixes throughout its life, and is therefore less stable than the mainline. (In releases prior to Cisco IOS Release 12.0, the P train served as the Technology train.)

- The S (Service Provider) train runs only on the company's core router products and is heavily customized for service provider customers.

- The E (Enterprise) train is customized for implementation in enterprise environments.

- The B (Broadband) train supports Internet-based broadband features.

- The X* (XA, XB...) special functionality train needs to be documented.

There are other trains from time to time, designed for specific needs, such as the 12.0AA train contained new code required for the Cisco AS5800 product.

Most Cisco products that run IOS also have one or more "feature sets" or "packages," typically eight packages for Cisco routers and five packages for Cisco network switches. For example, Cisco IOS releases meant for use on Catalyst switches are available as "standard" versions (providing only basic IP routing), "enhanced" versions, which provide full IPv4 routing support, and "advanced IP services" versions, which provide the enhanced features as well as IPv6 support.

Each individual package corresponds to one service category, such as

- IP data

- Converged voice and data

- Security and VPN

This brief overview helps make sense of the Discovery output that contains some of the Cisco IOS revision information. Older products are also analyzed as part of the Discovery and have a version string as well. The operating systems that are part of the Discovery output include the following:

- *IOS* report gives details on every device.

- *CatOS* report gives details on every device.

- "Other Devices" report the gives details on every device not running *IOS* or *CatOS.*

## Cisco EnergyWise Technology

A new innovation in green IT is Cisco EnergyWise, which uses the corporate network to manage power consumption of the IT infrastructure. In the IT community, much attention has been placed upon individual devices and data center power consumption in an effort to reduce carbon footprints and energy cost. Although these activities deliver real results in both power consumption reduction and savings, Cisco's EnergyWise technology is a broader network-based approach to address power consumed outside of the organization's data center.

The approach to power management is based upon the simple fact that future network devices will obtain their power from network switches using Power over Ethernet (POE.) Today, a typical device that uses the network as its power source includes wireless LAN access points (AP), IP phones, IP-based speakers, IP-based wallboards, and IP-based video surveillance cameras. For example a standard 48-port switch, on average, may provide power to 30 phones with PCs attached, 5 wireless access points, and perhaps some miscellaneous computers and printers. Adding up the power consumed by all the varying devices, a 48-port switch has the opportunity to manage and control some 740 watts of power, with an average of 15.4 watts per port. For a large organization, a Cisco EnergyWise-empowered network has the opportunity to manage millions of watts of power across the enterprise. In effect, a network switch is not only managing IP traffic, but also the energy consumed by connected devices.

In addition to power consumption information gathering and reporting, Cisco EnergyWise provides the means to control energy consumption by time of day. With a simple energy policy of shutting down devices for an average of four or five hours a day, a company gains significant power-usage savings. It makes sense that when the office lights are out for the evening or the weekend, not to keep all the devices running at full power.

Consider a 5,000-employee business all equipped with IP phones and 500 WLAN APs. By simply powering down IP phones and WLAN AP for ten hours per evening plus holidays and weekends, this firm saves about $51,000 per year by reducing its electrical energy consumption by 423,500kW, assuming 12 cents per kWh. That is the $CO_2$ equivalent of planting 200,000 trees or preventing some 12,000 mid-size automobiles from emitting annual emissions into the atmosphere.

Cisco EnergyWise is the most innovative approach to corporate energy management. The intellectual and engineering sophistication of the IT industry has stepped up to solve a difficult problem with sufficient scope and scale to deliver meaningful results.

## Summary

The simple advancements made to the large and small closets in this chapter have both green and technological advantages over the old solution. Many network environments have grown incrementally over the years and the old electronics needs to be updated.

The next chapter covers the case study Discovery example.

# CHAPTER 13

# Existing Network Analysis with Discovery

This chapter covers several topics related to analyzing the existing networking environment. The Discovery process evaluates many aspects of the existing network environment and reports on potential problems.

In general, Discovery reports support and security holes that exist. Discovery uses SNMP and Cisco Discovery Protocol (CDP) to identify network devices on a network. Discovery looks at the all the Cisco hardware and software found in the network. With the hardware results, Discovery checks existing support contracts and reports on the contract status of each device. With the operating systems (all operating systems are described in this chapter), Discovery checks for any known security vulnerabilities that exist in those software versions. Discovery also reports on the life cycle of both the hardware and operating systems. All these topics are discussed in this chapter. This information is provided in this chapter. I selected a subset of material in the Discovery output for a specific client example and included them in this chapter.

Some of the Discovery information is revealing, especially as it relates to Cisco *SmartNET* devices under support, because clients don't usually know what networking components they have in place. Comparing the Discovery output to *SMARTnet* support devices resulted in a significant number of discrepancies on every client case study on which my firm has worked.

The first section covers the prerequisites before Discovery can be run.

# Cisco Discovery Prerequisites Overview

Before a Cisco Discovery can be run, some prerequisites must be met. My firm has run hundreds of Discovery assessments, and the following are some basic prerequisites that I have found ensure that the Discovery is successful:

- **Network connection for the pre-connected laptop**. A working local area network (LAN) connection is required to attach a CDI pre-provisioned laptop for running the Cisco Network Collection (CNC) tool.

- **Internet access**. Internet access to www.cisco.com from the pre-concerted laptop is required to start the Discovery. Upon completion of the Discovery the collected data is to be uploaded to Cisco which in turn an Inventory Profile Report (IPR) is then generated.

- **Management network access**. The Cisco Network Collection (CNC) tool must be placed into a network segment that is capable of reaching all networking devices across the entire network that Discovery will analyze. The Cisco Discovery process requires network devices to be Cisco Discovery Protocol (CDP) reachable and the Simple Network Management Protocol (SNMP) enabled in order to facilitate the exchange of management information between network devices.

- **Network addressing**. In advance of initiating the Discovery, a complete and comprehensive list is required for all /24 network addresses in current production. This list expedites the Discovery process and provides seed addressing for the Cisco Network Collection tool. The list of subnet addresses may be in Excel (.xls) or comma-separated value (.csv) format.

- **Community strings**. In advance of initiating the Discovery a complete and comprehensive list is required for collection information about the discovered network devices. The Cisco Network Collection tool utilizes Simple Network Management Protocol (SNMP), community (Read Only or Read Write) strings to perform an inventory for IOS, CAT OS, or PIX OS network devices. The list of SNMP strings may be combined with the subnet addresses list or provided separately.

This list of prerequisites has helped us ensure that we run the Discovery with minimal assistance from our clients. There may be other special requirements for networks with unusual configuration; however, these prerequisites apply to all networks and help us get the Discovery run quickly.

The next section includes information from the *Discovery* executive summary.

## Discovery Executive Summary

Discovery produces an executive summary that includes the following information:

- A summary of the networking devices found including a total, those with SNMP access, and the number of Cisco devices.
- Advanced technology devices found, such as wireless.
- A summary of the IOS devices (see the previous chapter for an IOS overview).
- A summary of the CatOS devices (see the previous chapter for a CatOS summary).
- Security alerts (PSIRT) for various IOS releases discovered in the environment.
- Router and switch hardware summary for both IOS and CatOS.
- A summary for non-IOS non-CatOS devices.

I include many of these summaries in this section. Figure 13-1 shows the total number of devices found during the assessment.

| Total Devices | 377 |
|---|---|
| Cisco | 330 |
| Non Cisco | 0 |
| Unclassified | 47 |
| Unreachable or Devices missing vendor name | 0 |
| **SNMP Access** | **377** |
| SNMP accessible | 377 |
| NOT SNMP accessible | 0 |
| **Total Cisco Devices** | **330** |
| IOS Devices | 283 |
| CatOS Devices | 26 |
| Non-IOS/Non-CatOS Devices | 21 |

Figure 13-1   Total Number of Devices

It's uncommon to know the number and type of networking devices in an environment because most networks grow over time and components are added as required. The 330 Cisco devices cited at the top of the figure are further classified by operating system at the bottom of the figure. The previous chapter included an explanation of the operating systems, including those listed in the figure.

The most important technical information to know about the Cisco devices is software-related. Figure 13-2 shows Cisco Internetworking Operating System (IOS)-related information.

| Train | Maintenance Release Count | Device Count | SW Exception Count |
|-------|---------------------------|--------------|--------------------|
| 11.2 | 1 | 2 | 2 |
| 12.0 | 6 | 29 | 19 |
| 12.1 | 16 | 42 | 17 |
| 12.2 | 23 | 85 | 15 |
| 12.3 | 16 | 62 | 59 |
| 12.4 | 12 | 63 | 0 |
| **Total** | **74** | **283** | **112** |

Figure 13-2    IOS Summary

The Trains in Figure 13-2 are software releases of IOS. Some of the Trains have a high software exception count, which could include such potential problems as a special release or end of sale or engineering. These exceptions are potential red flags that require additional investigation.

The next software summary in the executive document is for the older Catalyst Operating System (CatOS), CatOS runs on many existing switches so, even though it pre-dates IOS, there is a lot of it running in existing environments, so knowing the profile of it in the environment is important. Figure 13-3 shows a CatOS summary.

| Train | Maintenance Release Count | Device Count | SW Exception Count |
|-------|---------------------------|--------------|--------------------|
| 7.2 | 1 | 6 | 6 |
| 8.3 | 1 | 3 | 3 |
| 8.6 | 3 | 17 | 15 |
| **Total** | **5** | **26** | **24** |

Figure 13-3    CatOS Summary

Figure 13-3 shows a substantial number of software exceptions in the CatOS devices, which also require more investigation.

The Trains in this figure are software releases of IOS. Some of the Trains have a high software exception count, which could include such potential problems as a special release or end of sale or engineering. These exceptions are potential red flags, which require additional investigation.

Security is a top concern on all IT components, including networking. Cisco's umbrella organization for security is Product Security Incident Response Team (PSIRT). This is a dedicated team that manages all aspects of security vulnerability-related information. Knowing information about potential PSIRT (www.cisco.com/go/psirt) vulnerability is important, and it is included in Figure 13-4 from the executive summary.

| Train | Device Count | PSIRT ALERT |
|-------|--------------|-------------|
| 11.2 | 2 | |
| 12.0 | 29 | P5,P14,P18,P19,P21,P22,P47,P57,P80,P88 |
| 12.1 | 42 | P5,P14,P18,P19,P21,P22,P38,P47,P48,P57,P80,P88,P106,P56,P3,P33,P34,P35 |
| 12.2 | 85 | P5,P14,P18,P19,P21,P22,P37,P38,P40,P44,P47,P51,P56,P57,P80,P88,P4,P9,P11,P20, P33,P34,P35,P36,P45,P46,P48,P54,P55,P79,P94,P95,P2,P6,P1,P106,P12,P28,P49,P53, P8,P3,P97 |
| 12.3 | 62 | P18,P22,P31,P32,P33,P34,P35,P36,P38,P44,P45,P47,P52,P54,P55,P79,P80,P88,P94, P95,P106,P46,P48,P98,P8,P9,P12,P14,P20,P25,P37,P19,P57,P23,P4,P5,P6,P10,P11,P21,P51 |
| 12.4 | 63 | P73,P79,P93,P94,P95,P96,P98,P100,P106,P44,P48,P55,P57,P12,P18,P22,P25,P32,P33, P34,P35,P36,P47,P54,P80,P88,P19,P20,P23,P31,P38,P43,P45,P50,P52,P91,P92,P24 |
| 4.7 | | |
| 7.2 | | |
| 8.3 | | |
| 8.6 | | |
| Total | 283 | |

Figure 13-4  *PSIRT* Summary

Of the many PSIRT entries shown for the 283 devices, some may be serious. Having this information gives the networking team a place to start in security updates.

In addition to the operating meeting and PSIRT information, it is useful to know about the networking hardware. The executive summary also contains information about the hardware.

Figure 13-5 summarizes the hardware running IOS.

| Series | Model Count | Device Count | HW Exception Count |
|---|---|---|---|
| Cisco 2600 Series Multiservice Platforms | 3 | 33 | 33 |
| Cisco 2800 Series Integrated Services Routers | 4 | 108 | 0 |
| Cisco 3700 Series Multiservice Access Routers | 2 | 6 | 6 |
| Cisco 3800 Series Integrated Services Routers | 1 | 5 | 0 |
| Cisco 7200 Series Routers | 2 | 3 | 1 |
| Cisco 7500 Series Routers | 1 | 1 | 1 |
| Cisco 7600 Series Routers | 2 | 3 | 0 |
| Cisco Aironet 1200 Series | 1 | 3 | 3 |
| Cisco Aironet 1240 AG Series | 1 | 1 | 0 |
| Cisco Catalyst 2900 Series XL Switches | 2 | 3 | 3 |
| Cisco Catalyst 2950 Series Switches | 1 | 2 | 2 |
| Cisco Catalyst 3500 Series XL Switches | 3 | 23 | 23 |
| Cisco Catalyst 3550 Series Switches | 3 | 24 | 24 |
| Cisco Catalyst 3560 Series Switches | 3 | 52 | 0 |
| Cisco Catalyst 4500 Series Switches | 1 | 1 | 0 |
| Cisco Catalyst 6000 Router Module | 1 | 3 | 3 |
| Cisco Catalyst 6500 Series Switches | 1 | 12 | 12 |
| **Total** | **32** | **283** | **111** |

Figure 13-5    Hardware Summary of *IOS* Devices

Figure 13-5 shows the number of routers and switch models in the environment running IOS. Shown in the figure are the number of different models represented within each series, and the number of devices deployed for each platform. The *HW Exception Count* shows the number of device models, which have a hardware exception that includes End Of Sale (EOS), Last Date of Support (LDoS, formerly EOL), and other exceptions.

Figure 13-6 shows the same hardware summary for one type of CatOS device family in the environment.

| Series | Model Count | Device Count | HW Exception Count |
|---|---|---|---|
| Cisco Catalyst 6500 Series Switches | 1 | 26 | 26 |
| Total | 1 | 26 | 26 |

Figure 13-6    Hardware Summary of CatOS Devices

The *HW Exception Count* for this device shows a one-for-one exception for all 26 devices. This may be the same exception for each device or several different exceptions which should be evaluated.

Cisco operating systems, other than IOS and CatOS, are summarized in Figure 13-7.

| OS Type | Series | Model Count | Device Count | HW Exception Count |
|---|---|---|---|---|
| AltigaOS | Cisco VPN 3000 Series Concentrators | 1 | 2 | 2 |
| NAM | Network Management Services Modules | 1 | 1 | 0 |
| SAN-OS | Cisco MDS 9200 Series Multilayer Switches | 1 | 1 | 1 |
| VxWorks | Cisco Aironet 1200 Series | 1 | 17 | 17 |
| | Total | 4 | 21 | 20 |

Figure 13-7    Hardware Summary of Non-IOS and Non-CatOS Devices

Figure 13-7 shows the operating system type that runs on each platform. These operating systems were not covered earlier, but all are Cisco operating systems that have a lot of *HW Exception Count* associated with them. The figure also shows the number of different models represented within each series and the number of devices deployed for each platform.

The information in the executive summary provides a good snapshot of the networking electronics and operating systems in the environment. The exception count indicates that some additional research needs to take place to ensure that no serious exceptions exist. The PSIRT entries indicate potential security problems. All this is important information and a starting point for researching networking aspects of the environment and making improvements.

The executive summary contains a wealth of high-level information, but the details are in the reports covered in the next section.

## Discovery Detailed Reports

Discovery produces not only the executive summary presented in the previous section, but also several documents, including the following:

- IOS report that details every device
- CatOS report that details every device
- "Other Devices" report that details every device not running IOS or CatOS
- Spreadsheet covering the details of every IOS device
- Spreadsheet covering the details of every CatOS device
- Spreadsheet covering the details of "Other Devices"

This book would be thousands of pages if I covered all these reports in detail, so instead, I cover some of the highlights. The documents are in the same form for different operating systems, so I give you a flavor for the layout and high points of the documents in the upcoming sections.

## Software Life Cycle Legend

Much of the data in the reports and spreadsheets are color coded to indicate the status of the software running on the electronics identified by Discovery. Although I can't show you colors in this book, Figure 13-8 shows the descriptions of the status used in the reports and spreadsheets.

| Warning Level | Color | Status Flags |
|---|---|---|
| Critical | Orange | LDoS - Last Date of Support (formerly EOL) |
| Major | Yellow | EOE |
| | | Special Release |
| Minor | Light Blue | EOS – End of Sale |
| Notice | Light Green | EOSA - End of Sale Announcement |
| None | White | Available/ Orderable |
| None | Green | Future EOX Milestone |

Figure 13-8    Software Life Cycle Legend

This life cycle information is embedded in many of the tables in the spreadsheet reports and documents, and the colors that appear in this table make it easy to quickly identify the level of attention required. Those devices for which a critical warning level exists, which require immediate action, appear in orange. The next most important warning level is yellow, then light blue, and so on. These colors are used consistently in the spreadsheet reports and documents.

The following are explanations for the Status Flags in the table directly from the Discovery document:

- **EOSA – End of Sale Announcement**. The date the End of Sale (EOS) and Last Date of Support (LDoS, formerly EOL) announcement is distributed to the general public and made available on www.cisco.com. This announcement indicates that a Cisco product will soon reach, or has already reached, End of Sale life cycle status, and will no longer be available for sale or download. The specific End of Sale date is available in the End of Sale announcement. Unless stated otherwise in the End of Sale announcement, the Cisco product is maintained by hardware and software maintenance contracts and is still supported by Cisco's Technical Assistance Center.

- **EOS – End of Sale**. The IOS Release has reached the end of general availability through regular sales channels. The End of Sale releases continue to be provided for download on CCO, regular maintenance releases continue to be provided until the release has reached End of Engineering, and support is provided until the End of Life for the specific release.

- **EOE – End of Engineering**. The IOS Release has reached the end of its maintenance schedule and no new maintenance releases will be produced. End of Engineering releases continue to be provided for download on CCO, and support is provided until the End of Life for the specific release. However, further software support to fix software defects will be provided by the next IOS train, and an upgrade to that release is usually necessary to resolve issues with additional software defects.

- **Special Releases**. Cisco IOS Special Releases introduce new hardware and new technologies to the market. These releases do not follow the same life cycles as Limited Deployment (LD) or Early Deployment (ED) releases, and usually have shortened life cycles, although some Special Releases have extended life cycles servicing particular hardware platforms or software feature deployments.

- **LDoS – Last Date of Support** (formerly EOL). After IOS Releases have reached Last Date of Support, Cisco TAC and other support is no longer available for this release, and the release is no longer available for download on CCO. In some cases, EOL releases remain posted for download on CCO; however, this in no way constitutes continued support of these releases.

In addition to specific Status Flags in the table, some background is helpful in understanding releases in general that are in the Discovery document, including the following:

- **GD – General Deployment**. Releases of Cisco IOS reach General Deployment (GD) when their quality has been proven through extensive market exposure in diverse networks, analysis of stability and software defect trends, and customer satisfaction surveys. General Deployment releases are continually improved utilizing post-GD maintenance releases schedules until they reach End of Engineering (EOE) in their deployment life cycles.

- **LD – Limited Deployment.** A Release of Cisco IOS is in the "Limited Deployment" phase of its life cycle during the period between initial FCS and the General Deployment (GD) milestones. Some number of release cycles occurs before software matures, and then is declared General Deployment (GD). Some versions of Cisco IOS are only released as Limited Deployment and do not ever become General Deployment.

- **ED – Early Deployment.** Cisco IOS ED releases are vehicles that bring new development to the marketplace. Each maintenance revision of an ED release includes not only software defect resolutions, but also a set of new features, new platform support, and general enhancements to protocols and the Cisco IOS infrastructure. In varying time frames, the features and platforms of the ED releases are ported to the next Cisco IOS train. Early Deployment versions of IOS are not scheduled to become General Deployment.

With an explanation of the terms in place, I now cover some of the reports generated with Discovery.

## IOS Detailed Report: Software, Hardware, and Security

The Discovery report detailing IOS has numerous sections covering software, hardware, security, and other status on IOS devices. The software life cycle legend in Figure 13-8 summarizes warnings with corresponding colors so the warning level is easy to identify. The detailed report uses the same warning levels and colors.

Figure 13-9 shows components that all have major warnings.

| Train | IOS Version | Model | Total | Status | IOS Release |
|-------|-------------|-------|-------|--------|-------------|
| 11.2 | 11.2(8.2)SA6 | catalyst2924MXL | 2 | N/F | Special Release |
| 12.0 | 12.0(4)T | cisco2621 | 5 | ED | EOE (Ref E1) |
| | 12.0(5.2)XU | catalyst3524XL | 1 | N/F | Special Release |
| | | cat3524tXLEn | 2 | N/F | Special Release |
| | 12.0(5.1)XP | catalyst3524XL | 1 | N/F | Special Release |
| | | catalyst2924XLv | 1 | N/F | Special Release |
| | 12.0(5.3)WC(1) | cat3524tXLEn | 2 | N/F | Special Release |
| | 12.0(5.4)WC(1) | catalyst3524XL | 7 | N/F | Special Release |
| | 12.0(5)WC3b | catalyst3524XL | 9 | ED | |
| | | catalyst3508GXL | 1 | ED | |

Figure 13-9    Partial *IOS Software Lifecycle Table* (Yellow: Major Warning)

Figure 13-9 shows a couple of software examples of major warnings, which are color coded yellow. As the software life cycle legend figure earlier described, a major warning is either a *Special Release* or *End of Engineering (EOE.)* Figure 13-9 shows examples of both of these in the *IOS Release* column.

Figure 13-9 shows a small subset of the *IOS Software Life Cycle Table,* which has in it many other warning levels including a lot of orange which are critical warnings.

The status of all hardware is also covered as part of the report and consumes most of the pages of the document because hardware is broken down in to low level components. Like software, there is a hardware life cycle legend, which is shown in Figure 13-10.

| Warning Level | Color | Status Flags |
|---------------|-------|--------------|
| Critical | Orange | LDoS - Last Date of Support (formerly EOL) |
| Major | Yellow | EOSWM - End of Software Maintenance |
| | | EOCR – End of Service Contract Renewal |
| Minor | Light Blue | EOSale – End of Sale |
| Notice | Light Green | EOSA - End of Sale Announcement |
| None | White | Available/ Orderable |
| None | Green | Future EOX Milestone |

Figure 13-10    Hardware Life Cycle Legend

As you can see, the Hardware Life Cycle Legend is similar to the legend for software. All the chassis and components within the chassis are evaluated and entries appear in many tables using the Hardware Life Cycle Legend. Of the 225 pages in this client example, document the hardware summary portion comprises roughly 200 pages. In some of the tables, there is a combination of both hardware and software exceptions, which can have different colors for software and hardware for a specific hardware component. Figure 13-3 shows an example of a chassis with a yellow *SW Exception* column (major) and an orange *HW Exception* (critical) column. This can't be seen without the color coding, of course, but Figure 13-11 is a good example of the detail included for one item in the report.

| Host Name | IP Address | Serial Number | Model | IOS Relese | Feature Set | Install Mem. | Install Flash | Req. Memory | Req. Flash | DEF Excp. | SA Excp. | SW Exception | HW Exception |
|-----------|-----------|---------------|-------|------------|-------------|--------------|---------------|-------------|------------|-----------|----------|--------------|--------------|
| NY, NY | 1.1.1.1 | (050443)(V) | cisco2621 | 12.3(19) | IP/FW/IDS PLUS IPSEC 3DES BASIC | 64 | 16 | 64 | 16 | N | N | EOE | LDoS(EOL)(H) |

Figure 13-11    Partial SW and HW Exception Example

Knowing these exceptions is key to having an operational and secure environment, which is easy to overlook with many networking components in your environment.

Thousands of such entries in the report require painstaking analysis. Each entry should be compared to the SMARTnet contract to identify discrepancies, which invariably uncovers savings because, in the case of my clients, there have always been items on SMARTnet that were not in the report and are no longer installed and should not be included in the SMARTnet contact. Conversely, there are sometimes installed components that are not on SMARTnet and need to be added.

Security is also part of the detailed report. There was some summary information on PSIRT alerts in the executive summary and substantially more detail in a detailed report. This detail on PSIRT-related information is produced on a device-by-device basis, as shown in Figure 13-12.

| Train | IOS Version | Model | Total | PSIRT ALERT |
|-------|-------------|-------|-------|-------------|
| 12.0 | 12.0(4)T | cisco2621 | 5 | P5,P14,P18,P19,P21,P22,P47,P57,P80,P88 |
| 12.1 | 12.1(9)EA1c | catalyst355024 | 2 | |
| 12.1 | 12.1(9)EA1c | catalyst355048 | 2 | |
| 12.1 | 12.1(22)E1 | catalyst6kMsfc2 | 1 | P3,P5,P14,P18,P19,P21,P22,P33,P34,P35,P47,P56,P5 |
| 12.1 | 12.1(20)EA2 | catalyst355024PWR | 4 | P5,P18,P21,P22,P80,P88,P106 |
| 12.1 | 12.1(20)EA1a | catalyst295012 | 1 | P5,P18,P21,P22,P80,P106 |
| 12.1 | 12.1(19)EA1c | catalyst355024 | 1 | P5,P18,P21,P22,P80,P106 |
| 12.1 | 12.1(18) | cisco2621 | 1 | P5,P14,P19,P21,P22,P38,P47,P48,P57,P80 |
| 12.1 | 12.1(17) | cisco2612 | 1 | P5,P14,P18,P19,P21,P22,P38,P47,P57,P80,P88 |
| 12.1 | 12.1(17) | cisco2621 | 1 | P5,P14,P18,P19,P21,P22,P38,P47,P57,P80,P88 |
| 12.1 | 12.1(14)EA1a | catalyst295012 | 1 | P5,P18,P21,P22,P80,P106 |
| 12.1 | 12.1(14)EA1a | catalyst355024PWR | 2 | P5,P18,P21,P22,P80,P106 |
| 12.1 | 12.1(14) | cisco2612 | 8 | P5,P14,P18,P19,P21,P22,P38,P47,P57,P80,P88 |
| 12.1 | 12.1(13)EA1a | catalyst355024 | 1 | P5,P18,P21,P22,P80,P106 |
| 12.1 | 12.1(13)EA1a | catalyst355024PWR | 5 | P5,P18,P21,P22,P80,P106 |
| 12.1 | 12.1(13)E12 | catalyst6kMsfc2 | 2 | P5,P14,P18,P19,P21,P22,P47,P56,P57,P80,P88 |
| 12.1 | 12.1(12c)EA1 | catalyst355024 | 1 | P5,P18,P21,P22,P80,P106 |
| 12.1 | 12.1(11b)EX1 | cat6509 | 1 | |
| 12.1 | 12.1(11)EA1a | catalyst355024 | 1 | P5,P18,P21,P22,P80,P106 |
| 12.1 | 12.1(11)EA1 | catalyst355024 | 1 | P5,P18,P21,P22,P80,P88,P106 |

Figure 13-12   Partial PSIRT Detail for All 283 Devices

Figure 13-2 shows that some components have multiple PSIRT alerts and others have none. The alerts are potentially serious business, so the more information you have about them, the better. The detailed report also includes URLs for the specific PSIRT alerts, as shown in Figure 13-13.

| PSIRT | Document id | Publish Date | URL |
|---|---|---|---|
| P1 | 63846 | 26-JAN-2005 | Crafted Packet Causes Reload on Cisco Routers |
| P2 | 61365 | 18-AUG-2004 | Cisco IOS Malformed OSPF Packet Causes Reload |
| P3 | 64439 | 06-APR-2005 | Vulnerabilities in Cisco IOS Secure Shell Server |
| P4 | 64424 | 06-APR-2005 | Vulnerabilities in the Internet Key Exchange Xauth Implementation |
| P5 | 61671 | 27-AUG-2004 | Cisco Telnet Denial of Service Vulnerability |
| P6 | 63708 | 19-JAN-2005 | Vulnerability in Cisco IOS Embedded Call Processing Solutions |
| P7 | 64347 | 06-APR-2005 | Cisco VPN 3000 Concentrator Vulnerable to Crafted SSL Attack |
| P8 | 66269 | 07-SEP-2005 | Cisco IOS Firewall Authentication Proxy for FTP and Telnet Sessions Buffe |
| P9 | 65783 | 29-JUL-2005 | IPv6 Crafted Packet Vulnerability |
| P10 | 50980 | 20-APR-2004 | Vulnerabilities in SNMP Message Processing |
| P11 | 65328 | 29-JUN-2005 | RADIUS Authentication Bypass |
| P12 | 68158 | 14-NOV-2005 | Multiple Vulnerabilities Found by PROTOS IPSec Test Suite |
| P13 | 68869 | 26-JAN-2006 | Cisco VPN 3000 Concentrator Vulnerable to Crafted HTTP Attack |
| P14 | 68793 | 18-JAN-2006 | IOS Stack Group Bidding Protocol Crafted Packet DoS |
| P15 | 70567 | 28-JUN-2006 | Access Point Web-browser Interface Vulnerability |
| P16 | 71141 | 23-AUG-2006 | Cisco VPN 3000 Concentrator FTP Management Vulnerabilities |
| P17 | 71255 | 20-SEP-2006 | DOCSIS Read-Write Community String Enabled in Non-DOCSIS Platforms |
| P18 | 68322 | 01-DEC-2005 | IOS HTTP Server Command Injection Vulnerability |
| P19 | 77859 | 10-JAN-2007 | DLSw Vulnerability |
| P20 | 72372 | 24-JAN-2007 | IPv6 Routing Header Vulnerability |
| P21 | 81734 | 24-JAN-2007 | Crafted IP Option Vulnerability |

Figure 13-13   Partial PSIRT URLs

Needless to say, it is important to be current on all security updates on all IT components, and networking is no exception. By the time you read this book, many of these will have been updated; but when Discovery is run in an environment, the URLs for PSIRT exceptions found are listed in the detailed report.

Additional reports are produced as part of Discovery. A CatOS and Other devices detailed reports are also produced. Depending on the number of such devices, these reports can be long and detailed. Also, spreadsheets are produced that have just the data on all components in them without the supporting explanations.

All this great information is only useful if it is applied. There are numerous ways this can be done, including the comparison of what is in place to SMARTnet to ensure the two jive, which I mentioned earlier, to address any potential PSIRT problems, and improving the existing environment by replacing outdated components with new ones.

## Summary

Discovery, like the other assessments run in the earlier sections, is most revealing. Knowing the status of all networking components is invaluable, especially if some of the components are older and you don't know if they are at end of engineering. Knowing the PSIRT alerts is also important so you can address any security holes.

The next chapter covers Voice over IP.

# Chapter 14

# Voice over Internet Protocol (VoIP)

This chapter covers the business drivers, solutions, and technologies involving Voice over Internet Protocol (VoIP) implementations. VoIP is one of the most misunderstood technologies I've worked with in my client base. VoIP has had a lot of publicity and fanfare recently and for good reason; it saves businesses money in a variety of ways that I describe shortly.

To begin, there are a lot of moving parts involved with VoIP which intimidates most of the experienced telecommunications technologists I interact with on a daily basis. Financial decision makers also have a lot to consider with VoIP because, in some cases, the payback is not crystal clear and requires some detailed analysis.

## Telecommunications Overview

Since the invention of the telephone, a normal phone call takes place by transmitting our voices electronically. It first started with sending pulses of electricity to a central operator whose phone rang and we told the operator who we were and who we wanted to talk to. The operator would in-turn send an electric signal to that destination phone number to make the phone ring. The phone on the other end would be answered and the operator would tell that person who was trying to reach them. Finally, the operator or sometimes a bunch of operators involving a long-distance call created a conference using a physical cable connection between the two sides of the line. This all worked fine until phones proliferated and this is where a phone system came into play. Whether at your local central office or in your business, there is an automated telephone switching system that simultaneously handles mass volumes of telephone conversations, controlling where the phone rings next, connecting people together and controls which services a phone gets, such as enabling a person to make an outgoing call (local vs. long distance), telling a person who is calling them (Caller ID), and enabling people to talk (conferencing). At home, this service is performed by your local telephone service provider, and at your office, this becomes a function of your internal phone system, also known as a private branch exchange (PBX.)

So now that I have the history out of the way, what is VoIP? Well, just like we learned in our short telecommunications lesson, there is a system that connects and controls our everyday communication, except in VoIP, our telephone conversation is digitized, packetized, and transmitted differently. Effectively, our conversations are transmitted on the IP rules-based network.

The next section covers the operation of VoIP.


## How Does VoIP Work?


In 1928, Henry Nyquist, while working at Bell Telephone Laboratories, discovered that to accurately represent an analog sound wave in digital form, that sound wave needs to be sampled by at least TWICE the amount of the highest perceived frequency. Basically, Henry measured that the human voice is perceived at 4,000 Hertz (4KHz) of audio frequency per second, and if we are to transmit it digitally and retain the quality on the other end, we need to digitize every second of our conversation to 8,000 Hertz (8KHz). Living in the world of digitization, our VoIP systems take that scale of 8,000 audio frequencies and codes them into 8 bit packets of 1s and 0s in a machine language. In short, each (11001010) bit represents a value in frequency of sound on Henry's scale. Each second of recorded conversation is then sliced into 10ms for lighter and faster transmission of packetized bits.

There are three distinct ways that consumers and businesses are using VoIP technology today. The following is a consumer solution, the second a business solution using traditional phones, and the third a specialized IP-based phone as described in the following bullets:

• **A consumer using a standard telephone and an adapter**. In this example, the consumer is using a standard telephone, a basic Internet connection, and a specially designed consumer VoIP adapter. This adapter converts the voice frequencies from an analog conversation into digital packets of data and transmits it over the Internet. It's easy to set up and it's becoming more common in the consumer Voice over IP marketplace. Figure 14-1 shows a phone, Analog Telephony Adapter (ATA), and a cable or DSL connection to the Internet to facilitate VoIP.

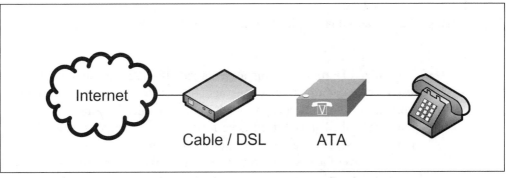

Internet

Cable / DSL      ATA

Figure 14-1    Consumer VoIP Using a Standard Phone and Adapter

• **Traditional business phone and an adapter**. For businesses with many users on traditional phones, the adapter becomes a specialized gateway that converts the analog voice frequencies into the packetized data. For example, when an employee in a New York office dials an extension in the Dallas office, the call is first routed through the phone system within the company's physical location. It is then extended to the organization's in-house IP-based network, gets converted to IP packets, and is then sent via the organization's internetwork to the Dallas office. Once received by the network in Dallas, the process is reversed and the phone call is connected using the local telephone system, as shown in Figure 14-2 depicting a phone connection between two offices.

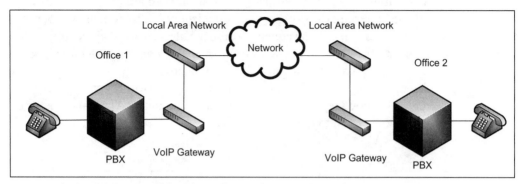

Figure 14-2    Traditional Business Phone and VoIP Using an Adapter

- **Specialized IP phone**. Using a specialized IP-based telephone, which resembles a traditional telephone but connects to the company's data network, a full IP solution is provided. There is no need for an analog to IP gateway, as the handset itself is performing that function. A specialized application server in an organization's back office is able to find and connect calls over the network from one VoIP-enabled phone to another. This option is becoming more popular, and manufacturers and service providers that specialize in managing this functionality have seen steady growth. This setup is shown in Figure 14-3.

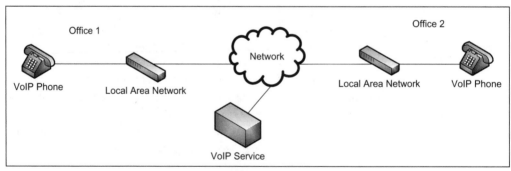

Figure 14-3    VoIP Using a Specialized IP Phone

- **"Soft phone" running on a computer**. This solution uses software on the computer, which emulates the physical VoIP phone. All that's needed is a reliable computer with a reliable network connection (a good headset also helps), and the ability to make and receive calls from anywhere and anytime makes a company's Business Continuity Plan (BCP) a very low cost reality. Figure 14-4 depicts the soft phone topology.

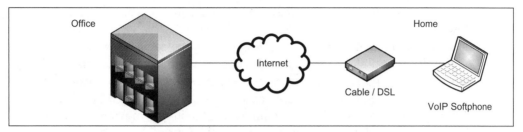

Figure 14-4    VoIP Using a Soft Phone

VoIP uses specialized technologies to digitize your everyday telephone conversation and dissect it into tiny computer bytes. Once these bytes are created, they are electronically transmitted across a network, whether that means it's the public Internet connection to your friend's house or your company's private network.

Typically, the electronic signals reach the other end of the conversation in fractions of a second and the VoIP technology is seamless. The same specialized technologies re-assemble the computer bytes to a normal and sensible telephone conversation. When combined on one network, voice and data together offer boundless opportunities for users and efficiencies for organizations.

## How VoIP Is Different from a Traditional Phone System

A traditional phone system utilizes Time Division Multiplexing (TDM), which is a method of multiplexing two or more signals or bit streams that take turns on a single communication channel. A common example of a TDM technology is a T-1 from a local telephony service provider. A T-1 is a dedicated connection supporting data rates of 1.544Mb per second. To support voice applications, the system divides that path into several recurrent time slots of fixed length, for a T-1 line is time-sliced into 24 virtual talk paths. There are many positive implications to this method, because each conversation is reserved in its own lane on the super highway, and we are assured a path for our conversation. Jumping lanes (crossed conversations) and data network interference become highly improbable. The drawback to TDM technology is that it is a highly inflexible and expensive technology; you are paying for this technology whether there are 10 or 20 conversations taking place. Additionally, this technology does not provide for much resiliency, because you have to purchase a second T-1 in case your first T-1 goes down.

A traditional phone system (PBX) utilizes the same TDM methodology. A PBX backplane uses TDM to support a variety of specialized and manufacturer proprietary system boards (blades). In turn, these boards use TDM to create dedicated electronic-based ports for voice. Each TDM board is highly customized to allow a certain number and types of phones to work. To give an example, some boards allow 8, 16, or maybe even 24 phones to work at a time. Some TDM boards only talk analog, some talk digital, some just T-1s, voicemail, and so on.

Basically, the phone system becomes housing for all these specialized TDM circuit boards, and the more people in an organization, the bigger the real estate. In a larger organization, it is common to find multiple refrigerator-sized phone system casings that take up a lot of dedicated space, power, and cooling. To make matters worse, if a company has more than one facility, the process needs to replicate all over again, each and every time.

As mentioned previously, with VoIP, conversations are transmitted over the standard IP rules-based network. VoIP in effect creates the need for commonality between the technologies while separating the application from the dependency on the physical topology. The next two examples compare a typical organization using a traditional (TDM-based) phone system, and a similar organization leveraging VoIP between their main offices, a branch office, and the corporate data center.

**Traditional voice and data network**. In this example, the business is using a traditional voice network approach and common data network components in connecting their users. The two technologies simply sit side-by-side at the user's desk. The data center hosts an organization's enterprise-wide applications, such as e-mail and financial services. This traditional environment is shown in Figure 14-5.

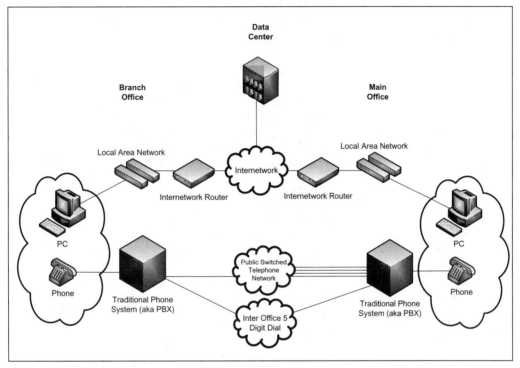

Figure 14-5    Traditional Voice and Data Network

**Converged voice and data network**. In this example, VoIP-enabled network components build convergence of the telephone and data systems. VoIP becomes an application on the corporate network that shares multiple common network paths.

The convergence of the two technologies enables a company to leverage their existing data center for housing a centralized telephone system, reducing the need for purchasing and maintaining a PBX at every office location. This is especially prudent in a retail and outpatient service organizations where space and funds are limited.

The convergence of the two technologies eliminates the need for private inter-office tie lines dedicated to four and five-digit interoffice dialing, because all calls between the two locations are first routed across the company's internetwork. If the internetwork becomes congested or unavailable, VoIP mechanisms in place re-route the calls during the outage using the public switched telephone network (PSTN) long-distance service.

The converged environment is shown in Figure 14-6.

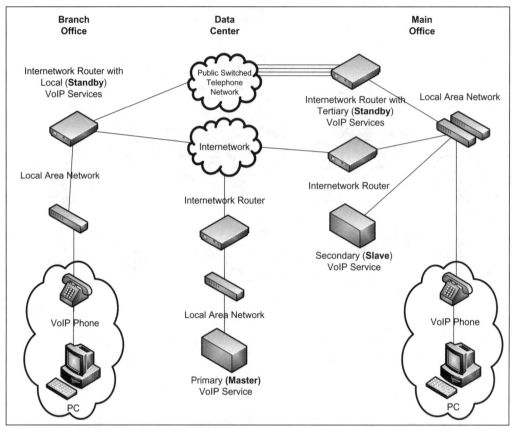

Figure 14-6    Converged Voice and Data Network

Figure 14-6 depicts that VoIP turns a voice conversation into an end-user application, which becomes a manageable and customizable resource. VoIP can be centrally managed while deployed from anywhere on the network. You don't need to operate two separate and dedicated networks for voice and data.

# VoIP, Green, and Cost Savings

Now that I've covered the background of VoIP, it's time to move on to the many ways that this technology saves money.

The next few examples are taken from clients with whom I've worked who used a traditional means of communication and then realized their Return on Investment (ROI) when they began leveraging VoIP-enabled technologies. I cover conferencing, data center consolidation, private networking, maintenance support optimization, and service contract optimization in these examples. I used examples from clients in different industries because VoIP is a technology that is useful in all industries, and these snippets of what has been implemented in each account will help with the positioning of VoIP capabilities.

## Audio Conferencing

One of the most compelling areas of savings supplied by VoIP is holding audio conferences in-house. One of my financial clients in NYC was spending $118K annually on his audio conference budget. Because the client was already VoIP enabled, an in-house conferencing system was presented, at a one-time cost of $70K. This resulted in a $284K ROI over the course of three years. Figure 14-7 depicts the high-level in-house conference system.

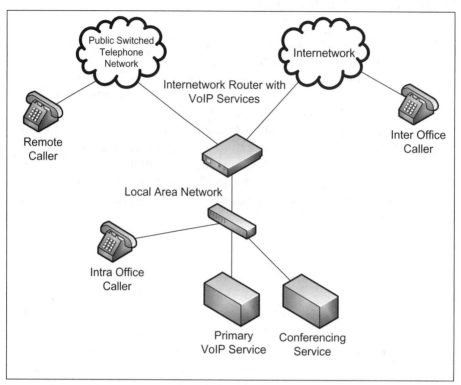

Figure 14-7    High-Level View of Diagram

In addition to the providing the client with the ability to host their own audio conferences, the system also came with desktop web and video conferencing abilities so the client did not have before deploying this solution Lastly, since the conferencing solution itself is VoIP based, integration with their corporate e-mail client was enabled, giving power and control to users themselves while removing the burden from the office manager.

## Video over IP

Video conferencing has a compelling ROI in that travel is typically reduced dramatically. One of my clients was a CIO of a worldwide R&D organization with seven direct reports located throughout the U.S., Belgium, Italy, and Mexico, was averaging a quarterly staff meeting with his direct reports.

Each meeting was held on a rotation and involved the CIO and staff managers traveling for three to four days every time. This technique was employed in building the team and reinforcing company policies, until video-conferencing technologies were introduced. With the implementation of video-enabled VoIP across the various locations, the CIO now had a readily available video conferencing solution, right from his office, and the face-to-face meetings with his direct reports were now literally just a phone call away.

VoIP technology brought right to its office desktop empowered the team to hold shorter and more frequent face-to-face meetings, immediately reducing travel for the IT executives by 50%, while saving the company $40K in the first year, in travel, expense, and lost productivity.

## Data Center Consolidation

Another firm with a large field sales force organization was supporting its outside sales work force of 7,000 people with a TDM PBX and voicemail system. With an estimated data center cost of $100 per square foot, the 15 cabinet solutions cost the company $25K per month. Figure 14-8 depicts the telephony footprint before VoIP was implemented.

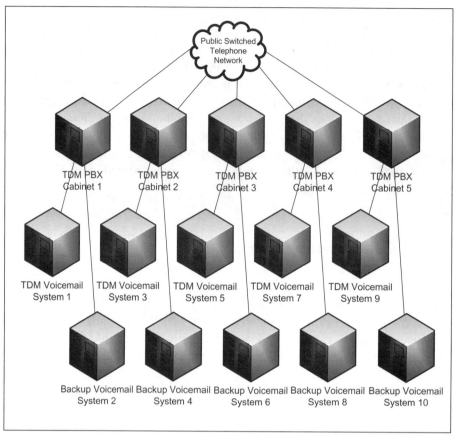

Figure 14-8    Telephony Footprint Before VoIP

After implementing VoIP, the organization reduced the telephony foot-print in the data center to just two data center racks, saving $264K in data center costs of space, power, and cooling in the first year. Figure 14-9 shows the reduced telephony footprint with VoIP.

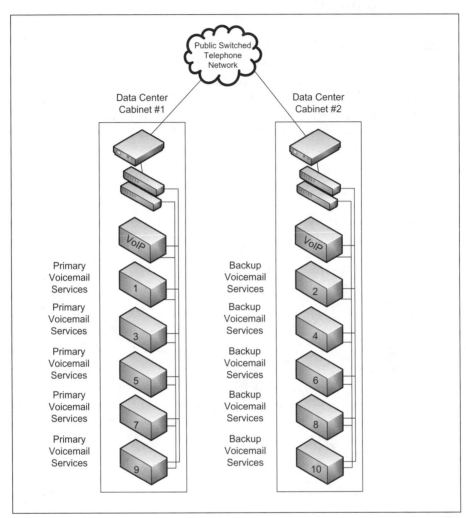

Figure 14-9    Reduced Telephony Footprint After VoIP

Figure 14-9 shows the two data center racks, which resulted in a greatly reduced footprint.

## Private Networking

Private networking helped a regional hospital. Inpatient and outpatient services with 11 facilities throughout the state was connecting their voice systems for 4-digit dial services between all locations, using dedicated voice T1s from their regional telephone company. With an average voice tie line costing $1,200 per month, the hospital was paying $158.4K annually for its private voice network. Figure 14-10 shows the hospital layout.

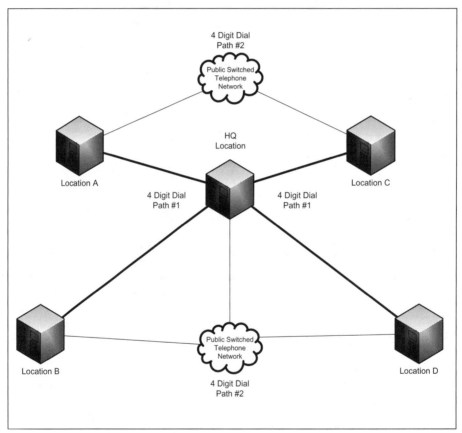

Figure 14-10    Reduced Telephony Footprint After VoIP

Because the organization already had a voice capable wide area network, after transitioning their telephony systems onto VoIP, the organization completely eliminated the dedicated voice tie lines, reducing the cost of its private telephony network by 100%. Figure 14-11 shows the private telephony network.

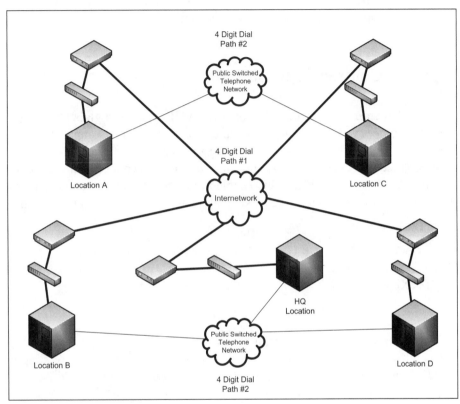

Figure 14-11    Private Telephony Network

Figure 14-11 shows the simple means by which VoIP was implemented on the network that was already capable of this service.

## Maintenance Support Optimization

By replacing its TDM key system equipment with VoIP-enabled technology, a nationwide retail organization reduced its telephony support budget by 50%. Switching to a VoIP solution no longer required dispatching local site technicians to program phones, change extension assignments, or manually program speed dials.

Additionally, the organization discontinued the practice of manually distributing monthly music on hold tapes to all 164 retail stores and began distributing them electronically. This action reduced the monthly service fee of $15 per tape, saving the company $30K annually.

## Service Contract Optimization

By implementing strategically regionalized VoIP systems, a global manufacturing company enabled the organization to streamline its support agreements from 37 locally managed service maintenance contracts down to 3 regionalized agreements, while standardizing on service levels and reducing maintenance costs by 30%. This enabled the organization to centrally manage and control its environments, keeping better track of costs, and reducing outages.

## What's Next for VoIP?

Over the last few years, IP Telephony has been synonymously used for VoIP; recently, a new term surfaced, dubbed "Unified Communications" or simply "UC," and over the last few years, UC has emerged as the primary driver for companies to move to VoIP.

UC means different things to different people. To an IT manager, it may mean having the phone system do something new. To an office worker, it may mean a cool new phone, the ability to check her voicemails right from her e-mail, or the ability to collaborate with coworkers using the corporate Instant Messaging system that allows them to control their phone and conferencing abilities. To a travelling worker, it may mean the ability to carry one smart device that acts as both an outside public cell phone and an in-house extension when he is in the office. To an executive, it becomes important to see presence of coworkers and direct reports, while having the ability to host a video conference right from his office. The common concept behind UC is that we as users now have control in choosing how, when, and where we are reached and by whatever means or applications we choose.

When Gartner asked early adopters of UC technologies to name three big benefits, answers included employee collaboration, employee productivity, and improved communication between geographically dispersed teams.

Today's telephony manufacturers, like Cisco, are making large R&D investments into VoIP and UC development, as well as enabling independent application developers worldwide to bring new technology to us every day.

The fact that most telephone service providers and manufacturers today have switched gears and are focusing on UC and collaboration using VoIP is a testament that the technology is here to stay.

## Summary

VoIP is an emerging technology in the sense that many firms are evaluating it to determine its potential savings and benefits. Many of my customers have implemented this technology and realized its benefits.

The next section covers many additional green topics, starting with SQL Server consolidation.

# Part IV
# General Green Topics

**Chapter 15: SQL Server Consolidation to Achieve Green Results**

**Chapter 16: The Green Data Center**

**Chapter 17: Cloud Computing**

**Chapter 18: Simple Power Savings and Other Green Tips**

**Chapter 19: Managed Services: Remote Monitoring**

# Introduction to Part IV

This part covers numerous green topics that my clients have used to streamline their environments to achieve both green and operational advantages. The following are some highlights in this section:

- SQL Server consolidation, originally written as an article by a Microsoft expert, is a case study of the way in which Microsoft approached the consolidation.

- My firm has done a lot of data center design and relocation, and this is a perfect opportunity to improve the overall green efficiency of your data center.

- Everyone is thinking about cloud computing, and Chapter 17 samples some cloud applications, such as laptop backup, that allows you to test the cloud to see if there are select tools and applications that you could be using in the cloud.

- There are countless simple green techniques that firms and individuals could be using that have an immediate green impact with minimal or no investment.

- Chapter 19 covers the service my firm has implemented for many of our clients, which help them make more informed decisions about their IT environments.

# Chapter 15

# SQL Server Consolidation to Achieve Green Results

This chapter is based on the article, "Green IT in Practice: SQL Server Consolidation in Microsoft IT," that appeared in the Microsoft publication *The Architecture Journal* (www.architecturejournal.net) written by Mark Pohto. This chapter focuses on all aspects of Microsoft IT to consolidate SQL Server. The chapter covers all the key points of SQL Server consolidation, including the following:

- Opportunities presented by SQL Server consolidation
- Initial SQL Server environment that Microsoft IT managed
- Desired SQL Server environment envisioned by Microsoft IT
- Approach taken by Microsoft IT to achieve the desired environment
- Solution implemented
- Results realized as a result of the solution
- Overall benefits of the undertaking

This chapter covers the Microsoft IT approach to SQL Server consolidation as a large case study starting with 100,000 databases on 5,000 SQL Server instances being reduced dramatically and many benefits being realized as a result.

# Opportunities

Strategies for lowering overall energy consumption include a broad range of activities that, when combined, could reverse the historical consumption trend. The study indicated that, if implemented, such activities could reduce data center electricity consumption by amounts equivalent to the power produced by as many as 15 new power plants. The savings correspond to carbon dioxide emission reductions of 15 to 47 million metric tons. (For more on data center energy consumption trends and recommendations, see the Report to Congress on Server and Data Center Energy Efficiency Public Law 109-431, listed in Resources.)

Microsoft IT has been engaged in various activities related to consolidation for several years. The efforts have targeted data centers, various layers of the application stack, and specific server workloads. Major consolidation efforts have included RightSizing, Storage Utility, Compute Utility, File Server Utility, and recently, the SQL Server consolidation initiative. Each effort has significantly reduced the data center footprint and has contributed to environmental sustainability. Areas of opportunity targeted by the SQL Server consolidation initiative include

- Energy efficient hardware

- Hardware consolidation

- Intelligent allocation of hardware resources

- Energy efficient data center design

- Intelligent placement of data center facilities

- Elimination of unnecessary hardware

- Enabling power management where practical

In addition to environmental sustainability benefits, SQL Server consolidation also presents clear business benefits, such as

- Reduce operating and capital expenses. New hardware has far greater computing power than hardware that is nearing end of life. Newer hardware generally requires less power and cooling.

- Environmental sustainability. For example, lower power and cooling requirements are the primary areas where the SQL Server utility addresses environmental concerns, but an overall reduction in data center space will also contribute over the long term.

- Provide business continuity, scalability, and availability. Requirements do not change for the SQL Server Utility; the goal is to find opportunities to standardize and improve best practices in these areas.

- Provide a standardized server build library. New technologies such as Hyper-V open new opportunities for standardization. Part of the vision of the SQL Server Utility is to eliminate or streamline many of the manual steps needed to build an application environment. This can be achieved by establishing Hyper-V guests, which are built with standard software configuration, including the operating system, SQL Server, tools, and approved configurations which can be provided for use in different phases of the software development life cycle.

The next section describes the initial SQL Server environment to be consolidated.

# Initial Situation

At the time of this writing, the Microsoft IT application portfolio consists of about 2,700 applications. There are approximately 100,000 databases on 5,000 SQL Server Instances, most of which are on dedicated hosts. Approximately 20% of those hosts reach end of life each year and are replaced. Average CPU utilization across these hosts is below 10%, indicating significant opportunity for host consolidation.

Fortunately, the landscape for SQL Server consolidation has changed dramatically over the past few months. New technologies, such as Windows Server 2008, SQL Server 2008, Hyper-V, System Center Virtual Machine Manager, and System Center Operations Manager, improved storage technologies and more powerful servers provide greater opportunities for consolidation than ever before.

In addition to server consolidation, other virtualization opportunities exist. Those benefits are not the focus of this chapter, but are described under General Benefits later in this chapter.

The next section describes the desired SQL Server environment.

## Desired Situation

The objective is to design and deploy a SQL Server utility service to reduce operating and capital expenses through consolidation and multi-tenancy. The SQL Server consolidation initiative will be based on the already successful shared service models of Storage Utility, Compute Utility, and File Server Utility. Each utility has contributed to standardization of the Microsoft IT infrastructure, and each provides a more predictable and reliable platform for other applications and services. The Storage Utility and Compute Utility will be discussed in more detail later, but they are both important to the SQL Server Utility design.

Not all SQL Server instances will be good candidates for consolidation. Initially, this solution will be developed with the most typical OLTP databases in mind. Multi-tenancy scenarios will also be supported for those customers who only want a single database. We expect that consolidation will be appropriate for thousands of instances and that multi-tenancy will be appropriate for hundreds of databases.

In fiscal year 2009, the goal is to engineer and provide a SQL Server utility that will reduce dedicated single instance SQL Server hosts by 10% and position Microsoft IT for continued consolidation.

The next section covers the approach to the SQL Server consolidation solution.

## Solution Approach

The solution mindset requires executive sponsorship, data-driven discussion, coherent storage and computing foundations, and an articulated consolidation strategy. Each of these needs to be addressed before you can embark on a serious SQL Server consolidation initiative. I cover all these topics in this section.

**Executive Sponsorship**. Executive commitment to maximize data center resource utilization and promote environmental sustainability is critical to the success of the project. Several activities described in this section provided the foundation needed for consolidation. None of these activities would have been likely to succeed without executive sponsorship and investment.

**A data driven discussion.** A data-driven discussion is also required as part of such a project. Microsoft IT developed the RightSizing initiative to ensure effective utilization of servers in the data center and in managed labs. Because significant underutilization occurs, one of the initiative's first tasks was for Microsoft IT to identify underutilized servers that might be good candidates for virtualization. The Capacity Management team relies on RightSizing data.

To accurately compare the performance of server platforms of varying architectures, Microsoft IT has developed a Compute Unit (CU) formula for each server platform that utilizes an industry standard, architecture-agnostic, benchmark suite from the Standard Performance Evaluation Corporation (SPEC). The SPEC benchmarks are developed in such a way to allow a repeatable test with strict result submission requirements. The Microsoft IT CU formula uses a baseline (not peak) benchmark that measures the rate of integer calculation work a server platform can perform in a given amount of time.

The servers available for purchase today represent a massive increase in performance over systems available in the past. Today's 2-way server provides the equivalent computing power of a 4-way from 12 to 18 months ago and even matches the Compute Unit capabilities of a 4-year-old 8-way server. By collecting information about current hardware and processor utilization, the RightSizing team can make recommendations on how to maximize server utilization.

Data center servers are underutilized, with an overall average CPU utilization of ~9.75%. As new server platforms are introduced with performance capabilities far surpassing their predecessors, this already low CPU utilization number will continue to fall.

A definition for processor utilization was crafted by Microsoft IT shown in Table 15-1.

**Table 15-1**   Server Temperature

| Server Temperature | Mean CPU% | Maximum CPU% |
|:---:|:---:|:---:|
| Permafrost | <<1 | <<5 |
| Cold | <=5 | <=20 |
| Warm | <=20 | <=50 |
| Hot | >20 | >50 |

Table 15-1 shows that for *Permafrost*, for instance, there is exceptionally low CPU utilization with a mean below 1% and a maximum below 5%. *Cold* is slightly higher, *Warm* is next, and *Hot* is the highest designation with a maximum utilization above 50%.

The next step was to measure the "temperature" of the active servers to determine under which designation they would fall, as shown Figure 15-1.

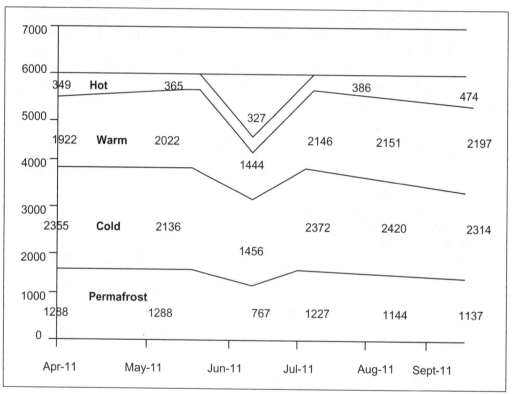

Figure 15-1    Server Temperature Sample Set

As Figure 15-1 clearly shows, there are few *Hot* servers compared with the other three categories. The *Permafrost* and *Cold* account for the majority of servers across the sample period.

**Storage Foundation.** The Storage Utility service provides shared or dedicated SAN storage to which data center servers can connect. The service provides the SAN storage and all hardware required to connect a server to the SAN, as well as all maintenance and management functions, but does not provide the server itself.

An effect of the Storage Utility was that instead of engineering and purchasing small, medium, and large servers with anticipated Direct Attached Storage (DAS) for SQL Server and other server types, Microsoft IT modified the standard builds so that minimal DAS was included in the purchase. This means that application support teams no longer had to anticipate disk capacity over the life of the server, which usually resulted in under utilization.

**Compute Foundation.** The Compute Utility strategy abstracts the services provided by hardware at Microsoft data centers as a computing foundation. Rather than having a business unit address its computing requirements by purchasing a server, in this approach, a business group provides its computing capacity requirements, and Microsoft IT then determines whether a virtual or physical server can meet those requirements and provides the service. The Compute Utility strategy sought to create this level of abstraction for business groups to encourage them to purchase computing power and storage without worrying about the server hardware.

Other utilities, such as the File Server utility, rely on RightSizing data and reside on Storage and Compute Utilities. SQL Server consolidation will further contribute to environmental sustainability and will also rely on these utilities.

**Consolidation Strategy.** There are multiple approaches to database consolidation strategy. More common approaches include instance consolidation and host consolidation. In instance consolidation, databases from multiple SQL Server instances are consolidated under fewer instances, and considerations range from CPU, memory, and I/O subsystem management to sort/ collation sequences to endpoint usage. In host consolidation, the host is partitioned (typically with Hyper-V or Windows System Resource Manager) and a larger number of instances are placed on each host. Each method of consolidation has its own considerations but many areas are much simpler to manage in a host consolidation approach.

Microsoft IT has compared consolidation approaches and has selected host consolidation for its ability to meet our consolidation objectives while introducing minimal risk. Since host consolidation still requires shared resources, such as CPU, memory, I/O, and network, selection of a manageable and flexible host partitioning method will have a significant impact on day-to-day operations. The General Benefits section describes some important advantages of using Hyper-V compared to Windows System Resource Manager and multiple named instances.

All SQL Server Utility offerings will leverage layers of the existing Microsoft IT utility stack as shown in Figure 15-2. Later phases of the consolidation initiative will consider other forms of consolidation and multi-tenancy.

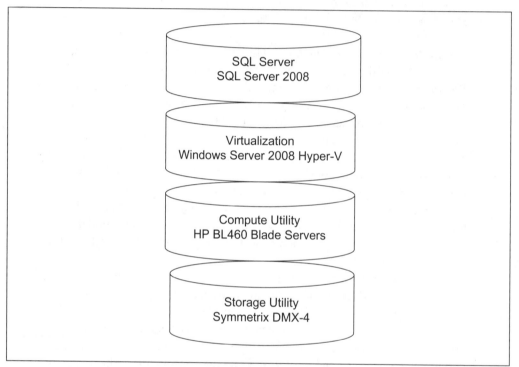

Figure 15-2    SQL Server Consolidation Stack

The stack in Figure 15-2 shows the building blocks for the SQL Server consolidation starting with shared storage at the bottom, blades servers next up the stack, virtualization on Hyper-V, and then SQL Server at the top.

Host consolidation requires that resources on a single host be managed to ensure that each instance receives predictable and reliable memory, processor, network, and I/O. Windows System Resource Manager and Hyper-V host partitioning technologies were evaluated; Hyper-V was selected for its manageability, scalability, and standardization benefits. Because Hyper-V on Windows 2008 scales to a maximum of four processors per guest (two processors for Windows 2003), consolidation of physical SQL Server instances will also be used to consolidate instances that require more than four processors. Physical SQL Server instances will be less manageable than virtual instances but will provide a consistent, proven approach to consolidation until Hyper-V scales to more than four processors.

The approach to host consolidation primarily targets servers that are approaching end of life. This provides minimal service disruption (because server replacement occurs with or without consolidation).

Multi-tenancy instances will also be deployed on Hyper-V and will be scaled to maximize host resources. As server and virtualization technologies improve, the Hyper-V approach to multi-tenancy will provide increasingly improved manageability and scalability.

Figure 15-3 depicts six end-of-life servers with 30 compute units each being replaced by equivalent Hyper-V guests on a single server.

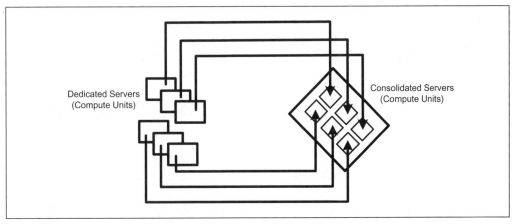

Figure 15-3    Host Partitioning: Hyper-V or WSRM

Figure 15-3 shows that substantial consolidating can be achieved going from dedicated to consolidated hosts.

Figure 15-4 depicts SQL Server utility offerings that cover different tenant needs. Hyper-V will be used to partition host resources for those tenants who need up to four processors and named instances either on a shared or dedicated server will be used for those who require additional processor or memory resources. As Hyper-V, hardware, and other technologies evolve, more and more tenant needs will be met using Hyper-V.

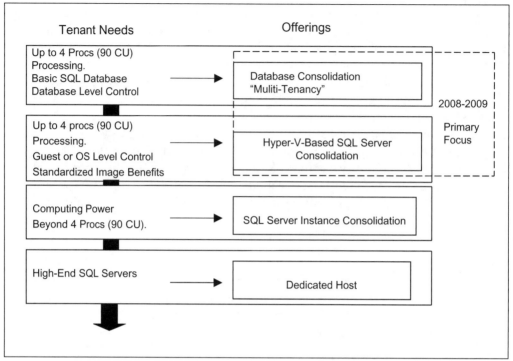

Figure 15-4    SQL Server Utility Offerings For Various Tenants

Depending on the needs of the tenant, Figure 15-4 shows that different options are available for the consolidation. The bottom of the figure shows, for instance, that high-end SQL Server environments will have a dedicated host, and the top of the figure shows that low-end servers can have high multi-tenancy on a server.

Table 15-2 shows the standard Hyper-V guest configurations that will be used in the SQL Server Utility.

**Table 15-2**   Guest Configurations

| Offering | Memory in GB | Number of Processors |
|---|---|---|
| Virtual Instance Low | 2-4 | 1 |
| Virtual Instance High | 4-8 | 2 |
| Virtual Instance Large | 16 | 4 |

Table 15-2 shows that, depending on the needs of the SQL Server instance, the memory and processor configurations vary.

The next section covers the solution implementation.


# Solution Implementation

The primary requirements of the SQL consolidation are to reduce operating and capital expenses by more effectively utilizing data center resources. System qualities, such as availability, that existed in the non-consolidated legacy environment are still requirements for the new consolidated environment. This architecture design followed basic IEEE-1471 guidance in identifying stakeholders, gathering and understanding requirements, and selecting and designing for specific architectural viewpoints. Architectural viewpoints were selected from traditional IT service management functions and were evaluated against Microsoft Operations Manager 4.0 IT service life cycle and current technology trends to anticipate future effectiveness of the design and to identify opportunities for improvement. Environmental sustainability has become an architectural consideration for business/home construction, automotive, and other industries; it is also a relevant architectural framework viewpoint for IT.

**Availability and business continuity** requirements provide the application development teams and operations teams with the flexibility to employ any SQL Server feature that is appropriate for an application. At the time this chapter is being written, SQL Server clustering on Hyper-V has not yet been approved as a supported implementation. However, database mirroring and log shipping are supported. SQL Server clustering will be introduced to the SQL Server Utility service as soon as that support is available. This project will be executed in phases, deploying implementations as support becomes available, so non-clustered deployments will be completed ahead of those that require clustering.

Figure 15-5 depicts Hyper-V SQL Server guests deployed from a standard build library with optional business continuity and high availability options. Tenant instances will be allocated and placed to distribute workload based on application business cycle requirements.

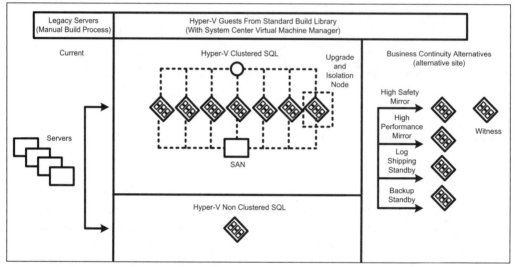

Figure 15-5    Hyper-V SQL Server Guests

**Manageability** in the consolidated environment is improved but similar to what it was in the non-consolidated environment. New and future solutions, like System Center Virtual Machine Manager, Data Protection Manager, and System Center Operations Manager, will help ensure continuous improvement in the area of manageability.

**Provisioning** is one key benefit of this consolidation architecture. This results in the ability to quickly provision new SQL Server guests. Because storage and host servers will be preconfigured, the turnaround time for providing a new SQL Server guest will be reduced by weeks when compared to the acquisition process for dedicated physical hosts.

Virtual Machine Manager Library, a standard build library, developed by Microsoft IT, with consistent Windows Server and SQL Server installation and configuration is another key manageability improvement for consolidation with Hyper-V, which will allow IT developers, testers, and production support teams to ensure a consistent experience across phases of the software development life cycle.

Imagine replacing less efficient build processes with a standardized and possibly automated deployment process. Colleagues with many years of experience in development and production support express excitement when contemplating the increased environmental consistency and stability offered by this approach.

Relocation of a virtual SQL Server instance is simpler and lower risk than the method of building a server, installing Windows Server and SQL Server, then migrating databases to the new physical SQL Server instance.

Basic database administration tasks for the consolidated SQL Server environment will continue to leverage the backup utilities that were written by Microsoft IT (see the September 2007 article on SQL Server Automation Scripts in *SQL Server Magazine*). Data Protection Manager has been deployed within Microsoft IT, and adoption for SQL Server backups is on the roadmap for this initiative.

Finally, the snapshot feature of Hyper-V will improve the ability to deploy and roll back host changes. You simply take snapshots at key points in your change deployment so that, instead of having to start from scratch and rebuild a server, you have the option to roll back. Although there is overhead associated with taking guest snapshots, as a tactical deployment tool, Hyper-V snapshots have advantages over a manual roll back.

**Performance** requirements and abilities in the consolidated environment are also similar to the previous environment. Because the Storage Utility had been implemented prior to SQL Server consolidation, a track record of performance from the storage layer already exists. In the consolidated environment, SQL Server operations teams will still be able to provide I/O performance expectations to the Storage Utility team and will be able to obtain Hyper-V guests with sufficient processor and memory from the Compute Utility team. Here are a few performance guidelines used in this consolidation effort:

1. Crawl, walk, run. Don't go for the maximum host consolidation ratio right away. Begin with the smaller workloads, validate your deployment, and refine the plan. Maximize your resource utilization in phases after establishing and evaluating your actual utilization.

2. Use Hyper-V pass-through disks or fixed Virtual Hard Disks (VHDs) for storage. Fixed VHDs offer some manageability benefits but provide slightly lower performance. Moving a guest to another host, for example, is simplified when using VHDs.

3. Do not over-commit processors for SQL Server guests. Begin with one logical processor for one physical processor. Verify your performance and refine your configuration as needed. At some point, this may include over committed, but begin without over committed to manage risks.

4. Avoid the use of emulated devices in Hyper-V. Favor synthetic/enlightened devices, which provide better performance and lower processor overhead.

5. Establish an Operating Level Agreement (OLA) with performance requirements for your storage provider if they are a separate service. Microsoft IT SQL Server utility has requirements for 1ms average disk/second read/write for log and 8ms for OLTP data.

Since Windows 2008, Hyper-V guests may use a maximum of four processors; native SQL instance consolidation is planned for workloads that require more than four processors. Native SQL instance resource management can be effectively accomplished using both SQL Server configuration and Windows System Resource Manager. Once Hyper-V scales to more than four processors, SQL instances that require more processing power will be deployed and managed on Hyper-V. (The recently published "Running SQL Server 2008 in a Hyper-V Environment - Best Practices and Performance Recommendations," offers more detailed Hyper-V guidance; see the list of resources at the end of this chapter.)

**Predictability and repeatability** can be improved by developing and adopting a configuration and deployment strategy that spans multiple phases of your software development life cycle. In today's environment, developers, testers, and production support teams build servers using standard install bits for the operating system, SQL Server, and additional tools. This time-consuming approach can sometimes result in inconsistencies between environments. These inconsistencies can ultimately result in unanticipated or unpredictable behavior once an application is deployed into production environments. Using Hyper-V, guests that are pre-configured with standard builds that the SQL Server Utility team expects will reduce or eliminate inconsistencies across the software development life cycle.

**Reliability** was a key concern for SQL Server consolidation tenants. The concern was that consolidated workloads and configurations would interfere with one another and that changes made for one application/tenant would impact others and cause additional application downtime.

Hyper-V provides operating system isolation so production support teams can prioritize their upgrade activities without dependencies on other application support teams. This greatly improves flexibility when it comes to test, change, and release and it improves overall reliability for applications because of fewer conflicts.

**Scalability and capacity management** are easier with virtualization. RightSizing teams and capacity management teams have greater agility when it comes to sizing up or down. If a tenant requests a medium-sized two-processor guest with 4GB of memory, but after deployment, learns that he underestimated his resource requirements, it is a simple matter to add memory and processors to the guest, even if it means relocating the guest to a host with available resources. This flexibility to reconfigure and relocate Hyper-V guests means that IT teams no longer have to over purchase hardware resources, which will result in less under utilization of data center resources.

SQL Server instances that require more than four processors will be in scope for consolidation but will be consolidated using physical rather than virtual instances. Windows System Resource Manager will be used in cases where multiple physical instances share a single host. Physical hosts will be dedicated to specific tenants for improved SLA management, security and customer satisfaction. Because Hyper-V supports an increased number of processors, more databases will be appropriately hosted in virtual instances.

**Physical Resource Optimization (PRO)** is achieved by using a variety of tools. With System Center Virtual Machine Manager 2008 and System Center Operations Manager 2007, administrators can assess historical performance data and intelligently place new SQL Server guests to optimize physical resource utilization and distribute workloads.

**Security** presents one of the greatest concerns. Microsoft IT production support teams have traditionally had access to host configurations. They are responsible and accountable for changes made to hosts and, although changes are made through established change control processes, these teams want to maintain the level of access and control that they've had historically. The Hyper-V approach to host partitioning provides production support teams with the flexibility to schedule, test, and apply changes and security patches in a timely manner.

Other methods of host partitioning, such as Windows System Resource Manager, meant that each instance on any given host would need to be on the same build of Windows Server and may need to coexist with other tenants who would likely have different service level agreements, maintenance windows, priorities, and application business cycles. Other partitioning methods also introduce security questions for data access, service account usage, certificates, logins/roles, and access to the operating system and hardware.

**Service monitoring and control** changes for this project are minimal in early phases. Monitoring requirements are somewhat increased by introducing an additional layer for virtualization, but since virtualization has been broadly adopted by other platform layers, such as for file servers and web servers, service monitoring and control is expected to become a standardized and effective part of our environment. Monitoring services currently provided using System Center Operations Manager 2007 by the Microsoft IT Enterprise Monitoring Team for the pre-consolidation environment will also be leveraged by the SQL Server utility. The SQL Server utility team believes that availability monitoring for databases and SQL Server services are a fundamental requirement for this service offering. Therefore, adoption of a database availability reporting/scorecard system and for improving the System Center Operations Manager SQL Server management pack rules are in scope for early project phases.

Another product that will be used to ensure consistent and optimal configuration is System Center Configuration Manager. Using this product with Desired Configuration Management, detection of configurations which have deviated or "drifted" from the known good and approved configurations will be much easier.

**Supportability** is important to application owners. The SQL Server utility project will not deploy unsupported configurations. We will, however, anticipate future supported configuration scenarios and posture accordingly.

The next section covers the results of the consolidation.

# Results

**Consolidation in the data center.** Operating costs are expected to drop sharply but not as dramatically as power and space. That is primarily because, even though we will have fewer physical servers, there will still be a cost associated with managing the Hyper-V guests. Annual operating costs for the SQL Server utility are expected to be $11 million/year lower than previously.

A typical end-of-life SQL Server host in the Microsoft data center occupies 6.8 rack units. Servers provided by the Compute Utility team occupy less than 1 rack unit and provide enough computing power to host five or six instances of SQL Server. This comes to a savings of over 33,000 rack units, or about 700 racks! This number does not even take into account that the DAS being replaced by SAN also comes with significant savings. On average, end-of-life servers use 369 volt amps while new servers more than 313 volt amps and can run at slightly higher temperatures. Similar power requirements exist for cooling. This means that there will be a dramatic reduction in power requirements, over 3 million volt amps, and eventually, there may be opportunities to modify data center cooling requirements to further reduce power consumption. Recycle costs for this project were estimated, but it is clear that deploying fewer servers has an impact on recycling and the environment. Figure 15-6 depicts the impacts of a 6:1 consolidation ratio for 5,000 SQL Server hosts (recycle costs were estimated).

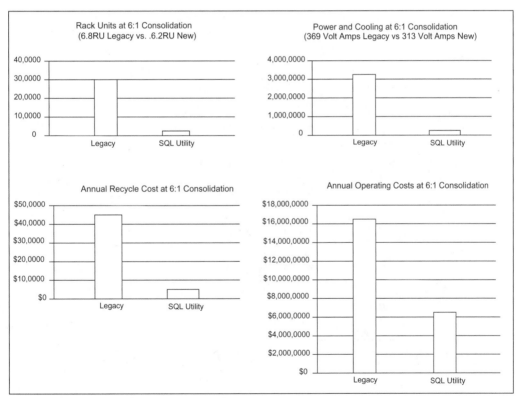

Figure 15-6     Positive Impacts of Consolidation

Figure 15-6 makes it clear that many positive impacts of consolidation have been realized in key IT areas. For instance, 97% less rack space and 86% less volt amps are consumed as a result of the consolidation.

**Consolidation across the software development life cycle.** Figure 15-7 depicts Hyper-V streamlined processes across the software development life cycle and well into production operations environments.

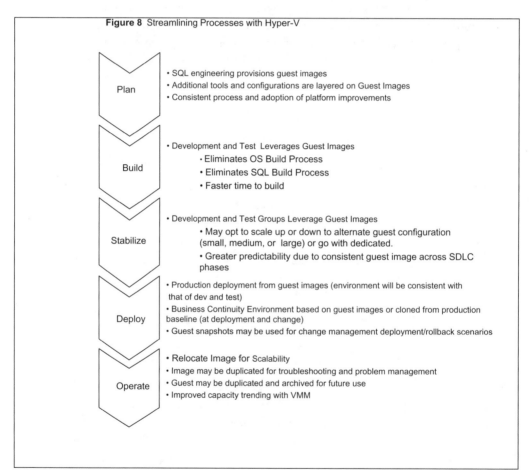

**Figure 8** Streamlining Processes with Hyper-V

**Plan**
- SQL engineering provisions guest images
- Additional tools and configurations are layered on Guest Images
- Consistent process and adoption of platform improvements

**Build**
- Development and Test Leverages Guest Images
    - Eliminates OS Build Process
    - Eliminates SQL Build Process
    - Faster time to build

**Stabilize**
- Development and Test Groups Leverage Guest Images
    - May opt to scale up or down to alternate guest configuration (small, medium, or large) or go with dedicated.
    - Greater predictability due to consistent guest image across SDLC phases

**Deploy**
- Production deployment from guest images (environment will be consistent with that of dev and test)
- Business Continuity Environment based on guest images or cloned from production baseline (at deployment and change)
- Guest snapshots may be used for change management deployment/rollback scenarios

**Operate**
- Relocate Image for Scalability
- Image may be duplicated for troubleshooting and problem management
- Guest may be duplicated and archived for future use
- Improved capacity trending with VMM

Figure 15-7    Streamlined Process with Hyper-V

This streamlined process includes many benefits that were not available in non-virtualized SQL environment. There are many general benefits to the virtualized environment, as shown in Figure 15-8.

| System Quality | Feature | Hyper-V | SQL Inst. |
|---|---|---|---|
| Manageability | Ability to build and provide canned environment | YES | NO |
| Manageability | Deploy/roll back benefits | YES | NO |
| Manageability | End-to-end (development through production) use | YES | NO |
| Manageability | Simple migration to new host during server retire/replacement | YES | NO |
| Manageability | Simplicity for instance scale up or scale down | YES | NO |
| Manageability | Simplicity for cloning a production environment (e.g., to test) | YES | NO |
| Security | Transparent to accomplish same level of security as with a dedicated host | YES | NO |
| Scalability | Dynamic sharing of processor resources | YES | YES |
| Scalability | Processors supported per environment | 4 | >32 |
| Performance | Acceptable performance | YES | YES |
| Availability | Clustering option (future ability for SQL Server on Hyper-V) | YES | YES |
| Business Continuity | Supports SQL business continuity features | YES | YES |
| Supportability | SQL 2005 and 2008 CSS support (not yet with SQL Server clustering) | YES | YES |

Figure 15-8   SQL Server Utility System Qualities

Figure 15-8 shows the benefits of consolidation on Hyper-V guests compared to using native instances of SQL Server in many key areas.

# Summary

Effective resource utilization within the data center has a significant impact on the global efforts to protect our environment. Beginning with the server build and through transportation to the data center, rack space utilization, power, cooling, and finally, to the eventual end-of-life recycle, each server deployed or not deployed impacts on efficient resource utilization and ultimately the environment.

Executive sponsorship is crucial to enterprise-wide consolidation projects. It is not difficult to make a business case for consolidation, particularly when you consider data center power and rack space benefits. The socialization, evangelism, and budget controls that executive sponsorship provides are vital to deployment and adoption.

Today, finding opportunities to consolidate various IT layers and functions is easier than ever. Windows Server 2008, Hyper-V, and SQL 2008 are a few of the products that are truly game changers when it comes to effective resource utilization and consolidation. The Microsoft IT SQL Server utility project is currently in progress and is expected to make a substantial impact on environmental sustainability while achieving many other virtualization and consolidation benefits.

This view into what Microsoft has accomplished has been done on a smaller scale by many of my clients and yields many of the same benefits as server consolidation.

# Resources

The following resources were used when this chapter was originally written as the article, "Green IT in Practice: SQL Server Consolidation in Microsoft IT."

Data Center Energy Forecast
http://svlg.net/campaigns/datacenter/docs/DCEFR_report.pdf

Microsoft IT RightSizing - Identifying Server Candidates for Virtualization
http://technet.microsoft.com/en-us/library/cc700692.aspx

Microsoft IT Showcase Virtualization Whitepaper
http://technet.microsoft.com/en-us/library/cc713312.aspx

Report to Congress on Server and Data Center Energy Efficiency
 (Public Law 109-431)
http://www.energystar.gov/ia/partners/prod_development/downloads/
EPA_Datacenter_Report_Congress_Final1.pdf

Running SQL Server 2008 in a Hyper-V Environment – Best Practices and
Performance Recommendations
http://sqlcat.com/whitepapers/archive/2008/10/03/running-sql-server-
2008-in-a-hyper-v-environment-best-practices-and-performancerecommen-
dations.aspx

SQL Server Magazine SQL Server Automation Scripts (September 2007)
http://www.sqlmag.com/Article/ArticleID./96463/
SQL_Server_Automation_Scripts.html

Standard Performance Evaluation Corporation
http://spec.org

# Chapter 16

# The Green Data Center

This chapter covers many topics related to the history of data centers as well as modern data center design. A history of servers, data center, cabling, cooling, racks, aisles, raised floors, and other relevant topics are covered. The focus of this chapter is on layout and cooling because of the green focus of the book but the other topics are also discussed.

My firm has done a lot of data center design and relocation, and I have acted as the lead on all these advanced projects. This chapter introduces some key data center-related topics and represents a small portion of what takes place when designing a new data center.

The first section covers the history of the data center.

## Traditional Data Center

The traditional data center layout has rows of racks all facing the same direction. The racks are arranged with just enough space in front and behind to service the equipment. The racks are two feet wide by three feet deep with an aisle in front and one behind for service access. The aisles are three feet wide to allow for installation of servers into the racks. The reasoning here was that a three foot deep rack could only hold equipment three feet deep or less, so a three-foot service aisle would be sufficient. The servers are physically bulky and not all were designed to be rack mounted, leading to many servers sitting on shelves in the racks. Most x86-based servers are powered with 110 volts from power strips mounted in the racks or run directly to outlets located under the raised floor. Figure 16-1 shows the vertical airflow.

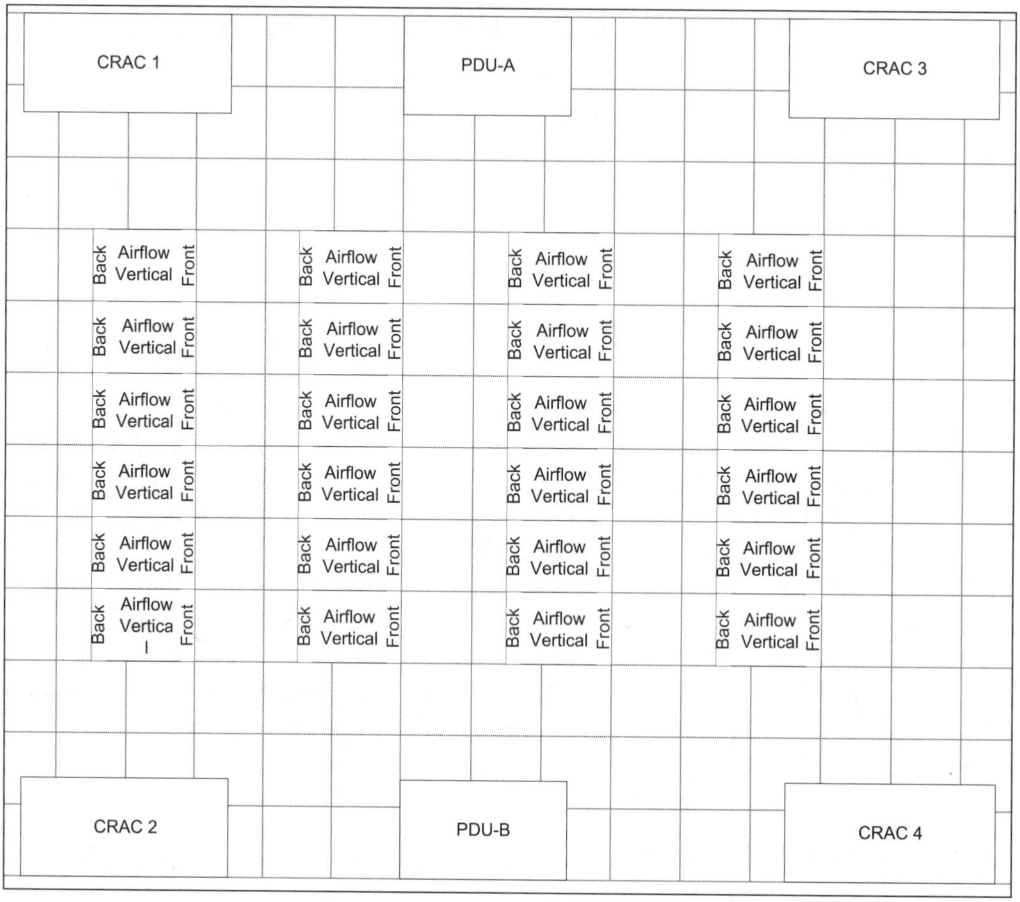

```
┌──────────────────────────────────────────────────────────────────────────┐
│ ┌──────────────┐           ┌──────────────┐           ┌──────────────┐    │
│ │   CRAC 1     │           │    PDU-A     │           │   CRAC 3     │    │
│ └──────────────┘           └──────────────┘           └──────────────┘    │
│                                                                            │
│  Back Airflow Front   Back Airflow Front   Back Airflow Front   Back Airflow Front │
│       Vertical             Vertical             Vertical             Vertical      │
│                                                                            │
│  Back Airflow Front   Back Airflow Front   Back Airflow Front   Back Airflow Front │
│       Vertical             Vertical             Vertical             Vertical      │
│                                                                            │
│  Back Airflow Front   Back Airflow Front   Back Airflow Front   Back Airflow Front │
│       Vertical             Vertical             Vertical             Vertical      │
│                                                                            │
│  Back Airflow Front   Back Airflow Front   Back Airflow Front   Back Airflow Front │
│       Vertical             Vertical             Vertical             Vertical      │
│                                                                            │
│  Back Airflow Front   Back Airflow Front   Back Airflow Front   Back Airflow Front │
│       Vertical             Vertical             Vertical             Vertical      │
│                                                                            │
│  Back Airflow Front   Back Airflow Front   Back Airflow Front   Back Airflow Front │
│       Vertica l            Vertical             Vertical             Vertical      │
│                                                                            │
│ ┌──────────────┐           ┌──────────────┐           ┌──────────────┐    │
│ │   CRAC 2     │           │    PDU-B     │           │   CRAC 4     │    │
│ └──────────────┘           └──────────────┘           └──────────────┘    │
└──────────────────────────────────────────────────────────────────────────┘
```

Figure 16-1   Phase 1: Vertical Airflow

Data cabling, in a traditional data center, is run under the floor right along with the power. The cables are long patch cables with the entire under floor space acting like a cabling trough. As new systems are installed into the data center, more patch cables are installed. Oftentimes, when older systems are decommissioned, the patch cables, and even the power cables, are left in place. They are left in place because, over time, the cables entangle with the new cables that are layered over them as new systems are deployed. Cables are rarely the correct length for the distance, so the excess cable remains coiled under the floor. As cables are pulled, they catch on these coils and create knots. This endangers production systems, especially if the power cords are part of the tangled mess. Over time, the space below the floor becomes congested with cable. Figure 16-2 shows the power cabling in a traditional data center.

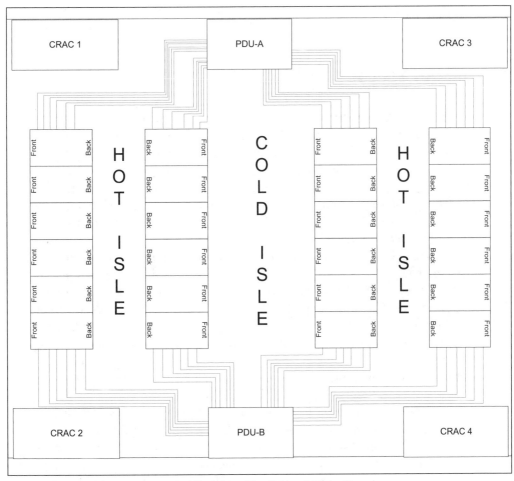

Figure 16-2    Power Cabling in a Traditional Data Center

Figure 16-2 shows the traditional power distribution in the data center. This figure appears again as Figure 16-9. The distribution has redundant power feeds (110v or 220v) to each rack. This example requires 24 dual pole circuit breakers in each PDU (48 breaker positions) to provide redundant 220 power to each rack.

Typical raised floor data centers use the space under the floor as a cool air distribution system for the room. Large Computer Room Air Conditioners (CRAC) are positioned around the room with air intakes at the top and the cold air supply being forced down under the floor. Proper airflow requires ample space so the air can flow under the raised floor. Large piles of data cables, piping, power cables, fire suppression systems, and sensors all take up space under the floor and restrict airflow.

## Rack and Air Flow History

Traditional data centers are normally packed with as many servers as could fit into a rack with as many racks as possible fit into a room. The servers limiting factor was its size. With the sprawl of x86-based servers and three-tiered application architectures coupled with a proliferation of web server farms, space is at a premium. Hardware manufacturers responded by improving the server form factor to smaller physical servers while improving the processor performance. Rack mount servers also became a predominant form factor for the data center.

Original x86-based servers were an offshoot of a desktop computer. As desktop computers became large, they were turned on their sides and placed next to or under the desk. This gave rise to the tower computer and became the form factor for the original Intel-based server. A typical desk is two foot six inches deep and a credenza is two feet or less, so the typical tower case needed to fit this form factor with room for air circulation and cables behind the case. The first rack mount servers were using the same sheet metal cases turned sideways with rack mounting rails and a new front bezel. Their depth was typically two feet to two and a half feet deep.

The rack mount form factor allowed for more servers per rack, which helped with the overall physical space difficulties. Although this improved the number of servers per rack, servers were still fairly bulky because of their storage requirements. One of the ways that the server manufacturers shrunk the size of the server was by increasing the depth of the server and putting the hard drive hot swap cage at the front. The server increased in depth to 34 inches, which made for a tightly packed server rack.

The form factor of the server, as it became slimmer and deeper, changed the fundamental airflow of a rack. The traditional airflow had always been from the bottom and front of the rack through the servers, out the back of the server, and out the top of the rack, as shown in Figure 16-3.

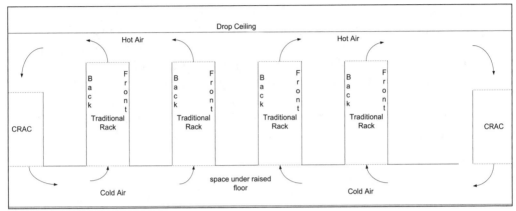

Figure 16-3   Traditional Vertical Airflow with Cold Air From Bottom

Many traditional racks had clear or smoked plastic doors on the front and back that did not permit airflow through the rack from front to back, but from the bottom to the top. Most racks were cooled with vented tiles located directly below the rack, and some were supplemented with fans in the top of the rack to increase airflow. The new server form factor and airflow requirements caused a change in rack design, which also caused a change to the typical computer room design.

The computer room rack evolved from a three-foot deep rack to a three-foot six inch rack to accommodate the newer, deeper servers and provide ample space for cable management. The new racks also needed to address the airflow issue created by the deeper servers. Racks could no longer be configured with solid front and rear doors because the airflow for the servers was designed to be from the front of the rack to the back. In a traditional computer room design, hot air was forced to the ceiling within the rack. With the new design, the hot air was blown out the back of the rack. As the processor power and densities increased, as memory capacities increased, and as hard drive sizes shrank while speeds increased, the heat that a server was generating per rack unit (RU) of height was exponentially increasing the amount of heat being generated by each server for the given form factor. The manufacturers compensated for the increase of heat by increasing the airflow through the server. This was accomplished by increasing the number of fans in a server and the speed of the fans.

The net result of the server squeeze allowed for more CPU cycles, hard drives, and RAM chips in the same physical space. The problem for the traditional data center rack layout was a change in the airflow pattern. As discussed earlier, the airflow in a traditional data center came from the bottom of a rack to the top, allowing hot air to accumulate at the ceiling where the CRAC units would have their hot air intakes. The new airflow in a data center is now horizontal in nature, feeding in the front of a rack and out the back with little or no vertical airflow. With a front-to-back rack layout, the hot air being blown out the back is aimed directly at the front of the next row of racks. Each subsequent row of racks receives hot air from the row of racks in front of it and passes the ever hotter air to the next row of racks, as shown in Figure 16-4.

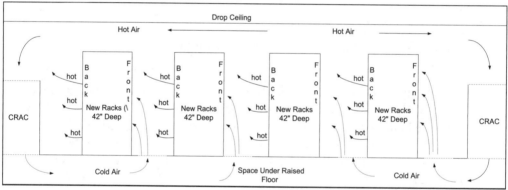

Figure 16-4    Traditional Rack Layout With Front-to-Back Airflow

Some air does rise to the ceiling, and each row of racks does have vented floor tiles in front of the racks, but the servers located on top of the racks receive little cool air, because most cool air provided at the floor level is sucked up by the servers on the bottom of the racks. Whatever cool air gets past the bottom servers is mixed with the hot air blowing out of the rack in front of it, causing the air to become hotter the further up the rack you go. Figure 16-5 shows the front-to-back airflow.

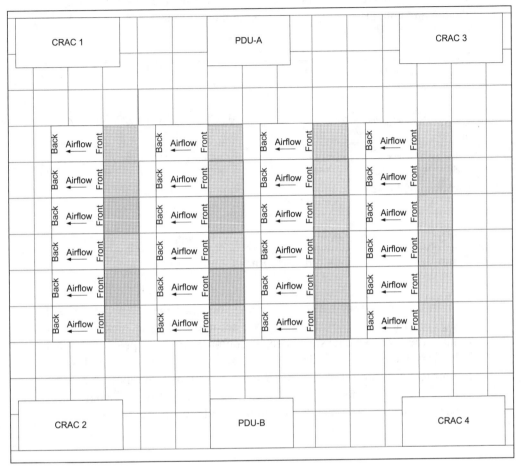

Figure 16-5    Phase 2: Front-To-Back Airflow

To compensate for the hotter and hotter aisles in the data center, data center managers began turning down the thermostats on the CRAC units. The effect of the change created both hot and cold spots in the computer room. The industry came up with a relatively low cost solution to the problem. Every other row of racks was rotated 180 degrees so that the backs of racks in one aisle faced the backs of racks in the next aisle. This consolidated the heat in a "hot aisle" and the cold air in a "cold aisle." The racks now received the cold air from the vented floor tiles in the cold aisle and blew hot air into the hot aisle, where it rose to the ceiling and drifted back to the large

CRAC units located at the perimeter of the data center. Figure 16-6 shows the hot and cold aisle approach to cooling the 42" racks.

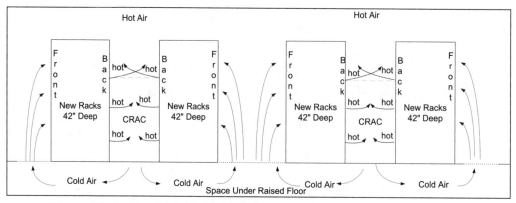

Figure 16-6    Hot Aisle/Cold Aisle Rack Configuration

In the process of rotating the racks, or when new data centers were being constructed, the new rack standard became a 42" deep rack. To accommodate these deeper racks and deeper equipment, and to provide for more cold air vents in the cold aisle, the cold aisles were increased from three feet to four feet at a minimum. The hot aisles were often maintained at three feet because most equipment is loaded into a rack from the front. The only access needed to the back of a rack is for cabling, as shown in Figure 16-7.

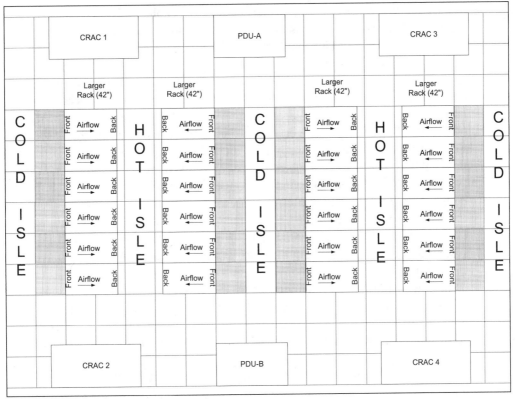

Figure 16-7    Hot and Cold Aisle Cooling

# High Density Racks

With the adoption of a hot aisle/cold aisle rack layouts, many existing data centers received a life extension of five plus years, but the additional density of computing platforms was just getting started. With the introduction of the blade server, even the hot aisle/cold aisle design could not keep up with the heat loads and power requirements. Traditional racks had migrated from 1Kw per rack with the traditional rack layout to 3–5Kw for a hot aisle/cold aisle design. With blade chassis, being loaded into racks with up to six blade chassis per rack, the heat load potential for a rack jumps to a staggering

24–30KW per rack. The apparent answer to this problem appears to be a design that decreases the density back to a manageable 3–5Kw per rack. It turns out that the cost per square foot for the real estate and construction costs to build a larger data center, at least in a metropolitan area, is so great that it negates the benefits of traditional cooling.

Typical data center raised floors are 18" or less. To provide adequate cooling in higher density environments, the floor height rapidly becomes a limiting factor. For example, to support a 24KW rack environment (400watts/square foot) you need over 4 feet of clear height under the raised floor. Using traditional CRAC systems, most data centers with 18-36" raised floors can expect to support a heat load of up to 6KW per rack with an average of 3—5KW. To move beyond this range requires a different approach to both cooling and power.

The two main factors in cooling data centers are temperature and air flow. CRAC units provide cooling and airflow as well as a humidity control system for adding or removing moisture from the air. It is important to have enough moisture in the air to prevent static electricity but not so much as to create the opportunity for condensation. Large CRAC units operate most efficiently when the airflow entering the intake on the unit is the hottest air in the room. The system is only capable of cooling the hot air that reaches it. All other air in the room is cooled by mixing the hot air with the cold air from the CRAC. If the hot air is not efficiently returned to the CRAC, but is allowed to mix with the cool air before reaching the intake, the CRAC will not operate at peak performance and may cycle on and off, causing wear and tear on the unit. The lower the temperature of a computer room, the lower the safe humidity level, because lower temperatures mean a lower dew point or point where humidity in the air will condensate. This can cause problems in a data center that has an uneven heat loads, causing the various CRAC units in the data center to operate at different temperatures. Oftentimes, one set of CRAC units will expend energy providing humidity to the room while another set, located in a different area, will be working hard at removing humidity from the air because it is trying to maintain a lower temperature to compensate for a high density section of the room.

The solution to cooling high density data centers varies marginally between the various cooling manufacturers, and the general approach is the same. The approach is to efficiently get the hot air coming out of the back of the racks to a cooling system without allowing it to mix with the cool air on the front side of the racks. All the solutions use a variation of hot air/hot aisle containment. The following is a list of four cooling options. Figure 16-8 shows option 1.

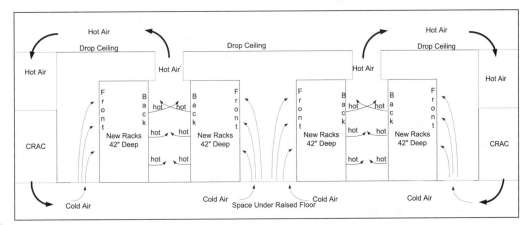

Figure 16-8    Hot Aisle/Cold Aisle with Hot Air Above Dropped Ceiling

- Option 1 involves creating a hot air return space above a raised ceiling. Each of the racks are run through ducts to the return space. The intake ducts on the CRAC units are extended up to the raised ceiling level so they receive all of their intake air directly from the hot aisle with no mixing of the hot and cold air. This solution produces hot air brought above the raised ceiling and then routed directly to CRAC units.

- Option 2 involves creating a microenvironment made up of two rows of racks. Each pair of racks contains at least two in row CRAC units capable of cooling the hot air being exhausted from the back of the racks. The hot aisle is typically sealed from the rest of the computer room, once again ensuring that the hot air and cold air do not mix. Figure 6-6 shows new racks with 36" deep servers using horizontal air flow through a 42" rack for cooling.

- Option 3 is a less strict version of option 2 in that small CRAC units are suspended from the ceiling or mounted to the tops of the racks that use the hot aisle air for their intake and supply cold air back to the cold aisle. The hot aisle is not sealed as with the first two options, so it is necessary to ensure that the overhead units are capable of enough airflow to ensure negative pressure in the hot aisle so that the hot air does not drift away around the ends of the racks or over the tops of the racks.

- Option 4 involves reducing the microenvironment to the rack level. This solution allows for high density cooling at the rack level with redundancy, but it also dictates the rack size, and each rack must be piped for coolant under the floor or overhead. This may be a viable solution for small environments with little or no raised floor and limited overhead space, but it is typically the most expensive solution because each rack requires full redundancy, offering net cost savings that can be obtained when using N+1 or N+2 redundancy.

All four options allow for adequate high density cooling. The selection process for identifying the most cost-effective solution for any particular data center environment depends on the site-specific details. A side benefit of the hot air containment solution is that the rest of the data center can be maintained at a comfortable working temperature. Because the hot air is captured and contained, the data center should maintain an even temperature throughout, eliminating the scenario where various CRAC units work against each other or are constantly cycling on and off.

## Green Data Center

Option 1 in the previous section offers several interesting options for conserving energy in a modern office environment. Data centers generate heat all year round, and to cool the heat requires air conditioners and various methods of heat rejection. During winter months in regions that require normal office heat, there are methods of using outside cold air and/or water to remove the heat. A better use of that heat would be to supplement the heating needs of the non-data center areas of the building, areas where people work, or that require heating and climate control for other reasons.

One of the difficulties with maintaining a clean data center is the quality of the air. It would appear that the simplest solution for climates that experience cold winter temperatures would be to "open the window" and let out the hot air and replace it with cold air. The problem with this solution is that you rapidly lose control of the air quality. Air quality, in this case, refers to the amount of dirt and humidity. You could filter the air, but that requires energy to force the air through the filters and frequent filter changes as the dirt from the outside world clogs the filters. During the cold winter months, the outside humidity is quite low and a significant amount of humidification would need to be provided to the data center to compensate for the low humidity in the outside air. Also, keep in mind that while the data center is running air conditioning, the rest of the building is typically being heated.

Rather than throwing away the heat from the data center, investigate ways to use the heat energy from the data center to heat other parts of the building. Various air to air and liquid heat exchangers are available that supplement the building heating system with the heat generated by the data center. This same type of system can be used in the hot summer months with outside air rather than air from the populated space of the building. Even on a 90 degree day, the air temperature in the hot air return space will likely be 10–30 degrees hotter.

## Unstructured Data Cabling

At the beginning of this chapter, I covered the issues with cable sprawl and buildup under the raised floor. In the past, there were many types of cable under the floor. Cabling for Ethernet category 3/5/6, single mode and multi-mode fiber, twinax, coax, various SCSI types, ESCON, serial, and various phone system trunk cables and station cables in 25–400 pair configurations. Today, many cable types have become obsolete, replaced with category 5/6 copper and fiber-optic cables. This greatly reduces the sheer volume and weight of cable in a data center. The one thing that can be counted on in a data center is change. Computer systems rarely last more than five years before they need to be upgraded or replaced.

As various new systems are brought into a data center, little or no thought is given to the cabling. As such, extra long patch cables are ordered because it is always better to have a cable that is too long than too short, right? Well, yes to a point, but ordering 10 meter fiber cables to connect a SAN switch to 40 blade servers in the rack next door makes for a large pile of fiber that needs to be stored someplace, and that someplace is almost always under the raised floor or on top of the rack because it will not fit in the rack and looks messy. When it comes time to move a system, the cables become tangled, and removing them from under the floor without impacting another critical system can be time consuming at best and result in unscheduled down time in the worst case. An option is to just abandon the cable under the floor and put more in for the new systems. I equate this to cleaning your house by sweeping the dirt under the couch.

How do we deal with change in the data center? Plan for it. Understand that systems are going to move. Plan on racks moving from one location to another. Expect that the space allocated to a rack holding 20 small 1U servers today may need to support a large SAN disk array next month.

## Structured Data Cabling

To provide a solution that is flexible, you must define criteria for the data center, such as the heat load and power that will be allowed on a per rack basis. This helps define how many servers will be permitted in a rack. Following the number of servers will be the number of network (LAN and SAN) connections required. Design areas of the data center that will be used for SAN and network consolidation points. This normally requires a careful LAN and SAN design process to identify current and future technologies that will be supported by the environment. Even with a modular design, there is a ridged structure supporting the environment that will involve more than a step ladder and some pre-terminated cable to adjust. Things like overhead ladder rack or under-floor cable troughs are disruptive to install and change. Recognize that no design will support every eventuality, but try to cover the ones that are most likely to occur in your environment. A properly designed ladder rack system allows for most changes with little or no re-work required and no downtime to make modifications.

## Future of Data Cabling

As computer systems continue to evolve, processors get faster and more functionality is being supported on smaller platforms. Virtualization of everything, servers, networks, storage, and desktops, are pushing flexibility at the infrastructure level. This flexibility requires large quantities of LAN and SAN bandwidth to allow for the peak demands that can be imposed by a virtualized computing world. The rapid adoption of 10Gigabit Ethernet and 8Gigabit Fiber Channel, with the promise of 40 and 100Gigabit Ethernet in the next couple of years, calls into question the viability of category 5/6 cabling as a method for connecting servers in the future. The size of category 6 enhanced cabling, along with its installation criteria, needs to be considered both from a financial investment perspective and from a physical implementation aspect. A rack full of blade server chassis will most likely be running over multiple 10Gigabit connections back to a network switch that may or may not be a hybrid LAN switch. What we do know is that the distance limitation of 10Gigabit Ethernet over copper will limit its use to within a rack or between several racks in a row. As fiber continues to expand in usage, the manufacturing price will continue to drop. The price of copper, along with the weight and size of the cables and its distance limitations, will become more of a factor in the data center. You can expect to provide fiber to every rack in the data center before too long so planning for it is a requirement. The new modular fiber systems offer a perfect solution for the data center that is subject to change. By using some of the modular fiber systems on the market today, you can install new fiber trunks in various densities quickly and with a minimum of tools. No special fiber-terminating skills or tools are required, as long as the data center has been designed to support this type of solution.

# Power Cabling

Providing power to the various racks of x86 servers in the past was fairly simple. Install a pair of redundant 20 amp 110 volt circuits, get a couple of rack mount power strips, and plug in your servers. You would run out of space in the rack before running out of power. With the higher density servers and the change in rack sizes, a flexible power distribution system for the data center has become more than a nice-to-have option. Although each city and state has their own electrical codes that must be adhered to, the basic limitations of past power systems are beginning to be addressed. This means that much like the data cabling systems being designed for change, the power distribution system can also be designed for change. Products like APC's InfrastruXure™ system provides a flexible, reconfigurable system for power distribution without having to run conduit in most areas of the country.

Other than the capacity of the power supply and battery backup system, one of the biggest limiting factors on data center flexibility is the sheer quantity of circuit breakers required. For example, a rack that used to take two 20 amp 110 volt circuits would require a single single-pole circuit breaker in each circuit breaker panel of a redundant system. On a panel that supports 42 circuit breakers, you could support 42 racks. With most equipment running auto-ranging power supplies, many data centers have moved to 20 or 30 amp 220 volt (more efficient) redundant feeds for their racks. Each 220 volt circuit requires a 2-pole circuit breaker, effectively reducing the number of racks that can be supported from 42 to 21, even if the power draw going to the racks is under the amount of available power. With blade servers running on 3-phase power, the most efficient way to deliver and power equipment, circuit breaker management becomes difficult. Each blade server chassis typically requires redundant 3-phase connections. Put six chassis in a rack and that is up to 12 3-phase connections. Just as the term 3-phase implies, it takes three circuit breaker positions in a panel. So, a fully loaded rack of blade chassis requires up to 36 circuit breaker positions. This leaves just six positions open in a 42 breaker panel. Many blade chassis manufacturers have recognized this problem and have developed a rack power distribution system to reduce the number of circuit breakers needed to support a rack of blade chassis. That said, you can expect to be supplying a redundant pair of 3-phase power feeds to each server rack in the not too distant future. This will reduce your typical 42 circuit breaker panel to supporting 14 racks, assuming that there is enough power feeding the panel, as shown in Figure 16-9 which also appeared earlier in the chapter.

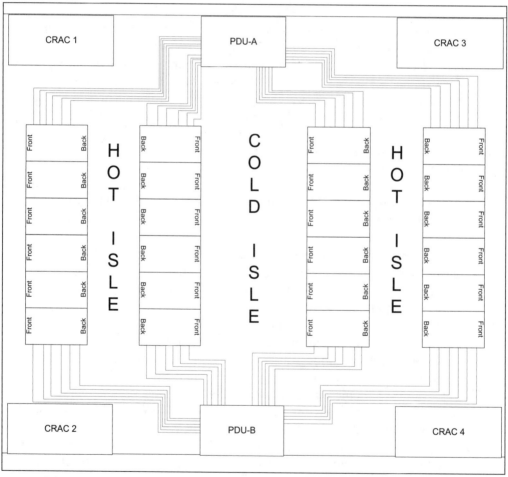

Figure 16-9    Power Cabling in a Traditional Data Center

The point is that where there used to be a pair of circuit breaker panels, you can expect to triple the quantity unless other methods of power distribution are adopted.

There are several alternatives to the traditional centralized circuit breaker panel solution. The first, and widely adopted solution for co-location centers, is a zone power distribution system where the power distribution is provided by zones sometimes as small as a row or pair of rows of servers. The Power Distribution Units (PDU) are located in close proximity to the racks to which it is supplying power. Its form factor is designed to fit in with a row of racks and compliment the airflow requirements of a hot aisle/cold aisle design.

Another option is a distributed bus system. A bus system is typically run overhead and will support up to 400 amps or more of 3-phase power. Figure 16-10 shows a distributed bus layout.

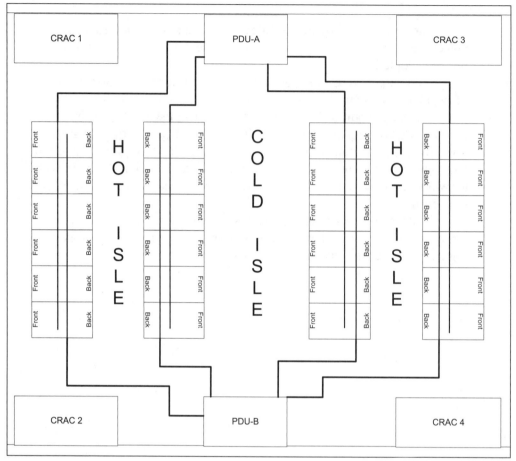

Figure 16-10    Cabling Using a Distributed Bus

Figure 16-10 shows the distributed bus system that facilitates various power requirements, improves flexibility, and reduces the large quantity of runs from each PDU to each rack. Distributed bus systems are available in various capacities, from 60 amp 110/220v through 400 amp 3 phase solutions. The larger the capacity, the more versatile the system. These systems are typically run overhead, which leaves more room under the floor for airflow.

Connectivity to the bus is done with special tap devices that can be configured with a variety of outlets to support the plug types required in each rack. For full redundancy, two bus systems can be run for each zone to be supported. The taps are configured with circuit breakers and monitoring systems to keep track of current and voltage. The feed to the bus system also has electronic monitoring to monitor phase loading and overall capacity. The advantage to the system is that it allows for easy reconfiguration of power provisioning to racks in any designated area of the data center without having to install more branch circuits and conduit under the raised floor or overhead bolted to the ceiling or ladder rack system. If a rack needs to be relocated and requires special power outlets and provisioning, it is a simple matter of disconnecting the taps and moving them with the rack. There is significant savings to be had in reducing the amount of cabling and conduit running from the PDU or the circuit breaker panel out across the floor to the racks. In a traditional installation, each three phase circuit requires four or five conductors – three for the power feeds, one for ground, and one for neutral. This means that 10 copper wire runs (5 for each circuit) must run from the panels to each rack. In addition, a power trough or individual conduit must also be installed. In some cases, long WIPs are installed, allowing for some flexibility in the outlet placement under the floor and reducing the amount of ridged conduit required, but the copper cable runs are still required.

## Summary

The topics presented in this chapter come in to play in all the data center designs and relocations in which my firm has been involved. A new data center is the ideal opportunity to implement improved airflow, power, and other enhancements.

The next chapter provides an overview of cloud computing, including some simple applications that may work in your environment.

# Chapter 17

# Cloud Computing

Cloud computing is becoming a popular alternative to conventional data center infrastructure and IT operations. Cloud computing, by definition, is the use of the Internet ("cloud") combined with a variety of computer technologies, such as software applications, servers, storage, and networking components. These components provide access to Software as a Service (SaaS), Web 2.0, and other common Internet-related services. In a nutshell, you can do almost anything in the cloud that you can do in your own data center with your own equipment and tools.

Cloud computing is now being used in a hybrid mode, whereby companies are splitting their workloads between their own data canter and the cloud. At this time, the vast majority of applications are hosted on-premises with only few applications used in the cloud. These on-premises applications can be run in a private cloud or in the traditional model of devoting resources to specific applications. More and more applications are being "picked off" and moved to the cloud. In general terms, cloud options are one of the following.

- Development platform service

- Infrastructure platform service

- SaaS

In the upcoming sections I cover private cloud considerations as well and general cloud computing.

# Private Cloud Considerations

The general benefits of cloud computing can be applied to private clouds by creating a cloud-like environment in your data center. Private clouds are pools of resources, rather than discrete units, that can be shared in a variety of advanced ways that make for a more efficient environment that is managed as one large unit. Among the technologies to consider when implementing a private cloud are the following:

- Virtualization Management of the private cloud(s)
- Charge back systems that track the consumption of IT cloud resources and charge accordingly
- Cloud Application Programming Interfaces (APIs) to foster cloud computing interpretability
- Self-service portals to assign resources as required
- "Elasticisty" or "flex" capabilities to grow and shrink the environment required
- Migration of virtual machines freely between blades or servers of like processors

A key objective of private clouds is to implement modular hardware that can grow and shrink dynamically, based on predetermined policies. Workloads can be shifted dynamically and the resources devoted to a workload are dynamic and controlled by tools. This "elasticity" is one of the most desirable aspects of private clouds.

Private clouds can have the capability of self-service portals whereby IT resources can be dynamically assigned as required by workloads. Lab manager products, for example, can be used by developers to provision resources by developers as their needs arise.

Industry Standard Servers (ISS) make a lot of this functionality possible. Migration of virtual machines is possible with blades or servers that have like processors. A lot of the elasticity comes from this migration capability and is now mainstream technology.

Many firms are determining whether to have one large private cloud or multiple smaller private clouds. Large firms may want to have a private cloud for major business areas such as manufacturing or finance rather than one large private cloud. All the same principals apply regardless of the number of private clouds.

The next sections cover public cloud applications.

## The Public Cloud

As shown in Figure 17-1, cloud computing provides web-based services through a grid architecture made up of servers connected through the Internet.

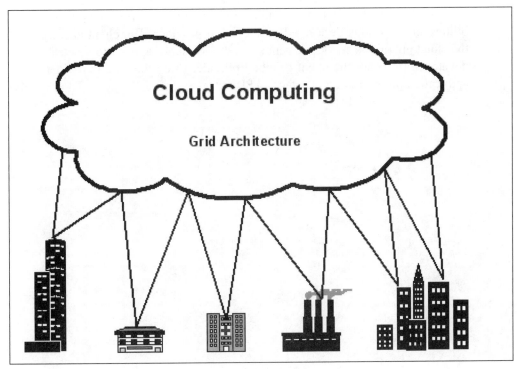

Figure 17-1    Basic Cloud Computing Architecture

Figure 17-1 shows various organizations connecting to the cloud through their local desktops and workstations. Internet-based servers are running applications that cache data accessed by local desktops and workstations at client locations. The servers and applications reside at the cloud provider instead of at the client locations. This is somewhat similar to a traditional Application Service Provider (ASP) model, where a client pays for a subscription service, with associated service levels, and does not incur the cost of infrastructure and operational support.

These cloud service providers have the necessary computing infrastructures, typically in a virtualized environment, and offer access to their cloud applications to clients via the Internet through a web browser or software application. They also have the internal expertise to manage and operate the cloud computing environments in a streamlined fashion. Many technologies described in this book are implemented by service providers; however, the client accessing the cloud uses these resources but does not have to manage them and know what happens "behind the scenes."

As illustrated in Figure 17-2, the cloud represents some of the responsibilities and functions performed by the cloud provider. The client accesses the cloud provider's services through a web browser or application interface developed by either the client or cloud provider using the cloud provider's application programming interface (API).

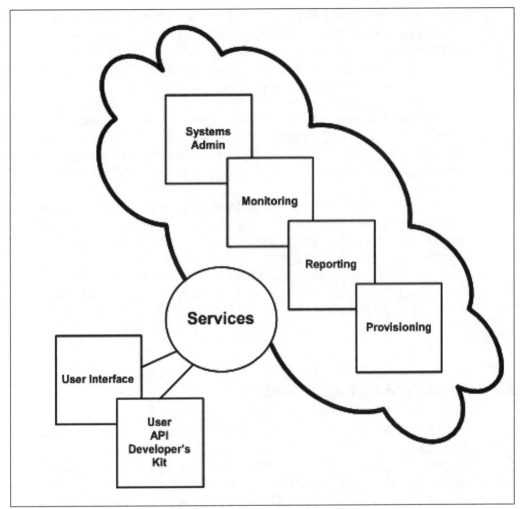

Figure 17-2    High-Level Logical Breakdown of Cloud Architecture

Some large client organizations will establish their own internal cloud computing environments, but typically, it is offered as an outsourced service. Because some cloud computing environments use server and storage grid architecture, cloud computing is sometimes confused with grid computing. In theory, cloud-computing is similar to utility-based computing or traditional outsourcing.

There are many benefits to cloud computing besides the reduction of infrastructure cost and operational support. Because the infrastructure resides at the cloud provider, capital expenditures are minimized. This includes data center real estate, electricity, cooling, server, storage, network technology procurement, and the cost of resources to manage the environment. Reducing time to market on the release of new applications is also a benefit. Some cloud providers offer a set of development tools that can reduce the time to develop a new application from months to weeks.

Cloud services providers realize the efficiencies of a virtualized environment with resource management to maximize resource utilization efficiencies. This workload management helps with multi-tenancy with distributed user workloads. Their environments are typically designed to scale for growth and have local redundancy, application availability, and redundant locations.

Some of the application services offered by a cloud provider are email, Microsoft online, and other web-based applications. The client devices used to access these types of applications consist of mobile, thin, and thick clients. Mobile devices typically consist of cell phones and Personal Digital Assistant (PDA) devices. Thin clients are terminals that depend on a central server where the operating environment resides and is managed and administered. Thick clients are traditional desktops and workstations that have a locally installed operating system.

## Sampling of Public Cloud Providers

There is an ever-growing cloud provider community developing now that cloud computing has reached critical mass. Some of the more prominent providers are Hewlett-Packard, Microsoft, Sun Microsystems, Salesforce.com, EMC, Amazon, and Google. I could never cover all the cloud providers, but some of the more widely used providers are discussed in this section.

HP offers a variety of cloud services. HP's strategy is the company's entrance into cloud computing with HP Adaptive Infrastructure as a Service (AIaaS), which lets customers host applications in HP data centers optimized for Microsoft Exchange, SAP applications, and other critical business applications. There is no capital outlay. The applications are deployed much quicker without the need for hardware and software procurement. The HP AIaaS provides application staging and on-boarding, application operations management, infrastructure operations management, and provisioning with pre-defined hardware and operating systems. Some additional cloud services from HP are covered in the following paragraphs.

CloudPrint is one of HP's cloud services. It is a free mobile service for your cell phone or mobile device. If you are on the road and forget to print a document for a meeting, as long as you have the document on your mobile device and have an Internet connection, you can access this cloud service to print your document. You can send the document or file to a CloudPrint Virtual Print Server and then go to a local printer service where the files can be printed. All this is done at the HP CloudPrint web site, including locating a local printer service provider.

Another example of an HP cloud service is called MagCloud. Mag-Cloud allows you to publish your own magazine online. All you have to do is upload your magazine content, and the cloud service provides the printing, mailing, subscription services, and so on. Printing on demand via this cloud service means no big print runs, with no pre-publishing expense.

A third example of HP cloud computing is a cloud service called Snapfish. Snapfish offers the ability to store photos online. In addition to storing photos, you can share your photos, order prints, and create personalized gifts, cards, mugs, and photo books. This cloud service helps you manage your photos and share them with others online. In addition to HP, Microsoft is also a cloud provider.

Another example of HP cloud computing is offered in conjunction with a business partner called NetSuite, Inc. Jointly, HP and NetSuite offer a business management solution that provides an integrated suite of applications to manage end-to-end business processes in real time. NetSuite's management suite includes the following services: accounting, enterprise resource planning (ERP), customer relationship management (CRM), and eCommerce. They also offer a dashboard technology that provides a view into up-to-date, role-specific, business information from a single pane of glass.

Microsoft offers a cloud service called Windows Azure, which is based on a set of discrete scalable services running on a managed code base. The Azure services platform is an Internet-scale cloud computing and services platform hosted in Microsoft data centers. The Azure Services Platform includes the infrastructure to support Windows Azure and provides a set of developer tools and services so clients can build their own application interfaces accessing Microsoft resources. Windows Azure is a cloud services operating system that serves as the development, service hosting, and service management environment for the Azure Services Platform. Clients download the Microsoft Software Developer's Kit (SDK) and develop their application interfaces to hosted Microsoft data center resources.

Figure 17-3 illustrates the Microsoft Azure Platform architecture and the relationships between the client and the Microsoft resources and services.

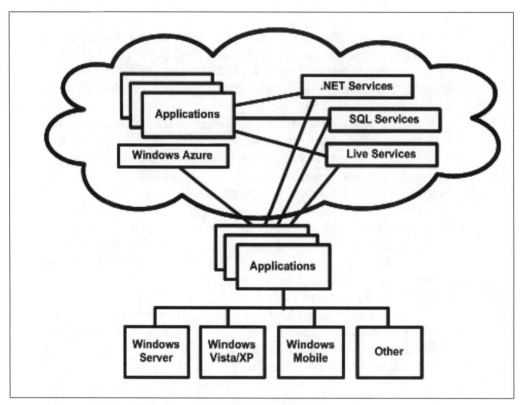

Figure 17-3   High-Level Microsoft Azure Platform

The applications, services, and storage space provided by Microsoft are accessed by the client via the Internet. Some of the tools provided by Microsoft consist of the.NET development platform, along with Microsoft SQL Server database services, and an online form of services through a live computing environment.

Sun Microsystems offers a cloud service based on the purchase of a Belgium-based company called Q-layer. Sun uses a Database Abstraction Layer (DAL) approach with a combination of server, storage, and network facilities along with a development language invented to operate in a virtual private data center (VPDC) environment in a cloud. Sun/Q-layer's NephOS software operates through existing virtualization hypervisor technologies, such as Microsoft, Sun Solaris containers, VMware virtual machines, and

Xen virtualized environments. The cloud providers use Sun/Q-layer's cloud development software and traditional virtualization technologies. Sun's offering is currently a development environment only.

In a Sun/Q-layer cloud environment, users provision their own virtual data centers through a web interface by specifying which virtualized resources are needed for the application they are seeking to provision. They select components like the server, storage, and network bandwidth needed. The purpose is to provide an application environment where the delivered services can be scaled up and down. The cloud providers offering these virtualized data center resources provide and manage the physical, commodity hardware-based infrastructure, while the client subscribers manage their own virtual data centers layered on the cloud provider's resources.

Figure 17-4 is a high-level depiction of Sun/Q-layer.

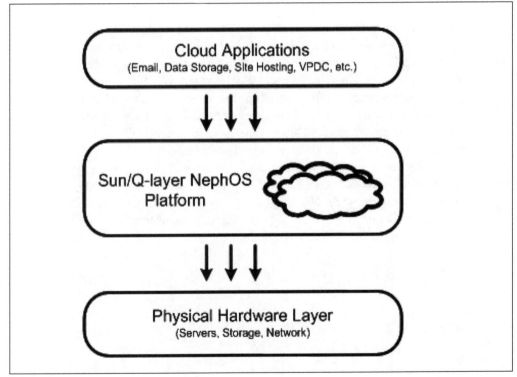

Figure 17-4    Sun/Q-layer Using Virtual Private Data Center (VPDC)

The architecture runs cloud applications on top of the Sun/Q-layer NephOS operating platform running on physical hardware that is virtualized.

Salesforce.com also offers a cloud-computing solution called Force.com. Application developers are using the Force.com platform to build core business applications, like enterprise resource planning (ERP), Human Resource Management (HRM), and supply chain management (SCM).

Because of its ease of development use, clients are developing, modifying, and deploying new applications on the Force.com platform much quicker than the traditional Software Development Life Cycle (SDLC). Client application developers connect to the Force.com Platform and use a tool to develop their on-demand applications and then run them on the Force.com platform.

## Backup in the Cloud

One of the most useful programs available in the cloud is backup. EMC offers a cloud service called Mozy. Mozy is an online backup SaaS. There are two offerings: a consumer product and a corporate enterprise version. The enterprise version, Mozy Enterprise, powered by EMC Fortress, offers secure and automatic offsite backup for client desktops, laptops, and Microsoft Windows servers. This cloud service is ideal for enterprise and remote-office environments. Mozy Enterprise is configured, deployed, and centrally managed via a web-based, multi-tenant administrative console.

Mozy software is available as a monthly subscription service, requires no hardware purchase because it is offered as a hosted solution, and requires minimal IT resources to manage it. Client data is backed up over the Internet via a secure connection, where it is stored for data restore and offsite data protection requirements, as shown in Figure 17-5.

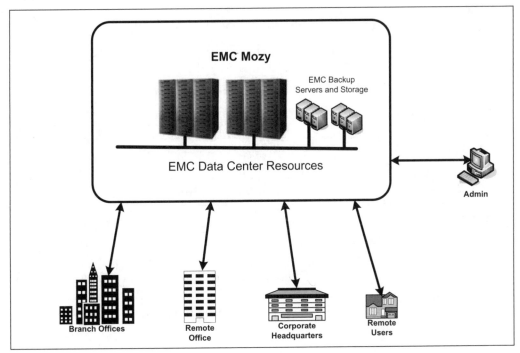

Figure 17-5    EMC Mozy Enterprise Backup Architecture

The Mozy Enterprise architecture illustrated in Figure 17-5 represents the components that make up the solution. The local agents transfer the backup data securely via the Internet to the Mozy Enterprise cloud, where it is stored in EMC data centers. The data is restorable from either the application software or web browser interface from anywhere on the Internet.

To provide an example of a Total Cost of Ownership (TCO) analysis of a cloud service, this next section contains an analysis generated with an EMC TCO tool specifically used for EMC Mozy Pro. For this use case scenario, ABC Company has an environment made up of 150 desktops currently being backed up in a traditional LAN-based manner using a small backup server with a small direct-attached autochanger library. It has a small IT staff in its central location and a few other small remote offices with no IT staff. The average amount of data backed up per desktop is 5GB.

Figure 17-6 is an example of the output generated from the Mozy Pro TCO tool provided by EMC Corporation.

## Laptop – Desktop Backup TCO Analysis

| | | |
|---|---|---|
| Number of Laptops or Desktops | | 150 |
| Average amount of GBs to be backed up per computer | | 5 |

| | Inhouse PC Backup Solution | MozyPro Online Backup Solution |
|---|---|---|
| Backup Software Package | $3,750 | Included |
| Server(s) | $1,500 | Included |
| Storage | $7,500 | Included |
| Networking Gear | $750 | Included |
| Data Center Power/Cooling | $3,750 | Included |
| Data Center Bandwidth | $15,000 | NA |
| Tech Support | $3,750 | Included |
| Training | $3,000 | Included |
| Management | $7,500 | Included |
| Offsite Solution (i.e. Iron Mountain) | $11,250 | Included |
| | | |
| Total 1 Year Costs: | $57,750 | $10,643 |
| **Customer Saves:** | | **$47,108** |

Figure 17-6    EMC Mozy Enterprise Backup TCO Example

You can calculate what you could expect in your environment by running the tool yourself. According to EMC, all costs were based on the number of clients being backed up and the industry average costs estimated per backup resource. The storage costs were based on a blended cost of tape and SATA disks. The networking costs were based on the number of cables needed for the backup clients and backup server to be connected to an existing network switch. The data center related costs were calculated using a percentage of the total annual spend for power and cooling and bandwidth coming into the data center. The cost for the Mozy Pro service was based on suggested retail pricing. You really want to run this analysis yourself to get a feel for an example of what a cloud application might save in your environment.

# Storage in the Cloud

Another EMC application is Cloud Optimized Storage (COS) called Atmos. EMC Atmos is designed to address the needs of cloud providers. It is massively scalable and globally distributed, but is managed as a single entity. Atmos utilizes metadata and policies to deliver petabytes of information. The metadata tags content and the policies automatically get the right information to the right location at the right time. EMC Atmos software runs on low-cost, high-density hardware. The hardware is configurable based on capacity and/or computer requirements.

EMC Atmos includes the following data services: replication, versioning, compression, de-duplication, and spin-down. EMC Atmos uses web service APIs, such as REST/SOAP for Internet-based application services and standard NAS protocols, such as CIFS and NFS for file-based services. Figure 17-7 illustrates how different cloud storage services can be provided over the Internet.

You could use cloud optimized storage as a repository for backup data, personal information, such as pictures and movies, and as a means to collaborate and share data with others.

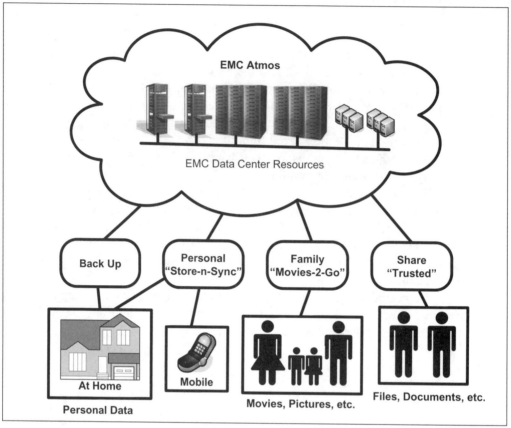

Figure 17-7   EMC Atmos Storage

## Other Cloud Applications

In addition to the applications covered in the previous sections, other applications are exclusive online service providers or retailers. Providers such as Google and Amazon offer cloud-computing solutions for e-mail, collaboration, and other web-related services.

Google has an application group called Google Apps. Google Apps cloud services such as e-mail and collaboration. These tools are available to subscribers and are completely web-based. A local client is not needed. In addition to e-mail services, Google Apps also offers voice and video chat, calendars, and instant messaging. It also offers a service to store documents, provide content management, and provide secure video sharing.

Amazon has a subsidiary company that offers web services. Amazon Elastic Compute Cloud (Amazon EC2) is a web service that provides resizable compute capacity in the cloud. Amazon EC2's web service interface allows clients to obtain and configure capacity. It provides control of computing resources, runs within Amazon's data centers, and is managed by Amazon's technical support staff. Amazon EC2 helps provision new server resources via the Internet without the hardware and operational expenses.

## Why Go to the Cloud?

Why go to the cloud instead of using traditional server and application provisioning? One scenario may be a small startup company seeking to introduce its products to market quickly and having little startup capital. By using the resources provided via a cloud provider, the development of its application interface or virtual storefront can be minimized and the infrastructure expense eliminated. This provides the company with the ability to focus on the business at hand and not worry about the establishment and management of its computing environment.

Another example of moving to the cloud is to reduce capital expenditures. Paying a cloud provider for the technical resources needed to run applications versus paying for the infrastructure servers, storage, and networking, and so on may provide a positive ROI. This also reduces the operational expense of administration and management by transferring that responsibility to a cloud provider in the form of a service level agreement.

Dynamic environments that can't predict how much scalability is required to run their applications can use a cloud provider that has more computing resources available. As their service demands increase, the cloud provider can adapt and adjust the amount of resources available to their applications. This can also work in the reverse. If the client experiences a slow period, he can cut back on the resources provisioned. The cloud provider can re-allocate those resources to another client.

The cloud is clearly growing in popularity for these, and many other, reasons, and many of my clients are experimenting with the cloud. Large companies have been starting with non-critical applications to test the model and may very well move other applications to the cloud.

In general, the benefits of the reduction and/or elimination of the cost of infrastructure and operational support, the reduction of time to market on the release of new applications, and using the skill sets of the cloud provider instead of growing in-house expertise make this an intriguing technology.

## Governance in the Cloud

Cloud computing is of a distributed nature, which means, in some cases, you're not sure where your data is located. For this reason, privacy rights and regulatory compliance are difficult to manage. In most cases, cloud-based applications are virtualized, which almost always employs a hypervisor. In this type of environment, it's difficult to ensure that virtual machines are altogether isolated because of the shared hypervisor.

Your cloud-based service may in fact be a "nested" cloud application because your SaaS application may be hosted on an infrastructure that is also cloud-based. A SaaS startup firm would likely employ this type of setup so it doesn't have to incur the cost of its own infrastructure. Now you have both the software you are using in the cloud and an underlying infrastructure in the cloud in yet another location. This makes it difficult to monitor and audit your data, its location, and its uses. Needless to say, this can be unnerving. You want to ensure that your security standards are being met by your cloud-based partner and consult with them regularly to ensure that their standards have not changed.

You also want to have a full understanding of the service level agreement (SLA) that will be in place with your cloud provider. Like in-house applications, there will surely be some down time associated with the cloud-based applications; however, in the cloud, you have both the application itself and Internet disruptions to consider.

If you have to conform to regulatory standards, such as Health Insurance Portability and Accountability Act (HIPPA) or Payment Card Industry (PCI) standards, you'll have other considerations with the cloud. You'll have to classify your data carefully and know where it's located and by whom it can be accessed in the cloud.

Governance in the cloud raises more questions than answers because this is an emerging way of working with applications and technology. To say it is evolving would be an understatement.

In some cases, these concerns may preclude some of your technology from existing in the cloud, at least initially, until more standards and regulatory issues can be worked out. Some applications, however, may be well suited for the cloud and allow you to reap the benefits of this emerging way of accessing applications and IT resources.

## Cautionary Note on Data Portability

Most applications covered in this chapter come from large firms that are long-time technology heavyweights. There are, however, many small firms with great cloud applications. There is a higher risk that these firms will close shop which, if you're using their tools, could leave you with no place to run your application. If you deploy an important custom application in the cloud, consider using a development platform that is portable, such as one that is Python-based. Your cloud provider will have to offer a portable development tool, so perhaps this should be a factor in your decision making regarding whether or not the cloud provider you are considering for your custom application is the right one.

You're entirely on your own when determining the long-term viability of the cloud providers you're considering, so being confident you'll be able to get your critical application(s) to another provider, or in-house systems, may depend on the portability of your applications.

## Summary

From the topics covered in this chapter, you can see that there are a wide variety of applications in the cloud, and I've only scratched the surface of what is available.

Depending on the type of application(s) you use in the cloud, there are many potential benefits. Some examples of the benefits are

- Reducing and/or eliminating of the cost of infrastructure
- Reducing the cost of operational support
- Reducing time to market on the release of new applications
- Using the skill sets of the cloud provider to embellish your own IT support staff

Starting small may be the ideal way to begin your work with the cloud and then expand to more critical applications.

The next chapter covers simple green techniques that can be implemented with little or no investment.

# Chapter 18

## Simple Power Savings and Other Green Tips

This book discusses many complex and advanced topics related to power and cooling, but there are also many simple ways to reduce power consumption. The following are some facts to consider related to power from an American Power Conversion (APC) study:

- In a typical desktop computer, nearly half the power coming out of the wall is wasted and never reaches the processor, memory, disks, or other components.
- The added heat from inefficient computers can increase the demand on air conditioners and cooling systems, making your computing equipment even more expensive to run.
- Even though most of today's desktop computers are capable of automatically transitioning to a Standby (also known as sleep) or hibernate state when inactive, about 90% of systems have this function disabled.
- Some 25% of the electricity used to power home electronics—computers, DVD players, stereos, and TVs—is consumed while the products are turned off.

These facts surprise a lot of people. In the upcoming sections, I cover more topics related to easy ways to save power.

# Turn Off Your Desktop Computer

The vast majority of my clients leave on their desktop computers all the time. They use password protection to ensure no one can log on to the computer, but their computers are always running. The following are some myths related to powering off desktop computers:

- You should never turn off your computer. Your computer is designed to handle 40,000 on/off cycles. If you are an average user, that's significantly more cycles than you will initiate in the computer's five-to-seven-year-life. When you turn your computer off, you not only reduce energy use, you also lower heat stress and wear on the system.

- Turning your computer off and then back on uses more energy than leaving it on. The surge of power used by a computer to boot up is far less than the energy your computer uses when left on for more than three minutes.

- Screen savers save energy. This is a common misconception. Screen savers were originally designed to help prolong the life of monochrome monitors. Those monitors are now technologically obsolete. Screen savers save energy only if they actually turn off the screen or, with laptops, turn off the backlight.

- Network connections are lost when computers go into low-power or Standby (sleep) mode. Newer computers are designed to Standby on networks without loss of data or connection. CPUs with Wake On LAN (WOL) technology can be left in Standby mode overnight to wake up and receive data packets sent to the unit.

- LCD monitors use less energy than CRTs, so therefore I should leave it on at all times. The average 17" LCD monitor uses 35 watts of electricity an hour. In a business environment where hundreds to thousands of LCDs are in use simultaneously, this adds up in cost. Again, use power-saving techniques, and look for a monitor that is an Energy Star qualified product. Energy Star products put the monitor into Standby mode if configured correctly. Remember, LCD monitors are considered to be "vampire energy users," meaning the display will still be drawing power, even in Standby mode. If the size of the monitor isn't necessarily a factor, consider purchasing a 14" LCD. You generate 40% less energy as opposed to a 17" LCD.

# Some Interesting Facts

Here are some interesting facts related to electricity use of computers:

- An average desktop computer requires 85 watts just to idle, even with the monitor off. If that computer were in use or idling for only 40 hours a week instead of a full 168, over $40 in energy costs would be saved annually.

- One computer left on 24 hours a day costs you between $115 and $160 in electricity costs annually while dumping 1,500 pounds of $CO_2$ into the atmosphere.

- A tree absorbs between 3 and 15 pounds of $CO_2$ each year. That means up to 500 trees are needed to offset the annual emissions of one computer left on all the time!

- If each household in a region the size of the metro Boston area turned off its computer for just one additional hour per day, it would save $3.2 million in electricity costs and prevent 19,000 tons of CO2 from heating the atmosphere.

- Electricity production is the largest source of greenhouse gas emissions in the United States, ahead of transportation.

# Some Tips for Saving Energy

Here are some tips to save energy:

- Turn off your computer at night so it runs only eight hours a day—you'll reduce your energy use by 810kWh per year and net a 67% annual savings.

- Plug your computer into a surge protector with a master control outlet, which automatically senses when the computer is not in use and cuts power to it and all of your peripherals.

- Purchase flat-screen monitors—they use significantly less energy and are not as hard on your eyes as CRTs.

- Purchase an Energy Star–compliant computer or laptop model, which uses much less energy than desktop units.

- Plan your computer-related activities so you can do them all at once, keeping the computer off at other times.

- Consider a smaller monitor—a 14-inch display uses 40% less energy than a 17-inch one.

- Enable the Standby mode and power management settings on your computer.

- Forgo the screen saver—it doesn't save energy or your screen unless you're using an old monochrome monitor.

- Review document drafts and e-mails on screen instead of printing them.

- Power off your monitor when you are not using it instead of using screen savers.

- Consider an ink-jet printer—although a bit slower than laser printers, ink-jets use 80 to 90% less energy.

- Buy vegetable or non-petroleum-based inks—they are made from renewable resources, require fewer hazardous solvents, and often produce brighter, cleaner colors.

- Turn off all printers and peripherals unless you are using them.

- Do not leave the computer running overnight or on weekends.

- Choose dark backgrounds for your screen display—bright-colored displays consumer more power.

- Reduce the light level in your room when you work on your computer.

- Network and share printers where possible.

- Print on recycled-content paper. Look for non-chlorine bleached papers with 50 to 100% post-consumer waste.

- Use double-sided printing functions.

- E-mail communications as an alternative to paper memos and faxing.

## Activate Desktop Computer Power Management to Save Energy

Saving energy at your desktop is easy. Your desktop computer has power-management features that are easy to configure. You can activate Standby settings through your operating system's power management control. The following descriptions help you determine which setting is right for you:

- **Standby mode** Use this mode if you're away from your computer for frequent short periods of time. Standby mode conserves energy by cutting off power to your display, hard drive, and peripherals. After a pre-set period of inactivity, your computer switches to a low power state. When you move your mouse or press any computer key, you exit Standby mode and your computer takes you back to its previous operating state. Standby mode is an especially effective way to conserve battery power in a laptop computer. However, if your computer loses power for any reason while in Standby mode, you may lose unsaved work. This is known as Sleep on Mac OS-X and Windows Vista and Suspend on Linux.

- **Hibernate mode**. Use this mode if you're away from your computer for an extended period of time. Hibernate mode saves energy and protects your work by copying system data to a reserved area on your hard drive and then completely turning off your computer. It also reduces wear and tear on your components. When you turn power back on, your files and documents appear on your desktop just as you left them. Be sure to set your system to automatically go into hibernate mode. This is known as Safe Sleep on Mac OS-X. On Linux this is known as suspend-to-disk.

These modes are easy to go into manually, from the Start menu, and by configuring Control Panel to automatically put you in to a power savings mode. The steps in Figure 18-1 show you how to go in to Standby mode on your computer from the Start menu.

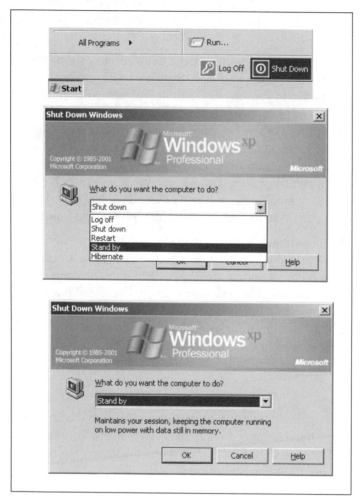

Figure 18-1    Going in to *Standby* From the *Start* Menu

From the *Start* menu, select *Shutdown, Stand by, OK,* and your computer goes into Standby mode and consumes substantially less power and maintains your current desktop so you can resume work where you left off the next time you power on your computer.

You can also automatically set up your computer to go into a power-savings mode, as shown in Figure 18-2.

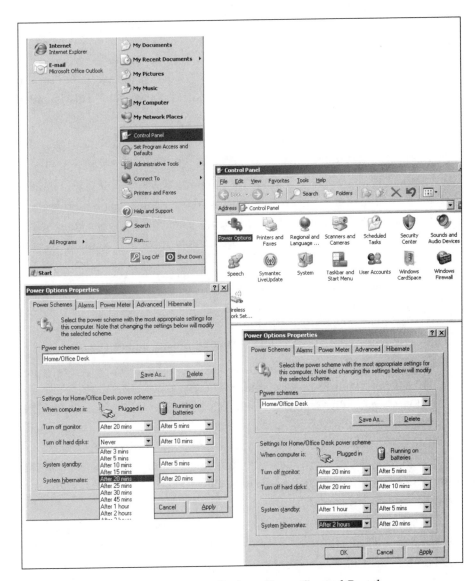

Figure 18-2    Configure Power Savings From *Control Panel*

To configure power savings, select *Start, Settings, Control Panel, Power Options* and any options you like. Figure 18-2 shows the monitor being turned off after 20 minutes and hibernating after 2 hours. This procedure is simple, and you can walk away from your computer knowing it will go into a power-savings mode.

# They're On Even When They're Off

Anything that uses a remote continues to consume power even when it's turned off—for example, when a TV is "off," it's really partially "on" so that the picture comes on quickly when you hot the remote. This is called "vampire energy use" or "phantom energy use."

In fact, there are probably several vampires in your home right now, sucking power from your electrical outlets and money from your wallet.

When your computer, plasma TV, or stereo is off, you probably think it is using as little power as possible. Fact is, these devices have high standby power use. What's more, all the peripherals connected to your computer—printer, monitor, USB hub, scanner, DSL/cable modem—continue to consume "idle current."

There may be as many as 20 devices drawing standby power in your home. These include any device with a remote control and external power supply (or adapter), permanently illuminated digital displays and LEDs, and many new larger appliances, such as air conditioners and refrigerators.

According to the Department of Energy, vampire energy loss represents between 5 and 8% of a single-family home's total electricity use per year. On average, that equals one month's electricity bill. Taken across the United States, it adds up to at least 68 billion kilowatt-hours of electricity annually—that's the equivalent output of 37 typical electricity-generating power plants, costing consumers more than $7 billion. The result of all this wasted energy? More than 97 billion pounds of carbon dioxide seeping into the atmosphere each year.

On a global scale, standby energy accounts for 1% of the world's carbon emissions, according to Alan Meier of the Lawrence Berkeley National Laboratory in California. So how do you combat those vampire energy loads? Fortunately, when it comes to your computer and electronics, there's an easy solution: a surge protector with a master control outlet. Simply plug your computer into the master outlet and your peripherals into the controlled outlets. The master outlet senses when your computer powers down or goes into Standby mode and automatically shuts down the controlled outlets. Your peripherals no longer suck up energy when they are in standby mode—and vampire loads no longer take a bite out of your monthly budget.

# Recycling Electronic Waste

A recent study by the EPA shows that electronics make up approximately 1% of the municipal solid waste stream. Research completed in Europe shows that electronic waste is growing at three times the rate of other municipal waste. Clearly, an essential part of green computing includes proper disposal of components that you no longer use.

Here are some interesting facts related to electronic waste:

- In a 2006 report, the International Association of Electronics Recyclers projects that with the current growth and obsolescence rates of the various categories of consumer electronics, approximately 3 billion units will be scrapped during the rest of this decade, for an average of 400 million units a year.

- Gartner estimates that 133,000 personal computers are discarded by U.S. homes and businesses each day.

- Each year, 130 million cell phones are retired.

- According to the EPA, we generated 2.6 million tons of e-waste in the U.S. in 2005, or 1.4% of total discards. Of this amount, only 12.6% was recycled.

- About 68% of consumers stockpile used or unwanted computer equipment in their homes.

Here are some tips to consider related to electronic waste:

- If you just bought a new computer, your old one may not be junk. If your old computer is less than five years old, chances are someone else can put it to good use. Donating electronics for reuse extends the life of valuable products and keeps them out of the waste-management system.

- Your old computer may be a full "system" with working peripherals. Remember that a functional, complete system, including monitor, wiring, printer, and software licenses, is preferable to a non-working, incomplete setup. Chances are, your recipient may not have the resources or expertise to make good use of a single component.

Donate your old computer to a school, non-profit organization, or a lower-income family. You may also be able to take advantage of tax incentives for computer equipment donations. Some organizations you may want to consider are the following:

- **Goodwill Industries**: Many Goodwills accept computer donations to help individuals with disabilities and other disadvantages upgrade their job skills and enter the workforce. **www.goodwill.org.**

- **Materials Exchange**: Many materials exchanges accept electronics. You'll find a state-by-state listing. **www.epa.gov/jtr/comm/exch-stat.htm.**

- **Reuse Development Organization (ReDO)**: ReDO is a non-profit organization that promotes reuse of discarded and surplus materials, including electronics. **www.redo.org.**

- If your computer cannot be reused, recycling it is your next waste—management option. Recycling electronics avoids pollution and the need to extract valuable and limited virgin resources. It also reduces the energy used in new product manufacturing. Contact your city or town to see if it offers computer and electronics collections as part of household hazardous waste services, or if there is a recycling drop-off center in your area. Also, check with TV repair shops, charitable organizations, an electronics recycling company, or even local electronics retailers—they may be your best option for recycling.

- To find an electronics recycling organization in your area, visit the following web site: **www.eiae.org**. EIA Consumer Education Initiative (CEI) helps you find environmentally responsible options for donating and recycling electronics in your community.

# Background on Electronic Waste

This section offers some interesting background on electronic waste, mostly from the EPA.

In 2007, the EPA reported that electronics make up roughly 1% of the municipal solid waste stream. In fact, there were 3,010 tons generated of selected consumer electronics in 2007 alone. Of this 3,010 tons, only 410 tons were recovered, or 13.6%. From this, you can see that electronic waste is a growing problem in today's generation. Electronic waste can be defined as a surplus of broken and/or obsolete electronic devices that were disposed of, rather than recycled properly. The growth of electronic waste, or e-waste, can be blamed on the rapid evolving technology in the world today in conjunction with the low costs it takes to produce these devices.

The Silicon Valley Toxic Coalition states that there are approximately 500 million obsolete computers in the United States alone. In 2003, an estimated 133,000 PCs were thrown out each day in U.S. homes and businesses. The EPA estimates that up to 40 million computers will be ready for end-of-life management each year. Of these 40 million, it is safe to say that only 10% will be recycled, contributing to our ever-growing e-waste problem. The growth of LCD TV use as well as cell phone use also plays a major role in our e-waste crisis. The EPA reported that in 2007, 26.9 million televisions and 140.3 million cell phones were disposed of. Only 18% and 10% were recycled, respectively.

So, why is e-waste any different from regular waste, such as food or paper? The reason we see so much concern for this type of waste is because of the harm it causes to our environment. Many of these products contain substances that are largely toxic, such as lead and mercury. These substances make leak into the ground and/or water streams, poisoning natural resources.

Another growing problem that we see in the U.S. is that e-waste that is actually recycled may consequently be shipped to impoverished countries for repair, only to see it burned, dumped into rivers, dumped into acid baths, in turn creating more problems for the people living in these countries.

So, why should we recycle at all? Not all recycling companies will ship your products off to another country. Many companies making an effort to properly recycle and dispose of this waste. Unfortunately, in some cases, this may come at a price. However, these are many other options to consider when recycling your outdated electronics. Consider donating your computer to schools, non-profit organizations, as well as less fortunate families. By doing so, you may be eligible for tax refunds. Remember, your old computer may still be more up-to-date than someone else's system. Even donating your computer's peripherals is acceptable. Printers, monitors, mice, and keyboards are all considered e-waste. Remember, by properly recycling or donating your electronic devices, you reduce the amount of waste entering the waste stream in your area.

If you are looking for places to donate or recycle your old equipment, check out the following organizations.

• Hewlett-Packard

**http://www.hp.com/hpinfo/globalcitizenship/environment/recy-cle/index.html**

HP recycling services provides an easy way to recycle computer equipment, printing supplies, rechargeable batteries, and other items, and in many cases, it is free.

• Environmental Protection Agency

**http://www.epa.gov/epawaste/conserve/materials/ecycling/index.htm**

Contains many options for donation and recycling in your area.

• Call2Recycle

**http://www.rbrc.org/consumer/**

This program has collected and recycled more than 42 million pounds of rechargeable batteries. There are now more than 50,000 convenient recycling locations nationwide. Check out this site to find a location in your area!

# Green Printing

One technology that has quickly advanced an eco-friendly way is printing. The following HP URL is an ideal place to start on saving energy, reducing waste, simple reuse and recycling, and other green printing topics:

**http://h71028.www7.hp.com/enterprise/us/en/ipg/eco-business-printing-solutions.html**

Printing is one of the technologies in which adopting green practices is easy. Such simple tips as duplex printing, consolidating old printers into new, efficient units, disabling color printing except when color is required, and using recycled paper are some of the easiest ways to go green. High-end HP printers give administrators control over printers with Webjet admin. Most green printing techniques are intuitive, so you may want to consider the following:

- **Use recycled paper**. By purchasing recycled paper, you reduce waste and energy consumption, and the quality of recycled paper is high.

- **Use duplex printing**. Duplex printing is the practice of automatically printing to both sides of the paper, reducing paper usage by 50%. Hewlett-Packard conducted an internal case study, which reported that switching to duplex printing reduces total paper volume by 800 tons.

- **Use black and white printing**. Use the black and white printer option when possible as opposed to color printing.

- **Consolidate your print infrastructure**. By doing this, you reduce the total space occupied by equipment and transition from personal printing to more centralized workgroup-level printing, which in turn significantly reduces costs and need for maintenance.

- **Use digitally stored documents**. Try storing documents digitally or using e-mail instead of snail mail. In some respects, you may find yourself more organized storing documents electronically rather than printing them and storing them in files.

These simple printing suggestions can make a difference. Many high-end printers, for instance, can be set to black and white and color can be enabled only when color jobs are required.

## Summary

Here are some key facts covered in this chapter:

- About 25% of the electricity used to power home electronics is consumed when the devices are turned off.

- It takes less energy to boot up a computer than it does to leave it running for more than 3 minutes.

- Plug functionally related electronics into a surge protector (or UPS) that features a master outlet/controlled outlet technology to avoid vampire energy use. For example, plug a computer into the master outlet and the peripherals (printer, speakers, etc.) into the controlled outlets. When the computer powers down, the master outlet automatically shuts off power to the peripherals.

- Use Standby or sleep mode on your personal computer.

- Use green printing tips, such as duplex printing, black and white printing, recycled paper, consolidate old printers, and store documents digitally.

- Recycle electronic waste (see the earlier URLs).

The next chapter covers managed services that many of my clients are using to gain key information about the operation of their IT environments.

# Chapter 19

# Managed Services:
# Remote Monitoring

This chapter covers remote monitoring and remediation of infrastructure. The detailed reports produced by this solution give insight into infrastructure that smaller clients had never had access to before monitoring was introduced to their environment. This means that more informed decisions about technology procurement and professional services needs can result in an overall more efficient environment. When trends can be identified for server and entreating components, for instance, then more informed and efficient decision making takes place, resulting in an overall better operational environment.

The service used in this chapter is my firm's IT Diagnosis, which uses *Onsite Manager* from *Level Platforms* as an underlying technology that discovers and reports on the environment. The key to success is the service my firm provides to monitor and remediate problems; however, the reporting the tool provides is key to understanding the operation of your environment and making informed decisions. I cover detailed inventory and reporting information in this chapter. This information is useful to my clients because it provides insight into the operation of IT environment.

The reports can be generated at any interval, and I typically provide the report to my clients on a quarterly basis.

The following are the reports produced and covered in this chapter:

- Executive overview
- Hardware inventory
- Site inventory
- Site health
- Software inventory
- Windows server health

## Executive Overview

The executive overview provides a summary of your entire network. The report shows a summary of Windows server and workstation health on the monitored network, as shown in Figure 19-1.

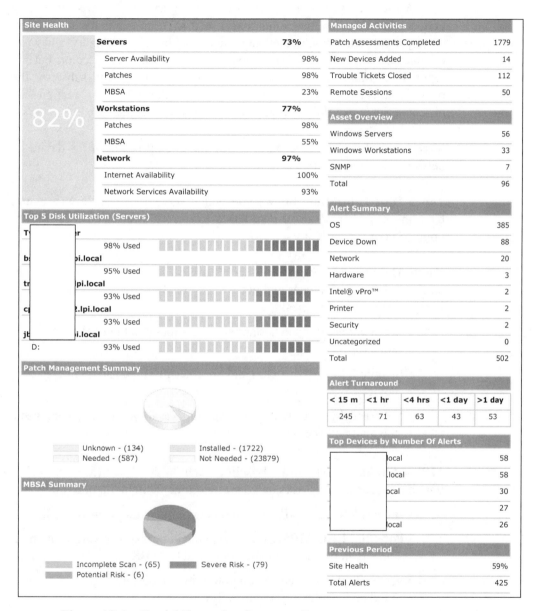

Figure 19-1   Partial Executive Summary Report

As you can see in the figure, several categories are covered, including network health score, patch summary, security scan summary, asset overview, top problem devices, alert summary, trouble ticket summary, and work completed. Some of the effect is lost because of the lack of color, but the report is a good at-a-glance summary. The figure is a small subset of the overall executive summary, which includes the following sections. (I obscured the name of the servers that appear in the original report.)

**Site Health Tab**. The percentage shows the overall health of the device or network over a given time period.

**Top 5 Disk Utilization**. Shows you which servers on your infrastructure have the highest amount of disk space usage. This tells you it is time to upgrade your system's storage space.

**Patch Management Summary**. Shows a pie chart listing your infrastructure's total security patches and hot fixes applied over a given time, including the following categories:

- **Needed**: Security patches and hot fixes found but not yet applied to the devices.

- **Installed**: Security patches and hot fixes installed and applied to the device.

- **Not Needed**: Security patches and hot fixes found which are not needed by the given device.

**MBSA Summary**. Microsoft Baseline Security Analyzer (MBSA) shows you the current security risks on your environment, including the following:

- **Incomplete Scan**: MBSA could not complete the security scan.

- **Potential Risk**: MBSA's reported potential risks affecting your environment (can be automatically addressed by MBSA).

- **Severe Risk**: Severe risks on your network detected by MBSA (these are handled by MBSA automatically).

**Managed Activities**. Activities performed for maintenance/patching during a given time period, including the following:

- **Patch assessments Completed**: The number of patch assessments completed by the Patch Management portion of Level's software.

- **New Devices Added**: Displays the number of new devices added to your environment within a given time period.

- **Trouble Tickets Closed**: The number of closed trouble tickets generated by Level platforms when problems on the environment occurred and were reported and resolved.

- **Remote Sessions**: The total number of times remote desktop sessions occurred in a given time period.

**Asset Overview**. Provides information such as the number of devices found on the network, including the following:

- **Windows servers**: Displays the total number of Windows Servers being monitored by Level Platforms.

- **Windows Workstations**: The total number of monitored devices running a Windows non-server operating system (Windows XP, Windows 98, and so on).

- **SNMP**: The total number of monitored SNMP devices on the network. SNMP includes routers, switches, ASAs, etc.

- **Total**: The total number of all devices being monitored on the network. This includes a total of Windows servers, Windows workstations, and SNMP devices.

**Alert Summary**. The number of total alerts generated on monitored devices in a given time period. Alerts are listed in the following categories:

- Operating system

- Devices reported as being down

- Network alerts

- Hardware alerts

- Intel's vPro alerts

- Printer alerts

- Security alerts

- Uncategorized alerts

- Total amount of all alert categories

**Alert Turnaround**. This section shows you the total number of alerts in a given time period and the following time periods it took to resolve the alerts:

- < 15 m: Number of total alerts resolved in less than 15 minutes.

- < 1 hr: Number of total alerts which took less than 1 hour to resolve.

- < 4 hrs: Number of total alerts which took less than 4 hours to resolve.

- < 1 day: Number of total alerts which took less than 1 day to resolve.

- > 1 day: Number of total alerts which took more than 1 day to resolve.

**Top Devices by Number Of Alerts**. This section shows you the most troublesome devices on your network that have generated the most alerts within a given time period.

**Previous Period**. This final category of the executive summary shows you the overall site health and total number of alerts of the last executive summary generated for your network. This allows you to compare your current summary with a previous summary to see if your environment has improved or become more troublesome.

These key areas provide a great snapshot of your environment.

# Detailed Hardware Inventory

A detailed hardware inventory is produced as part of the report. There is a summary of all the hardware in the environment and a detailed server-by-server description. In the client example, the server summary shows the following types of servers in Table 19-1.

**Table 19-1** Device Summary

| Type of Hardware | Qty |
|---|---|
| Windows Domain Controller | 1 |
| Windows Member Server | 4 |
| Windows Workstation | 2 |
| SNMP | 2 |
| Others | 2 |

Detail is provided for each device monitored, as shown for the domain controller in Figure 19-2.

| OS Description | | |
|---|---|---|
| Microsoft(R) Windows(R) Server 2003, Enterprise Edition | | |

| OS Version | Service Pack | Role |
|---|---|---|
| 5.2.3790 | 2.0 | Domain Controller |

| IP Addresses |
|---|
| 192.168.10.2 |

| Service Groups | Site Groups |
|---|---|
| Windows 2003 | |
| IIS 6 Web Server | |
| Domain Controller | |
| Symantec Antivirus | |

| Hardware Information | | | |
|---|---|---|---|

| Manufacturer | | Model | |
|---|---|---|---|
| KM266_ | | AWRDACPI | |

| CPU | | Version | Clock Speed |
|---|---|---|---|
| AMD Athlon(tm) XP 2100+ | | Model 8, Stepping 1 | 1728MHz |

| Logical Disk | Capacity | Used | Free |
|---|---|---|---|
| C: | 78153MB | 7067MB | 71086MB |

| CD Drive | Manufacturer |
|---|---|
| D: | (Standard CD-ROM drives) |

| Physical Memory |
|---|
| 2039MB |

| Video Card | Color Bits | Resolution | Driver | RAM |
|---|---|---|---|---|
| S3 Graphics ProSavage DDR 8D04 (Microsoft Corporation) | 32 | 1024 x 768 | 6.13.10.1075-13.93.41 | 8MB |

| Network Card | DHCP Enabled | MAC Address | Driver | Driver Version |
|---|---|---|---|---|
| Realtek RTL8139 Family PCI Fast Ethernet NIC | False | 00:50:BA:CB:D5:74 | Realtek RTL8139 Family PCI Fast Ethernet NIC | 5.396.530.2001 |
| WAN Miniport (PPTP) | False | 50:50:54:50:30:30 | WAN Miniport (PPTP) | 5.2.3790.0 |
| WAN Miniport (PPPOE) | False | 33:50:6F:45:30:30 | WAN Miniport (PPPOE) | 5.2.3790.0 |

| Monitor |
|---|
| Default Monitor |

Figure 19-2    Partial Listing of Device Detail for the Domain Controller

The hardware detail is long and only a small subset of the report is shown in the figure. The hardware inventory covers the following categories:

- OS version

- Current service pack installed

- Machine's role in network environment

- Machine's IP address

- Current service groups running

- Manufacturer and model of the machine

- CPU speed

- Hard drive capacities total/remaining

- CD drives

- RAM installed

- Machines video card includes

    Color depth
    Resolution
    Driver version
    Video RAM

- Installed network cards

- Network card information,

    DHCP enabled yes/no
    Network card's MAC address
    Driver name and version

- Current monitors applied for monitoring by the management tool on the machine

Not all these categories are shown in the figure, but they are part of the detailed report.

The software detail is covered in the next section.

## Detailed Software Inventory

A detailed software inventory is produced as part of the report. The software discovered in the monitored environment is listed, including the quantity of the number of devices on which the software runs.

The software discovery shows a list of all machines being monitored and all the software found, including operating systems and every piece of software installed on each machine. Figure 19-3 shows a partial software report.

| SW Inventory By Application | | Device Count |
|---|---|---|
| **Marvell Miniport Driver** | | 1 |
| ☐ | | |
| **Microsoft .NET Framework 2.0** | | 1 |
| ADSERVER | | |
| **Microsoft .NET Framework 3.0** | | 2 |
| ADSERVER | ☐ | |
| **Microsoft Baseline Security Analyzer 2.0.1** | | 1 |
| ☐ | | |
| **Microsoft Internationalized Domain Names Mitigation APIs** | | 6 |
| ADSERVER | GEN2 | |
| GEN3 | GEN4 | |
| ☐ | ☐ | |
| **Microsoft Kernel-Mode Driver Framework Feature Pack 1.5** | | 1 |
| GEN2 | | |
| **Microsoft National Language Support Downlevel APIs** | | 6 |
| ADSERVER | GEN2 | |
| GEN3 | GEN4 | |
| ☐ | ☐ | |
| **Microsoft Office 2003 Web Components** | | 1 |
| IPMISERVER | | |
| **Microsoft SQL Server 2005** | | 3 |
| GEN2 | ☐ | |
| ☐ | | |
| **Microsoft SQL Server 2005 Backward compatibility** | | 1 |
| ☐ | | |
| **Microsoft SQL Server 2005 Express Edition (SQLEXPRESS)** | | 2 |
| GEN2 | ☐ | |
| **Microsoft SQL Server 2005 Reporting Services** | | 1 |
| ☐ | | |
| **Microsoft SQL Server 2005 Tools** | | 1 |
| ☐ | | |
| **Microsoft SQL Server Management Studio Express** | | 1 |

Figure 19-3   Partial Listing of Software Detail

On the right, Figure 19-3 shows the number of devices on which the software is running. On the left is the software name and the specific devices on which the software is running. (I obscured several of the host names.)

## Site Inventory

One of the most revealing aspects of managed services is the full site inventory. For every client I've run the inventory, there were a lot of surprises regarding what they had installed. It's difficult to do your job and keep track of everything procured and installed over the years.

There are a variety of ways that an inventory can be performed because *Level* scans based on different options. Level can scan an IP range, individual IP addresses, or an entire subnet for servers, workstations, printers, and any network devices that contain an IP and/or SNMP strings.

Figure 19-4 shows a partial listing of a software inventory.

| Operating System Inventory | |
| --- | --- |
| **Operating System** | **Count** |
| Microsoft Windows XP Professional | 1 |
| Microsoft(R) Windows(R) Server 2003 for Small Business Server | 1 |
| Microsoft(R) Windows(R) Server 2003, Standard Edition | 1 |
| Microsoft(R) Windows(R) Server 2003, Web Edition | 1 |
| Microsoft® Windows Vista™ Business | 1 |
| Microsoft(R) Windows(R) Server 2003, Enterprise Edition | 3 |
| **Total** | **8** |

| Software Inventory | |
| --- | --- |
| **Application** | **Count** |
| Acronis Backup Server | 1 |
| Acronis True Image Enterprise Server | 1 |
| Acronis Disk Director Server | 1 |
| Acronis True Image Server | 3 |
| Adobe Flash Player 9 ActiveX | 4 |
| Adobe Flash Player ActiveX | 1 |
| Adobe Reader 7.0.9 | 1 |
| Adobe Reader 8 | 2 |
| ATI - Software Uninstall Utility | 1 |
| ATI Control Panel | 1 |
| ATI Display Driver | 1 |
| ATI HydraVision | 1 |
| Camtasia Studio 4 | 1 |
| DFE-538TX | 1 |
| GDR 1406 for SQL Server Database Services 2005 ENU (KB932557) | 1 |
| GDR 1406 for SQL Server Integration Services 2005 ENU (KB932557) | 1 |
| GDR 1406 for SQL Server Reporting Services 2005 ENU (KB932557) | 1 |
| GDR 1406 for SQL Server Tools and Workstation Components 2005 ENU (KB932557) | 1 |
| Intel(R) Graphics Media Accelerator Driver | 1 |
| Intel(R) PRO Network Connections | 1 |
| Intel(R) PRO Network Connections 11.2.0.69 | 1 |
| iReasoning MIB Browser (remove only) | 2 |
| LiveUpdate 3.2 (Symantec Corporation) | 1 |
| Managed Workplace Onsite Manager | 6 |

Figure 19-4    Partial Listing of Software Detail

This software listing goes on for several pages and includes all software that can be identified. The software included in the inventory is both operating system and applications and, depending on the size of your environment, can be a long listing.

The hardware inventory pages include servers, networking electronics, and other devices. Figure 19-5 shows a partial listing of a hardware inventory for computers.

| Page 8 of 10 | | | | Site Asset Inventory |
|---|---|---|---|---|
| **Processor Inventory** | | | | |
| **Processor** | | | | **Count** |
| Intel Celeron processor | | | | 1 |
| Genuine Intel(R) CPU | @ 2.40GHz | | | 2 |
| AMD Athlon(tm) XP 2100+ | | | | 2 |
| Intel(R) Pentium(R) 4 CPU 3.00GHz | | | | 4 |
| **Total** | | | | **11** |

| **Physical Memory by Device** | | | | |
|---|---|---|---|---|
| **Device** | **Operating System** | | | **Memory** |
| | Microsoft(R) Windows(R) Server 2003, Enterprise Edition | | | 997MB |
| | Microsoft Windows XP Professional | | | 190MB |
| | Microsoft(R) Windows(R) Server 2003, Enterprise Edition | | | 319MB |
| | Microsoft(R) Windows(R) Server 2003 for Small Business Server | | | 3063MB |
| | Microsoft(R) Windows(R) Server 2003, Enterprise Edition | | | 991MB |
| | Microsoft(R) Windows(R) Server 2003, Standard Edition | | | 1023MB |
| | Microsoft® Windows Vista™ Business | | | 502MB |
| | Microsoft(R) Windows(R) Server 2003, Web Edition | | | 495MB |

| **Hard Drive Capacity by Device** | | | | |
|---|---|---|---|---|
| **Device** | **Disk Letter** | **Used Space** | **Capacity** | **Used** |
| | | | | |
| | C: | 43974MB | 157066MB | 28.00% |
| **Total** | | **43974MB** | **157066MB** | **28%** |
| | | | | |

Figure 19-5   Partial Hardware Inventory Listing for Computers

This listing of the servers starts on the previous page and goes on for several additional pages. (I obscured the host names.)

Figure 19-6 shows a partial listing for some of the networking electronics.

| Network Card Inventory | |
|---|---|
| **Card Name** | **Count** |
| WAN Miniport (PPPOE) | 8 |
| WAN Miniport (PPTP) | 8 |
| Realtek RTL8139 Family PCI Fast Ethernet NIC | 5 |
| Packet Scheduler Miniport | 2 |
| RAS Async Adapter | 1 |
| Realtek RTL8029 PCI Ethernet NIC | 1 |
| Realtek RTL8139/810x Family Fast Ethernet NIC | 1 |
| SiS 900-Based PCI Fast Ethernet Adapter | 1 |
| 1394 Net Adapter | 1 |
| 3Com 3C920 Integrated Fast Ethernet Controller (3C905C-TX Compatible) | 1 |
| Intel(R) 82566DM Gigabit Network Connection | 1 |
| Intel(R) PRO/1000 PL Network Connection | 1 |
| Microsoft Tun Miniport Adapter | 1 |
| **Total** | **32** |

| CD Drive Inventory | |
|---|---|
| **CD** | **Count** |
| (Standard CD-ROM drives) | 5 |
| (Standard CD-ROM drives) | 2 |
| (Standard CD-ROM drives) | 1 |
| **Total** | **8** |

| SNMP Devices | | |
|---|---|---|
| **Device** | **SNMP Name** | **Description** |
| | Training Switch | Cisco Systems Catalyst 1900,V9.00.00 |
| | SBS Switch | Cisco Systems Catalyst 1900,V9.00.00 |

Figure 19-6    Partial Hardware Inventory Listing for Networking Electronics

Networking is one of the easiest areas for companies to lose track of electronics, because networking is usually viewed as "hands-off"after it is installed and operational.

# Site Health

The overall health of your site is important to know. The managed services solution in this chapter provides a detailed report on your environment.

Figure 19-7 shows a partial output of alerts identified in the example environment.

## Alerts

The number of self-healed alerts are indicated by the brackets.

| | Network | OS | Uncategorized | Application | Total |
|---|---|---|---|---|---|
| Switch | 96 (0) | 0 (0) | 0 (0) | 0 (0) | 96 (0) |
| Performance Counters | 0 (0) | 16 (79) | 0 (0) | 0 (0) | 16 (79) |
| Uncategorized | 0 (0) | 0 (0) | 0 (0) | 0 (0) | 0 (0) |
| Resources | 0 (0) | 0 (0) | 0 (0) | 0 (0) | 0 (0) |
| Firewall | 0 (0) | 0 (0) | 0 (0) | 0 (0) | 0 (0) |
| Appliance | 0 (0) | 0 (0) | 0 (0) | 0 (0) | 0 (0) |
| Security Events | 0 (0) | 0 (0) | 0 (0) | 0 (0) | 0 (0) |
| Application Events | 0 (0) | 0 (0) | 0 (0) | 0 (0) | 0 (0) |
| System Events | 0 (0) | 0 (0) | 0 (0) | 0 (0) | 0 (0) |
| Total | 96 (0) | 16 (79) | 0 (0) | 0 (0) | 112 (79) |

### Top Devices by Number of Alerts

| Device | Count |
|---|---|
| | 50 |
| | 46 |
| | 4 |
| | 4 |
| | 4 |
| | 2 |
| | 1 |
| | 1 |

### Alerts Resolution Time (based on Trouble Ticket Resolution)

| Ticket Id | Title | Device | Time Of Alert | Resolution Time |
|---|---|---|---|---|
| 985 | Warning | amtintel3.SBSR2.local | 1/23/2008 4:09:57 PM | 1 days, 21hrs 31mins |
| 994 | Memory  Available MBytes | amtintel3.SBSR2.local | 1/24/2008 3:06:30 PM | 22hrs 34mins |
| 986 | Warning | sqlwhite.sbsr2.local | 1/23/2008 4:09:57 PM | 1 days, 21hrs 31mins |

Figure 19-7   Partial Output of Alerts in Site Health

In addition to the alerts, numerous charts and graphs summarize the health of the environment, including uptime of servers and Internet connectivity. (I obscured the device names.)

In addition to the reporting, this application also improves uptime. The solution uses Microsoft Security Baseline Analyzer, for example, to provide alerts when there are patches and security updates for your servers and workstations. It also generates reports and informs you of security risks.

# Windows Server Health

The Windows Server Health report provides details on all aspects of Windows servers. This service collects usage statistics of the CPU, RAM, paging file, and hard disks. Reports are then generated over any given time, and conclusions can be drawn as far as upgrading server RAM, CPU, and hard disk. Figure 19-8 shows the summary page of Windows Server Health report.

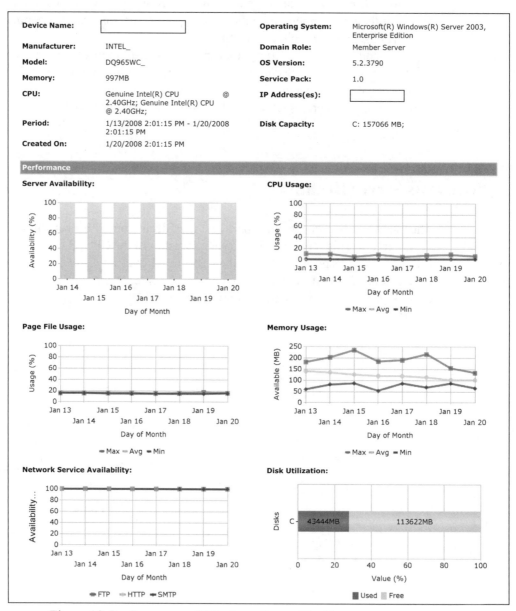

Figure 19-8    Summary of Windows Server Health

As you can see in this figure, over the period of 1/13 to 1/20, the availability was 100% and the CPU usage was low. The low CPU usage was covered in detail in the first section, which focused on server consolidation. (I obscured the device name and IP address.)

Also reported are alerts caused by the following occurrences on servers:

- Logon failure
- Account expired
- Denied logon attempts
- Accounts locked out
- Dr. Watson errors
- Duplicate network names
- IP address conflict
- Windows update failure
- Event log full
- Service or driver has stopped responding or failed to start
- Service terminated unexpectedly
- Logical disk manager can not read disk
- NTFS write failure
- NTFS file system corruption
- Unexpected system shutdown
- Bad block reports

The next section covers the underlying tool used as part of the monitoring service.


# Underlying Tool

As previously mentioned, the tool used for this service is *Onsite Manager* by *Level Platforms*. Onsite Manager is a lightweight web-based program that collects data via Windows Management Interface (WMI) and Simple Network Management Protocol (SNMP). Onsite Manager then reports the information back to my firm's Network Operations Center (NOC) and the technical experts monitoring client installations.

During the setup phase of Onsite Manager, a range of IP addresses is specified for discovery. Onsite Manager then scans your entire network with the given IP range and finds all the network devices with the SNMP string given, then populates a data base in the NOC. After the discovery takes place, the following features are available with the service:

- A monitor set (i.e., events, services, applications, logs, syslog, SNMP, WMI, web sites, etc.) that allows for the monitoring of any entity that falls within your service agreement.

- Alert rules and thresholds that can be modified.

- Performance and availability monitoring for devices, services, software, and web sites.

- Integrated monitoring and alerting against Managed Workplace features (i.e. Patch Management and MBSA).

- Over 100 predefined best-practice management templates available make the tool useful upon setup.

- Modification of alerts, alert categories, views, and groups.

- Cross-site monitoring and extensive collaborative services.

This service is customized to suit our client's needs and produces useful reports that can be used to make IT-related decisions.

## Summary

Having all this valuable information about your IT environment is invaluable in making informed decisions and preventing potential problems. If these reports are combined with the right services to maintain your environment, you can prevent many problems that may adversely impact your business.

# Index

## Symbols

% CPU Utilization, 29
Tape0, 124

## Numerics

10,000 RPM, 148
10/100 MBit switch, 162
10/100 POE switch, 162
10/100/1000 MBit switch, 162
15,000 RPM, 148-149, 152
2,500 IOPS, 151
220 volt, 251
2D, 79
2-pole circuit breaker, 251
3D, 79
3-phase, 251
3-phase power, 42
42" rack, 244
7,200 RPM, 148

## A

Account Expired, 307
Adaptive Infrastructure as a Service, 262
ADIC, 119, 124
Administrative costs
    BURA, 135
ADSL, 169
AIaaS, 262
Air conditioning, 12
Air flow, 238, 242, 246

Aisle
    air flow, 243
Aisle (in data center), 237
Akorri, 44
Amazon, 262, 270-271
    EC2, 271
Amazon Elastic Compute Cloud, 271
AMD, 43
American Power Conversion, 275
Amps, 34
Analog Telephony Adapter, 197
APC 251, 275
Application programming interface
    (API ), 93
Application Service Provider, 260
Archive, 92
    operation, 93
    solutions, 93
Array-based, 145-146
ASP, 260
Asset Overview, 293
Association of Electronics
    Recyclers, 283
ATA, 197
ATM, 168, 170
Atmos, 269
Availability, 225
Avamar, 114-115
Azure, 263
Azure Services Platform, 263

**B**

Backup, 111
   ADIC, 120
   analysis, 108
   call home, 126
   case study, 87
   clients, 102
   clone, 95
   daily backup, 104
   encryption, 114
   implementation, 125
   initiating, 123
   jobs, 106
   licenses, 128
   Management Console, 117
   metadata, 114
   NetWorker Server, 114
   number of jobs, 102
   reduced time with archive, 93
   replication, 95
   resources, 105
   SAN clients, 121
   success rate, 102
   tape barcode, 120
   Target ports, 121
   throughput, 107
   time and hours, 103
   VCB, 128
   VMware, 128
   zones, 126
Backup (*see also* BURA), 86, 131
Backup activity, 102
Backup and recovery, 111
Backup Assessment, 99-104, 111, 131
Backup Assessment Using Quick Scripts,
      99, 111, 131
Backup results, 125
Backup servers, 101
Backup size, 127
Backup (Replication), 118

BalancePoint, 44, 45
BCP, 199
Bell Telephone Laboratories, 196
BL460c, 32, 34
Black and white printing, 287
Blade, 32, 33, 34
Blade PC, 75
Blade workstation
   administration, 83
   benefits, 81
   dynamic resources, 83
   provision, 81
Blades, 57
BladeSystem, 22, 32, 40, 42
BTU
   definition, 12
BTU/hr, 34
BURA, 132
   benefit, 132
   TCO, 132
Bus system, 253
Business Continuity, 225
Business Continuity Plan, 199

**C**

c7000, 34, 39, 40, 41
Cable, 197
Cable sprawl, 249
Cabling trough, 238
Call2Recycle, 286
Capacity Management, 219, 229
Capacity Planner, 19-22, 31, 38, 50
Carbon emissions, 282
Carbon footprint, xvii
CAS, 92
CAT OS, 178
Catalyst Operating System (CatOS), 174,
      179, 181, 183-185
   HW Exception Count, 184
c-Class, 39, 40, 58, 126

CCO, 187
CDP, 177, 178
Celerra Replicator, 146
Centera, 92, 146
Central Backup Server, 114
CIFS, 269
Circuit breaker, 251
Circuit breaker panel, 255
Cisco, 163, 186, 211
   EnergyWise, 174
Cisco Discovery, 158
Cisco Discovery Protocol (CDP), 178
Cisco Network Collection (CNC), 178
Citrix Xen, 13
CLARiiON, 145
Cloud,
   AIaaS, 262
   Amazon, EC2 271
   Azure Services Platform, 263
   benefits, 273
   CloudPrint, 263
   EMC Atmos, 269
   Google Apps, 270
   hypervisor, 272
   make portable apps, 273
   Mozy Enterprise, 267
   Mozy Pro, 267
   Python, 273
   Snapfish, 263
   software application, 260
   Sun/Q-layer, 265
   thin clients, 262
   Web 2.0, 257
   web browser, 260
Cloud computing (see Cloud), 257
Cloud Optimized Storage, 269
Cloud service, 260
CloudPrint, 263
CNC, 178
Converged platform, 164

$CO_2$, 174, 277
Color depth, 297
Compliance
   archive, 92
Compute Utility, 221
Computer room (*see* data center), 243
Computer Room Air Conditioner, 240
Condensate (data center air), 246
Consistency group, 62
Consolidation, 22
Consolidation Stack, 222
Consumer Education Initiative
   (CEI), 284
Content addressable storage, 92
Continuous Access, 146
Control Panel, 279
Converged platform, 164
Converged switch, 164, 167
Cool air, 240
Cooling
   rack level, 247
Cooling techniques, 247
COS, 269
CPU, 22, 221
CPU Queue, 29
CPU Speed, 297
CPU usage, 306
CPU utilization, 217
CPUs, 32
CRAC, 240-247
CRT, 276
Cumulative backup, 95
CX array, 60
CX4-240, 59

**D**

DAL, 264
DAS, 221, 231
Data
   static, 92

Data (*continued*)
  storage, 148
  unchanged, 92
Data cabling, 238
Data center, 237
  air flow, 238
  air quality, 248
  aisle, 237
  blade chassis, 245
  cable, 249
  cables, 238
  CRAC, 242, 248
  hot air, 246
  hot aisle, 245
  humidity, 246
  power, 251
  zone, 253
Data Center Energy Forecast, 234
Data Protection Manager, 226
Data Store, 114-115
Database, 149
Database Abstraction Layer, 264
Databases, 215
De-duplication, 91, 114, 118
  BURA, 131
  results, 125
Denied Logon attempts, 307
Department of Energy, 282
Desktop
  access, 75
  benefits, 67
  benefits of VMware, 69
  check out, 76
  encapsulated, 69
  end users, 66
  Gold Master, 72
  gold master image, 72
  isolated, 69
  management, 70
  policy setting, 67

  printers, 75
  ROI/TCO, 79
  storage, 73
  virtualization, 65
  VM, 67
Desktop, 276-277
  IT needs, 66
Desktop virtualization
  TCO/ROI, 78
Desktop virtualization, 65, 78
Desktops
  hosted, 69
Device Summary, 295
DHCP, 297
Differential backup, 95
Digital Subscriber Line, 169
Direct Attached Storage, 221
Discovery, 158, 173, 178
  life cycle, 186
  PSIRT, 192
  Status Flags, 186
Disk
  archival, 148
  technologies, 148
Disk library, 118
  implementation, 126
  operation, 117
Disk queue, 29
Disk speed, 148
Disk Utilization, 29, 292
DiskXtender, 93
DL360, 9, 10
DL3D, 111, 117
DMX, 146
Documentation, 61
  backup, 127
Domain Controller, 296
Driver Version, 297
DS3, 168
DSL, 169, 197

Dual uplinks, 164
Duplex printing, 287

**E**

Early Deployment, 187-188
ECC, 150
Eco-friendly printing, 286
ED, 187, 188
EDL, 111
Elasticity (in private cloud), 258
Electricity, 275
Electronic waste, 283
Email, 169
Email archiving, 93
EMC, 93, 262, 268
    Atmos, 270
    Mozy, 268
EMC Atmos, 269
EMC Centera, 92, 93
EMC NetBackup, 125
emissions, 277
End of Engineering, 187, 189
End Of Sale (*see* EOS), 183, 187
End of Sale Announcement, 186
End-user computers, 65
energy, 277-278
Energy efficient hardware, 216
Energy Star, 276-277
energystar.gov, 234
EnergyWise, 174-175
Enterprise Disk Library, 111
Enterprise Virtual Array, 146
Environment, 231
Environmental Protection Agency, 286
EOE, 187, 189
EOL, 183, 186, 187
EOS, 183, 187
EOSA, 186
EPA, 283, 284
ESCON, 249

ESX, 13, 15, 21, 38, 39, 57, 60-64
    backup, 115
    TCO, 50
Ethernet, 43, 249
EVA, 146
Event Log, 307
e-waste, 283-285
Extended Remote Copy, 146

**F**

Fabric-based replication, 142
FATA, 148
Fax boards, 6
FC, 32, 148-149, 155
    speed, 148
FC3, 121
FCS, 188
Fiber optic, 249
Fibre Channel, 32
Fibre channel, 59, 117, 148
Firewall, 169
Flash disk,148, 150
Flat-screen monitors, 277
Floor
    cabling, 238
    raised, 240
Footprint
    telephone system, 207
Force.com, 266
Full backup, 94
Full-height, 41

**G**

Gartner, 283
GD, 187, 188
General Deployment, 187, 188
Goodwill Industries, 284
Google, 262, 270
    Apps, 270
Governance, 272

Graphics-intense applications, 82

Green Tips, 275

Greenhouse gas emissions (GGE), xvii

## H

Half-height, 41

Hardware alerts, 293

Hardware inventory, 290

HBA, 22, 32, 60

Health Insurance Portability and Accountability Act, 272

Henry Nyquist, 196

Hertz, 196

Hewlett Packard, 286

Hibernate, 275, 279

High read demand in desktop, 72

High-data-rate DSL (HDSL), 169

HIPPA, 272

Horizontal air flow, 247

Host Bus Adapter, 22, 32

Hot air return, 247

Hot fixes, 292

Hot spots (in data center), 243

Hot-pluggable, 42

HP CloudPrint ,263

HP LTO-3, 119, 122

HP Power Calculator, 7-12, 34-35

HP SIM, 58-64

HRM, 266

http

//sqlcat.com, 235

//svlg.net, 234

//technet.microsoft.com, 234

//www.energystar.gov, 234

//www.sqlmag.com, 235

Human Resource Management, 266

Humidity, 246

Hyper-V, 13, 217, 222-228, 234

guest configurations, 224

Hypervisor, 14, 264

## I

I/O, 6, 44, 221

I/O per second, 148

ICE, 40

IEEE-1471, 225

Ignite-UX

Initial load, 23-30, 52, 101-107, 138

ILM, 92

iLO, 40, 59

Implementation

blades, 58

data replication, 62

Knowledge Transfer, 61

shared storage, 59

Site Recovery Manager, 63

View, 64

VMware, 60

In-band, 115

Incremental backup, 95, 108

Industry Standard Servers, 3

InfiniBand, 42

Information lifecycle management, 92

InfrastruXure, 251

Integrated Control Environment, 40

Integrated Lights Out, 40-59

Interconnect bays, 42

Internal Rate of Return, 55

International Organization for Standardization, 169

Internet, 169, 170, 269

Internetworking Operating System (*see* IOS), 180

IOPS, 148-156

calculation, 149

IOS, 171-173, 178-185, 187-188

Software Lifecycle Table, 189

IP, 197, 198

IP Telephony, 210

IRR, 139

BURA, 137

definition, 55
desktop, 78
iSCSI, 43
ISP, 169
ISS, 4, 13
ISV, 93
IT Diagnosis, 289
Itanium, 43

**J**

Job backup, 101

**K**

Kilowatt hours, 12
kWh, 174

**L**

Lab Manager, 16
Ladder rack system, 250
LAN, 170-171, 178
Last Date of Support (*see* LDoS), 183
Latency, 152
Lawrence Berkeley National Laboratory,
    282
LCD monitor, 276
LD, 187-188
LDoS, 183, 186-187
Level, 300
Level Platforms, 289
Library, 134
Life Cycle Legend, 190
Limited Deployment, 187-188
Linked clones, 72-73
Linux, 279
Local Area Network, 170, 171
Local tape drives, 89, 96
Logical Units, 38
Logon Failure, 307
LTO-3, 120

LUN, 60, 62
LUNs, 38

**M**

MAC Address, 297
Mac OS-X, 279
MagCloud, 263
Manageability, 226
Management
    desktops, 69, 70
Mark Pohto, 215
Master control outlet, 282
Master images for desktop, 72
Materials Exchange, 284
MBSA, 292, 308
Media savings, 135
Media server, 89, 126
Memory
    size, 27
    utilization, 25
Meta-data, 269
Mezzanine, 43
Microsoft, 262-263
Microsoft Active Directory, 64
Microsoft Azure Platform, 264
Microsoft Baseline Security
    Analyzer, 292, 308
Microsoft Exchange, 45, 262
Microsoft IT, 215-217, 221
Microsoft IT RightSizing, 234
Microsoft Security Baseline Analyzer, 305
Microsoft Software Developer's Kit, 263
Mirrorview, 145
Modem, 169
Monitor, 278
Mozy, 266
Mozy Enterprise, 266
Mozy Pro, 267, 268

## N

NAS, 43, 146
   backup, 118
Navisphere, 59
NephOS, 264
Net Present Value
   definition, 55
Network alerts, 293
Network Bytes Per Second, 29
Network Cards, 297
Network Interface Card, 6, 22, 32
Network Operations Center, 308
Network Router, 169
Network Virtualization, 11, 21-22, 32, 35,
      50-51, 138, 164, 167, 219, 225, 295
NetWorker, 114, 124
   implementation, 127
   licenses, 127
   patches, 128
Networker Server, 114
Networking
   cooling, 165
   power, 165
Networking switch (*see* switch), 164
NFS, 269
NIC, 19, 22, 32, 38, 39, 43
NOC, 308
Non-Virtualized, 5
NPV, 139
   BURA, 137
   definition, 55
   desktop, 78
NTFS, 307

## O

Obsolete servers, 30
Offline Desktop, 77
OLA, 228
OLTP, 151, 228
Onboard Administrator Module, 42

Online transaction processing, 151
Onsite Manager, 289, 307, 308
Open System Interconnection, 169
Operating Level Agreement, 228
OSI, 169
Out-of-band, 115
Overhead ladder rack, 250

## P

P2V, 61
Packets, 169
Pages Per Second, 29
Patch
   desktop, 73
Patch Assessments, 292
Patch cables, 238
Patch Management, 308
Patch Management Summary, 292
Payback, 139
Payback Period, 54
   BURA, 138
Payment Card Industry, 272
PBX, 196, 200, 201
PCI, 43, 272
PDA, 262
PDU, 13, 253, 255
Peer-to-Peer Remote Copy, 146
Peripherals, 283
Permafrost, 220
Personal Digital Assistant, 262
Physical hosts, 229
Physical Resource Optimization, 229
Physical-to-Virtual, 61
PIX OS, 178
POC, 81
POE, 164, 167, 174
Power,
   40,000 on/off cycles, 276
   $CO_2$, 277
   dark backgrounds, 278

desktop, 78, 275
disk, 152
DSL/cable modem, 282
electronic waste, 283
Energy Star, 276
Hibernate, 279
laptops, 276
LCD, 276
light level, 278
master outlet, 282
paper memos, 278
peripherals, 278
printers, 278
screen saver, 276
Standby, 276, 279-280
tree, 277
Power and Cooling, 34, 35
Power cables, 40, 239
Power Distribution Unit, 253
Power Management, 278
Power Savings, 281
Power supply (switch), 164
PPRC, 146
Primary Backup Server, 89
Printer alerts, 293
Printing, 75, 286
consolidate, 287
digitally stored documents, 287
Driver-free, 75
Private Branch Exchange, 196
Private cloud (*see* cloud), 258
Private networking, 208
PRO, 229
Processor
frequency, 24
switch, 164
utilization, 25
Processor utilization, 21
Product Security Incident Response Team
(*see* PSIRT)

Proof Of Concept, 81
Provisioning, 226
desktop, 67
PSIRT, 182, 191-193
PSTN, 170, 201
Public Switched Telephone Network, 201

**Q**

Q-layer, 264
Queue (backup), 106

**R**

Rack, 241
air flow, 241
Rack layout, 237
Rack level cooling, 247
Rack Unit (RU), 241
RAID, 59, 149
1+0, 149
5, 149
RAID, 5 154
Raised floor, 240
RAM, 22, 32, 297
Random Access Memory, 22, 32
Random read misses, 151
RDP, 79
Recover Point Appliances, 62
Recoverpoint, 142
Recovery, 111
case study, 87
Recovery Point Objective, 96, 142, 147
Recovery Time Objective, 96, 142-147
Recycle, 231
Recycled paper, 287
Recycling Electronic Waste, 283
Recycling electronics, 284
ReDO, 284
Regulation
archive, 92
Regulatory compliance, 92

Remote Desktop Protocol, 79
Remote Graphics Software, 80
Remote monitoring, 289
Remote Physical PC, 75
Replication, 58, 62, 141, 142
    backup, 114
    host-based, 144
    out-of-band, 142
Replistor, 144
Resolution, 297
REST/SOAP, 269
Restore
    environment, 107
    jobs, 106
    success rate, 107
Retention policy, 127
Return on Investment
    definition, 54
Reuse Development Organization
        (ReDO), 284
RGS, 80, 81
Robotics controller, 126
ROI, 139, 271
    BURA, 137
    definition, 54
    desktop, 78
    telephone system, 203
Router, 173
Routing tables, 169
RPA, 62
RPO, 96, 142, 147
RRM, 151
RTO, 96, 142, 147
RU, 241

S

SaaS, 257, 272
Salesforce.com, 262, 266
SAM, 80, 81, 82
SAN, 5, 38-43, 58, 60, 142, 144, 146, 231

SAN port
    savings, 135
SAS, 42, 148, 155
SATA, 148, 155, 268
SATAII, 148
Scalability, 229
Screen saver, 276
SDK, 263
SDLC, 266
SDSL, 169
Security, 229
    desktop, 67
Security, 169
Security alerts, 293
Security patches, 292
Sequential
    tape, 94
Serial attached SCSI (SAS), 148
Serial attached technology attachment
        (SATA), 148
Server (in rack), 237
Server Temperature, 219, 220
Service Level Agreement, 90, 126, 272
Service Monitoring, 230
Service Pack, 297
Session Allocation Manager, 80, 82
Shared storage, 5, 15, 59
Shared tape libraries, 90
Silicon Valley Toxic Coalition, 285
Simple Network Management Protocol,
        178, 307
Single instance storage, 72
Single log in, 83
Single phase, 42
Site health, 290
Site Health Tab, 292
Site inventory, 290
Site Recovery Manager, 16, 58
SLA, 90, 96, 126, 127, 272
Sleep, 275, 276, 278

SMARTnet, 191, 193
Snapfish, 263
SnapView, 59, 60
SNMP, 178, 293, 300, 307, 308
Soft phone, 199
Software as a Service, 257, 266
Software Detail, 299
Software Development Life Cycle, 227, 232, 266
Software inventory, 290
Solid state disks (SSD), 148, 150
SONET, 169, 170
Source-based, 114
SourceOne, 93
SP, 15
spec.org, 235
Special Release, 189
SQL Server, 215, 218, 222-224, 227, 228, 233, 264
   clustering, 225
   Consolidation, 217
   Guests, 226
   management utilities, 230
   reduction from consolidation, 231
   scaling, 223
   security, 229
   Storage Utility, 220
   Utility Offerings, 224
   utility stack, 222
SQL Server Consolidation, 215
SQL Server Utility, 217
SRA, 63
SRDF, 145
SRM, 16, 58, 63
SSD, 148
SSL encryption, 67
Standby, 275-280
Standard Performance Evaluation Corporation, 235

Storage
   desktop efficiency, 67
   tiers, 147
Storage Area Network, 5, 58
Storage Node, 89, 113, 114
Storage processor, 15
Storage Replication Adapter, 63
Storage tiering, 92
Storage Utility, 218
Subnetworks, 170
Subscription service, 260
Sun Microsystems, 262
Sun Solaris Containers, 264
Sun/Q-layer, 264, 265
Surge protector, 277
Switch, 162
   48-port, 164, 167
   redundancy, 166
   slot-based chassis, 164
Symantec Volume Replicator, 144
Symmetrix Remote Data Facility, 145
Synchronous Optical Network, 169
syslog, 308
System Center Configuration Manager, 230
System Center Operations Manager, 226
System Center Operations Manager 2007, 230
System Center Virtual Machine Manager, 226
System Center Virtual Machine Manager 2008, 229

**T**

T-1, 199
T-3, 168, 170
Tap (power bus system), 255
Tape, 134, 268
   reliability, 136
Tape backup, 114

Tape library, 114
   implementation, 126
Tape media, 94
Tape storage
   cost, 135
Target-based, 114
TCO, 49, 51, 267
   blades, 50
   BURA, 131
   Capacity Planner, 50
   Data Center, 53
   disk, 154
   ESX, 50
   three year, 52
   VMware, 50
TCO/ROI
   desktop, 79
TDM, 199, 200, 205, 209
Telephone, 195
Temperature, 219, 225, 246
Test and Acceptance Plan, 63
Thermal
   network switch, 167
Thin client, 68, 80
Three phase power, 255
Tier 1 storage, 148
Tier 2 storage, 148
Time Division Multiplexing, 199
Top-of-rack switches, 42
Total Cost of Ownership, 49, 267
Train, 172, 173
Travel expense reduction, 205
Trouble Tickets, 293
Trough, 250

**U**

UC, 210
Unified Access, 75
Unified Communications, 210
Uninterruptable Power Supply, 161

Uplink, 163, 166
UPS, 13, 161, 287
Utilization, 6

**V**

Vampire energy loss, 282
VC, 16
VCB, 67, 128
VDM, 64
VDSL, 169
Very high DSL, 169
VHD, 227
VI, 15-16
Video conferencing, 204
Video RAM, 297
View (*see* VMware View), 64, 68
   printing 75
View Composer, 67
View Manager, 67, 70
View (virtual desktop), 16
Virtual Center, 16, 61
Virtual Connect, 43
Virtual Desktop Manager, 64
Virtual Hard Disks, 227
Virtual infrastructure, 15
Virtual Machine File System, 38
Virtual Machine Manager Library, 226
Virtual Private Data Center, 264
Virtual tape drives, 117
Virtual Tape Library, 100, 107, 111, 117
VirtualCenter, 63, 64
Virtualization
   background, 13
   TCO, 53
Virtualized, 33
Virutal tape libraries, 118
VMFS, 38
VMotion, 38, 67
VMware, 13, 28, 31, 44, 49, 50, 57, 61
   ESX, 38, 39

Lab Manager, 57
TCO, 50, 51
VMware Consolidated Backup, 67
VMware TCO/ROI Calculator, 78
VMware View, 67
   components, 68
   economies, 69
VMware View (*see* Desktop), 66
VMware Virtual Infrastructure, 75
VoIP, 170, 195, 196, 199, 200, 205, 209, 211
VPDC, 264
VPN, 173
VTL, 100, 107, 111

**W**

WAN, 81
Watts, 34, 276
Web, 169
Webjet admin, 286
Whitepaper, 234
Windows 2003, 223
Windows 2008, 222, 228
Windows Azure, 263
Windows Domain Controller, 295

Windows Management Interface, 29, 307
Windows Server 2008, 234
Windows server health, 290
Windows System Resource Manager, 229
Windows Terminal Server, 75
Windows Vista, 279
Windows Workstation, 295
Windows XP, 293
Wiring closet, 161
WMI, 29, 307, 308
Write once read many (WORM), 92
www.cisco.com, 186
www.cisco.com/go/psirt, 182

**X**

x64, 13
x86, 13
xDSL, 169
Xen, 265
XP, 146
XRC, 146

**Z**

Zone power distribution, 253

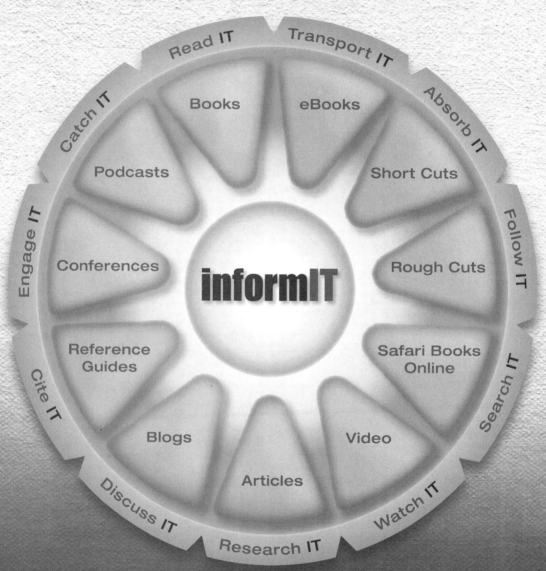